Souls Collide

Collide Series

Book Three

Kristina Beck

ISBN-13: 978-3-947985-03-6

To Mom

I know you're smiling down at me from your beach chair in heaven.

I wish I could share my books with you.

Chapter 1

Alexa

The teenager behind the counter, with severe acne and tall as a beanpole, keeps staring down my shirt. He hasn't looked at my face since I ordered. I don't know what he sees, because the front isn't cut low and I don't have big boobs. He'll never get a girlfriend if he makes it that obvious.

He hands me my order and mumbles how much it costs. I wave a ten-dollar bill in front of his face. "Hello! Up here. I didn't hide it down my shirt."

Clearly flustered, he drops the money on the floor and almost bangs his head on the open cash register drawer when he stands up again. His face burns so red that it's almost purple.

I turn around and roll my eyes. "All I want is my favorite Asian wrap. Is that so difficult?"

"I guess it is," Natalie says and giggles along with another woman who's standing in line.

"I'll go find us an empty table. Hopefully, somewhere quiet so I can tell you about my horrible date the other night."

"Oh man. I can't wait to hear about this one. I have to live vicariously through you."

"Believe me—you're better off," I say over my shoulder as I walk away. "I'm ready to close up shop."

While grabbing a stack of napkins, I zone in on an empty table for two in the corner. Perfect. I shimmy between the tables and sit facing away from everyone. I hate to see how people eat. Most of the time I lose my appetite.

Natalie comes up behind me as I hang my coat off the back of my chair. "I'm kinda pissed. No one behind the counter tried to look down my shirt. I think I need to talk to the manager."

"That's what happens when you wear turtlenecks all the time. It's only October, and it's still warm. How are you not sweating?"

She shrugs her shoulders and opens her bottle of Diet Coke.

"It wouldn't matter what I wear when you're next to me. I could be naked, and the guys would still flock to you."

"Shut up. You're beautiful, and you know it. Even with the turtlenecks."

She tilts her head to the side as I wink at her.

Natalie is attractive, but she has this one snaggletooth that practically pokes you in the eye when she smiles. She complains about it, but she refuses to get it fixed because she's deathly afraid of dentists. I understand what it's like to have a phobia, so I don't push her.

Just as I take the last bite of my wrap, my phone chirps like a bird and vibrates in my coat pocket. I grab a napkin to wipe off my hands. *Chirp*. Let me guess who it is.

I twist in my chair to pull it out, and I stiffen in annoyance when I read the screen.

"Your face is priceless. You always purse your lips when you're annoyed. Who's sending you messages?"

I ball up my garbage and push it to the side. "Joker the Poker."

She covers her mouth, preventing the soda from shooting out her lips.

"I'm going to kill you." She smacks my hand while laughing. "It almost came out of my nose. Who is he, and what the hell does 'Joker the Poker' mean?"

"Who do you think? He's the next one crossed off my list."

"This is going to be a good one. I can already tell." She relaxes into her chair.

I give secret names to guys, like Joker the Poker, Tony the Tiger, Corkscrew, or Bendy Barry. As for Bendy Barry, believe me—no one should know why I call him that. It's not pretty.

"We met up at a restaurant near the movie theater. He thought he was a comedian every time he opened his mouth. His laugh was so obnoxious that I wanted to crawl under the table. I guess alcohol can do that to you. I had only one glass of wine, and he had three beers."

Natalie leans forward. "So why did you go out with him?"

"He wasn't like that the first time I met him. His friends were with him, so we were interacting in a group. He was funny in a goofy kind of way. But I thought it was because he was tipsy. We were all laughing, so I didn't think much of it."

Chirp.

I purse my lips to the side and ignore it. "Anyway, I couldn't wait to see the movie because I wouldn't have to listen to him anymore. While we waited in line to buy the tickets and get our drinks, he stood behind me and proceeded to poke me in the ass with his third leg."

Natalie bursts out laughing. "You have to stop, or my ribs are going to snap."

Someone giggles at the table next to us. I lay my hand on the older woman's table. "Sorry. I get loud when I'm emotional."

"No problem, dear. You're very entertaining. Thanks for the laugh."

I sway my hand. "Hence, Joker the Poker. I should give up on the whole dating scene. I'm finished with men."

The woman stands up from her table. "You two are beautiful and still young. Your prince charmings will show up when least expected. Don't give up yet."

"I'm not sure about that," Natalie mutters as the woman walks away.

"Anyway, he keeps calling, and I keep ignoring him. I told him after the movie I wasn't interested in another date. You know me, Natalie. I'm always up front with guys. They just don't get it."

She glances at her watch. "Oh. It's one thirty. I need to go. But before I do, to give you a heads-up, I'm sending out an email today about a meeting we'll have in New York City to meet the other sales reps for the first time. You'd better make sure you're working hard to learn everything you can about oncology. I was told again there will be layoffs. I won't be the only one making the decisions on who'll be let go."

"I'm on my way to the library after this."

"Why don't you study at home with sweatpants and a sweatshirt on? I would."

"You know I like libraries. One of the most respected cancer institutes is a twenty-minute walk from my apartment. If I need to study about oncology in order to keep my job, I'm going to do it in their huge modern medical library."

She wraps her magenta scarf around her neck. Like she really needs one. "Good. Gotta run. See you on Friday. Don't forget to dress up. Watch out for the Poker." She giggles as she walks toward the exit.

I love libraries. I practically lived in one when I was in graduate school. Because I have blond hair, big green eyes, and a bubbly personality, people, especially men, assume I'm a dumb blonde. If I go on a date, I show my true colors, but most guys aren't interested. They only want to jump in bed. Poker is the latest.

When I walk out of the café, a strong gust of cold wind almost knocks me over. It was sunny when I arrived, but now there are black stormy clouds overhead. I'm glad I grabbed my hooded raincoat when I left my apartment. Maybe I should have worn a turtleneck like Natalie, but I hate things around my neck. I swiftly put on my coat as I walk to the hospital.

My phone goes off again, but I ignore it. Will Darren never get the point?

I turn right onto the next street. It's eerily quiet. A raindrop lands on my nose, so I pick up speed since I don't have an umbrella. I stop short as a grungy black cat jumps in front of me with a haunting snarl. It stands still, his spooky orange eyes daring me to pass. The stand-off lasts only a moment, until a car honks its horn. The cat twitches and skitters off. I let out my breath as my heart pounds.

"What the fu—" I stop before I swear. I promised my four-year-old niece, Felicia, I'd put twenty-five cents in a jar every time I swear. She doesn't understand why, but her parents aren't happy that I curse so much in front of her. I try to be good, but the F-bomb slips out more than it should. If they had more than one child, I'd be broke.

"You know it's bad luck when a black cat crosses your path?" cackles someone behind me.

Chills run up and down my spine. The scratchy voice sounds like the wicked witch in *The Wizard of Oz*. I spin around slowly, afraid I'll see a green woman wearing a black pointy hat. I'm relieved she isn't green, but I'm shocked to see she's dressed up as a witch. Her eyes are jet black with no whites showing. I hate those contacts that people wear when they dress up. Don't they hurt? And how can you see through them?

"Well, good for me since I have extra luck to spare," I joke. "At least my family thinks so."

She invades my space and hisses, "You're gonna need it, Blondie." She flicks my hair over my shoulder.

I slap her hand away. "Back off, you fucking freak. Halloween isn't for a couple of days. Why don't you go fetch another bottle of alcohol," I snap as I wave my hand in front of my nose. "Or several mints." Her breath is rancid.

She snickers and staggers off as more raindrops fall from the sky.

I take a deep breath and shake my head.

What if my luck does run out?

Chapter 2

Kent

This hospital is my second home, and I hate it. *Hate* is too nice a word. Despise? Nope. I'd rather lose my left ball than come back here and watch another family member suffer. When will it ever end? I don't think I'll ever see the light at the end of the tunnel.

My sister begs me to stop being so angry and cynical. She tries to convince me her illness is different from Mom's. How can they be different when they're the same? I don't know how she remains so cheerful and positive after all we've been through. All *she's* been through.

There are only two people who take priority in my life. My sister and my partner, Vince. He's been my partner since we graduated from the police academy. Vince keeps me grounded when we're on the job. No need for me to become the next angry cop in a video going viral on the internet. I keep my cool, but I'm not sympathetic. If someone's car registration has expired, ticket. If someone drives over the speed limit, ticket. If someone swerves while driving, alcohol test. No excuses and no warnings.

I'm on my way to work now. The hospital lobby is full of kids dressed in ridiculous Halloween costumes. Don't they know it's in a couple of days? Why would they ever want to be in a hospital for fun? I walk through the first set of sliding doors but am blinded by a flash of golden light. Then someone collides with my chest. I stumble backward and grab on to the person.

"I'm so sorry. I didn't see you. It's like you came out of thin air," babbles a woman's voice with annoying cheer. "I thought I ran into the door—you have a chest of steel."

I blink to adjust my eyes. The woman pulls off her red hood, and her hypnotizing, brilliant seafoam eyes lock with mine. Her full red lips match a candied apple. My chest tingles as I take a deep breath, inhaling what feels like a beam of sunlight exuding from her. A warm, tingling sensation rushes through my lungs, zaps my icy heart, and continues through my blood until my fingers and toes release an ounce of the negative energy I've been harboring. I don't move or say anything. This is the first pure breath of fresh air I've taken after holding it in for so many years. *I don't like it.*

"Are you okay? Cat got your tongue?"

I snap out of whatever spell she has me under and increase the distance between us. My face tightens, and my wall shoots straight back up. "I'm fine. Next time you should watch where you're walking."

"Yes, sir!" She chuckles. "I tried to go to the hospital library, but the entrance was closed. It directed me to this one. Then it started to pour, and I followed your group of kids in." She brushes the rain off her jacket.

She proceeds to wipe down my shirt with her well-manicured hand, which increases the blood flow to a specific part of my body.

"You're all wet now too, and I marked it with my red lipstick. A little gift from me to you."

Seriously? Is she touching me? I grab her hand and am surprised by the warm sensation. I drop it like it's poison. "Don't touch me."

Her beaming smile fades as she steps back. Regret tries to seep in, but my wall prevents it.

"Man. What's your problem? I said I was sorry." She pulls her hand through her long, shiny blond hair.

"Did you ever hear of personal space?"

"Can you hold this for me, please?"

"No," I say curtly.

She ignores me and shoves a paper bag with the name of a café my sister loves into my hands. Who the hell does she think she is? I'm sure she gets her way with everyone, with the brightness that emanates from her.

She searches through her bag and tugs out a red rubber band.

"Can you hold my handbag too?"

"Are you kidding me? Can't you just put the strap over your shoulder? Or do all strangers do what you want? I need to get to work."

"Forget it. You need to lighten up," she growls as she steps around me. "Life's too short to be so pissy."

I don't move or respond.

"Hey," she yells at me from behind.

What the hell now? I glance back at her as the costumed kids filter past me and outside.

"For someone who works with kids, you've got a sh—" She covers her mouth and glances at the kids. "*Bad* attitude. But I'm sure the other teachers *love* seeing you with that police costume on." Her eyes trail up and down my body.

The same tingle from before teases me.

"It sure made my day." She blows me a kiss, then turns away.

Wait. What? She thinks I'm a teacher dressed up like a cop? I can't respond because a little boy grabs my hand and pulls me out the door and into the rain. Why is this happening today?

The boy lets go as soon as we get outside. It feels good to have rain splash on my face. I need to wake up from whatever just occurred in there. But if it's raining, what was that blinding light I saw when I neared the door? I'd thought the sun reflected off something.

Was it lightning?

A camera flash?

Little Red Riding Hood?

Chapter 3

Alexa

Wow. I gently rub my lower abdomen with my hand. Can ovaries twitch? I watch him let rain drip down his perfect face. Yup, mine do. Man, he was beyond hot. He might have been a total jerk with his badass attitude, but if I were a mother, I'd request a parent-teacher meeting every day. Or I'd ask if I could sharpen his pencil. I can't imagine working with a guy who looks like that, and a teacher no less. Tall, dark, and lickable. What a head of hair. Overgrown dark-brown thick wavy hair that was all disheveled on the top and short in the back. His eyes were like pools of milk chocolate. I'm surprised I didn't feel his long eyelashes brush against my cheek.

I hear a grinding sound and jerk forward. I don't get far because my handbag gets stuck in the electronic sliding doors. When they finally open, I lose my balance and bang into another person. What the hell? I feel like I'm in a pinball machine today. I inspect my Gucci bag for damage.

"Alexa Kramer?" a man says as he skims my arm with his fingers.

I'd know that slimy voice anywhere. I yank my arm away as I shiver, like a spider skittered across my skin. Who knows where his fingers have been. Actually, I do know. He's a proctologist. I back up to increase the distance between us.

"Hello, Dr. Wanker. I mean Walker."

His left eyebrow shoots up.

"I haven't seen you at the clinic in a while. No sales meetings lately?" he says as his creepy eyes wander down my body and land on my knees.

I'm so glad I wore jeans today.

"Nope." I glance around to ensure other people are near us. I can't stand being alone with this doctor.

"I hope you're not sick."

He reaches his hand out to touch my arm again, but I dodge it and say, "I'm fine. I'm on my way to the library."

"I hope to run into you again sometime soon," he calls out, then has a hacking fit.

I pretend not to hear him and walk faster before I almost vomit. I slip around a corner and then lean against the cold wall across from the elevator. Why is he at this hospital? I've only seen him at a clinic in Manhattan where some of my old clients were.

I've been in the pharmaceutical arena for a long time. I'm surrounded by doctors and other medical professionals every day. But Dr. Wanker disgusts me with the way he undresses me with his eyes and his obsession with my knees. The hair on my arms stand at attention when he's near me.

He wasn't a client, but he worked at that clinic and was always around when I had sales appointments there. It's as if he knew my schedule. I'm glad I don't have clients there anymore.

I take a deep breath and focus. Where is the library? I'm not familiar with this section of the hospital. A nurse marches out a random door into the hallway, her arms full of files.

"Excuse me," I say.

She stops in her tracks but doesn't smile.

Does this hospital piss people off or something? "Can you please tell me where the library is? The library entrance by the parking deck is closed off. It said to come this way and follow the signs."

She looks at her watch and huffs. "Go to the elevator. Turn left and then an immediate right. Go all the way to the end. Look for the signs that are hanging everywhere," she says with a flat tone and bustles off.

I continue forward, wondering what world I'm in. This has to be the most bizarre afternoon. First the cat, then the witch, then the frigid teacher, then Dr. Wanker, and now the crabby nurse. They all need a dose of laughing gas. This weekend can't get here fast enough.

I repeat the directions to the library in my head. I stop and do a double take. A young woman leans against the wall while laughing with a nurse. I'm taken aback by how beautiful she is. No one could miss the bright-orange scarf on her head. It makes me think of a sunset. She wears it like it's a fashion statement. The nurse is dressed in a pea soup–green uniform and has big Jersey hair. Horrible. It reminds me of the eighties.

My phone dings to remind me I have an appointment tomorrow. I try to mute my phone, but it interrupts them. The woman looks in my direction, and we smile at each other before she turns back to the nurse.

I continue my search for the library and finally see some signs. An older man walks hand in hand with a little boy who is pale as a ghost. Clumps of hair are missing from his head. The more I learn about cancer, the more my heart bleeds for the sufferers. Why does anyone have to go through such torture?

My mind wanders back to the woman with the head scarf. Why am I so fascinated with her? Is it because of the scarf? But why would I be excited about that? Maybe it's because she's beautiful and looks happy even though she's sick. It's not like I'm attracted to her.

The pharmaceutical company I work for acquired another big pharma that focuses on the discovery and development of cancer treatments. There are talks my division might be sold off and the company will focus on oncology. With my lack of oncology experience, I could lose my job when layoffs begin.

I'm not too worried I'll be let go. This has been my best year in sales. I have an excellent track record. When it comes to my job, I make sure I know everything I can. That's why I'm good at it. When people meet me, they think I'm just a pretty face. When they give me a chance, they find out I'm clever and know what I'm talking about.

The same thing with guys—they never take me seriously. Every time something intelligent comes out of my mouth, they ignore it or laugh. No one believes I'm smart. I lose interest in guys quickly because I can't act like myself. Just because I'm bubbly, like to dress well, and am blond doesn't mean I'm a ditz. That's why I'm ready to give up on finding love. I'm content on my own.

Just as I see the doors to the library, the delicious smell of freshly baked cake surrounds me. It's better than the smell of disinfectant. I turn around and see a sign for the hospital café. It makes me crave the éclairs I bought this morning. I search through my bag and scrunch my forehead. The prickly teacher walked away with my damn éclairs. How rude! No. It's even better. I hope they make him think of me all day and how much of a beast he was.

I'll be thinking about him. More about his chocolate eyes and uniform than his personality. That would only ruin my fantasies.

Chapter 4

Kent

I hate Halloween. My sister and I never had real costumes when we were little. Mom always rushed around the house searching for something we could use, but that sucked all the fun out of it.

Tonight I'm bartending at Vince's uncle's bar because he's low on staff. Unfortunately, he loves Halloween and is having a party there. I was told to look at least a little dressed up. Pumpkin-orange T-shirt and black jeans are about as close as I get.

As I walk in, a hanging skeleton with glowing red eyes greets me at the door. I don't need the reminder that my mom looked like a skeleton when she died.

Two guys dressed like zombies from *The Walking Dead* saunter by and sit at a table near the bar. The crowd isn't too thick yet, but it's Friday. It'd better get busier, because I need to make extra cash.

Medical bills are piling up. Abby's insurance only pays so much of her expenses. She doesn't earn her regular salary since she's on sick leave. I convinced her to move in with me until she's finished with her treatments and can finally go back to work, *if* she can go back to work. I take on extra jobs like bartending and small house repairs. My grandfather worked in construction and showed me how to do almost everything.

"Hey, Kent," Joe greets me as he shakes my hand. "Thanks for helping me out tonight."

I shrug. "No problem. You're lucky I didn't have to work. Money's tight, so you know I'll help out when I can."

"How's Abby? Is she doing okay?"

"You know Abby. She's as cheerful as can be. You'd never know that she's sick or having a bad day. I was with her this week for her normal checkup with her oncologist. Last round of chemo is in about three weeks, and if all goes well, she'll be finished."

Joe pats me on the shoulder. "That's great news. I told you she'd pull through. Her cancer was caught early enough. Be thankful she's always in a good mood. Most aren't when they've gone through cancer treatments."

"Like my mom."

He lifts his hands up in front of him in peace. "Okay, before you get all pissed off like you always do when you talk about Abby or your mom, get behind the bar and work. Get your mind off it for at least one night." He pats me on the shoulder. "Oh, and try to be friendly."

I squint my eyes at him.

"I said *try*. You'll make more tips."

A couple of hours fly by. I've had hardly a chance to take a break. Not everyone is dressed up, but some people either are creative or take Halloween way too seriously. The Blue Man Group is gathered in one corner. Luke Skywalker and Chewbacca talk to some Trekkies. A woman is dressed as an angry emoji. Maybe I should wear that costume.

I squeeze a cold lime into a bottle of Corona Light and place it on the bar in front of a customer. From the corner of my eye, a soft glow catches my attention. To the right of the bar is a woman playing with her phone. The room is suddenly quiet. People nearby talk and walk around the bar in slow motion, but my entire body fixates on her. *Her*.

After I left the hospital that day, my body hummed for hours. I refused to acknowledge it. Now she's standing there again, and it's like the sight of her is a drug. The tension and anger I hold in seeps out. I search to see if anyone else notices her. Maybe she's an illusion.

"Hey, Kent!"

I twitch, and the moment is over. The music is loud, and the people chat like normal. I glance her way again, and her eyes connect with mine. She lays her chin in her hand. One corner of her mouth lifts up.

"Kent," Vince yells while knocking on the bar.

"What?" I snap.

"What's up? You're staring at that blonde like she's a goddess."

She is. "No." I clear my throat. "I was looking at something behind her. Two guys looked like they were ready to fight."

Dani, Vince's girlfriend, appears from behind him. She's one of the hospital nurses who sometimes takes care of Abby. She's dressed like an angel, with massive white-and-silver wings and very little else. Every time she moves, her wings bang into people and chairs. She must have taken a shower in sparkles. Her dark Italian features contrast with the white costume.

She's a nice person and would do anything for Abby. She's been dating Vince for about a month or so. I'm not sure it's the healthiest relationship, but I don't get involved. I'm the last person to dish out advice.

"Who looks like a goddess? Me?" Dani says as she puts her arm around Vince's shoulder and kisses him longer than I care to witness.

"Don't you love my costume, Kent? I'm a Victoria's Secret Angel." She rotates back and forth.

I throw some dirty napkins into the garbage can. "You know I'm not into Halloween, but I guess it's nice."

"That's a compliment, coming from you." She beams. Her bleached teeth match her white wings.

"He was staring at the one dressed in the red costume at the end of the bar." Vince motions with his chin.

Dani squints her eyes, and then they bulge. She pulls her head back. "I think I know her." Her head stretches forward again. "If she's who I think she is, she was one year ahead of me in high school. The guys followed her around like puppy dogs. My brother, Dominic, included. He was obsessed with her for years. It's probably why he only dates blondes.

"She was the prom queen, valedictorian, and captain of the cheerleading squad. She was the most down-to-earth person though. I'm sure she landed herself a sugar daddy. I'm going to see if it's her. She probably won't remember me."

"Seriously? Why do you need to talk to her?" I say with annoyance. I don't want her any closer to me.

She rolls her eyes. "What's the big deal?"

Vince and I watch as Dani makes her way down the bar. Her wings shed feathers as she moves, leaving a trail behind her. She reaches the blonde. Seconds go by as they smile and giggle, so I guess it's her.

After a few minutes, they come and stand next to Vince. *She's* dressed in a snug red devil costume. It's tight enough that it's safe to assume she has nothing on underneath it. Her long golden hair is pulled back in a tight ponytail, and horns stick out of a headband, convincing me she really is the devil. Her fiery-red lipstick enhances her perfect full lips, which pisses me off even more.

"I was right, guys. This is Alexa Kramer from my high school. We both grew up in Cleartown."

Just like the other day, Alexa's smile radiates through me. Vince shakes her hand, and then Alexa looks at me with an evil smirk but doesn't say anything right away. She leans slightly on the bar.

"So. A teacher by day and bartender dressed like a deranged pumpkin at night." She leans in a bit further. "You owe me two éclairs, by the way." Her devilish grin matches her costume perfectly. "Did you like the salted caramel one? It's my favorite."

Dani's gaze shoots from me to Alexa. "Kent?" She clears her throat. "You know Alexa?"

Alexa chuckles. "Kent? As in Clark Kent? Superman? Were your parents into superheroes? Superman was my brother's favorite. Please don't tell me your last name is Clark."

Vince and Dani stifle their laughs, then stop because they know I avoid talking about my parents, especially to strangers.

"His last name is Hayes," Dani tells her.

Alexa Hayes.

I shake my head. What's gotten into me? I vigorously wipe down the bar counter, as if I'm waxing a car, to cool my heated blood.

"So how do you know each other?" Vince asks.

Without looking up, I say, "We bumped into each other the other day. We never exchanged names."

"Why did you say *teacher*?" Dani asks Alexa.

"He was with a group of kids. They wore adorable costumes. Superman over here wore an awesome police costume. It was quite convincing," she says, then winks at me. "It was so sweet when a kid grabbed his hand and dragged him outside."

Vince chokes on his beer, and Dani is about to say something, but I subtly shake my head. She nods in understanding. I don't want Alexa to know anything about me.

I raise my voice. "I can't talk anymore. I need to work. Does anyone need a drink?"

Alexa raises her hand. "I'm waiting for someone to meet me here, so I'd like to order something. The martini special sounds yummy. The Autumn Blossom please," she says with pure, sickening delight.

How can someone be so peppy all the time? Her happiness grates under my skin. She probably gets her way any time she flashes her mesmerizing smile. I shake the martini vigorously several times, pour it into a glass, and place it on the bar in front of her. Before I can get my hand away, her fingers graze mine as she picks it up. That soothing warmth dances up my fingers, through my hand, and up my forearm. I jerk my hand away and scratch my arm to make the unwanted sensation stop.

"Does he hate when people touch him, or is it just me?" Alexa asks Vince and Dani, as if I'm not even here. "I don't have cooties."

Vince waves his hand. "Nah. He hates everything and almost everyone. Don't take it personally."

I fill orders and avoid their conversation, though I wasn't talking to them to begin with. Not that I care what they chat about anyway.

"So, Alexa, what have you been up to? Are you married?" Dani asks.

I lose my grip on a white wine bottle but catch it with my other hand.

Okay. Now I'm interested.

Chapter 5

Alexa

I swallow my first sip of the sweet, refreshing martini. "No*pe*." I pop the *p* emphatically.

"No prince charming swooped you off your feet years ago? No kids?" Dani delves deeper. "I don't buy it."

Vince taps Dani's arm. "Don't be so nosey." She swats his hand away.

"Hey, she was the prom queen of high school and most likely to succeed. We all bet she'd become a millionaire, find her prince, and have tons of babies."

I wiggle my fingers on my left hand. "No wedding ring here and never has been. It seems princes don't like women with actual brains, their own opinions, or successful jobs. They want trophy wives who will do what they say. I'm not settling for that. I'd rather end up a spinster with twenty cats. Relationships are a pain in the ass anyway. I don't need the drama anymore."

I reach for my drink and notice Superman observing us. I wonder if I'm sweating because of this tight polyester costume or because I'm around him. His eyes lock on mine, and it's unnerving. They are dark, suspicious, and bitter. His face is carved out of stone, lacking emotion. What is he hiding behind that mask? Or does he think I'm lying?

"What's the problem, Superman? Did I say something wrong?" I inch forward so my arms rest on the bar. "Oh, let me guess. You didn't think I had a brain when you met me the other day. That's a pity. Judging a book by its cover. Tsk-tsk. There's a lot to discover about me."

He leans closer and whispers, "I actually read people very well. But *you* are not a mystery I'd ever want to solve." His voice drips with disgust as he pushes off the bar.

He grumbles to Vince and Dani, "I'm taking a break. I'll see you in a little while."

Both of their mouths drop.

I face away from the bar and rest my elbows on it. "Jeez. Is he always so uptight? He needs to lighten up."

"Yup. Dani, Kent's sister, and I are the only ones he gets along with."

No mention of his parents. He acts like my brother, James, did when Jessica and the baby died. His anger and disgust for all humankind wafted off him like a bad smell. He only spoke to my parents and me, until Lisa walked into his life and changed everything. I should tell Superman my sister-in-law is a psychologist. It sounds like he needs one.

"Enough of Superman. Dani, what are you doing now? Are you living in Hoboken or just hanging out tonight?"

"I moved back from San Francisco about a year ago for a new job. I needed a change. My twin brother, Dominic, lives here too. Do you remember him? He had such a crush on you. He's meeting us here later. My parents moved to Arizona for the warmer weather. We're on our own over here."

I nod even though I don't have a clue who her brother is. Well, I don't remember her either. Since I've moved away from home, I'm not in contact with many people from Cleartown.

"I'm a nurse at LCCI, the Long Center Cancer Institute. It's a great job, but working with cancer patients can be mentally and emotionally draining. I've learned to handle it over the years, but the emotions still sneak up on me."

"That's funny. That's where I ran into Kent. I'm a cardiovascular sales rep at the pharma company Quadro, and I might take on oncology in the future. I've been studying my ass off to learn everything I can about cancer therapies and medications."

Vince bumps elbows with Dani, and they give each other a cryptic look, as if there's a secret I'm not supposed to know.

"We should exchange numbers," Dani suggests. "I can help you if you have any questions. Maybe even show you around the hospital. But I'm not allowed to tell the staff you're a sales rep. Conflict of interest, which I'm sure you already know."

I nod.

"We can hang out or get a bite to eat," she suggests.

I grab my phone. "Sure. Give me your number, and I'll call you so you have my information." She repeats her phone number as I punch it in. I ring her number, then put my phone on the bar.

Dani smiles. "Cool. I'm excited. It's nice to know more people here. Most of my friends are married with kids. They don't come out to Hoboken often. It's harder to make friends in our thirties."

"Hey, what about me? I'm your friend," Vince jokes.

"You're not a girlfriend. You're a guy I'm dating. Big difference." She kisses his shaven head as he wraps his arm around her thin waist, almost getting tangled in her ridiculous wings.

Dani points to the door with excitement. "Dominic is here. He's going to get the shock of his life when he sees you."

I notice Vince roll his eyes.

"Dominic," she yells over the loud crowd while waving her arms around. A couple of loose feathers land on Vince's black shirt.

Dominic zones in on us and waves back. He's cute. Tall with light-brown hair. Nice smile. Superman is hotter though.

My phone vibrates and lights up. I check the number. Finally. It's Natalie from work. "Sorry, guys. I need to take this call. I'll be right back."

21

Glued to the screen on my phone, I zigzag through people. I pass someone with a thick stench of garlic. I despise that smell on people. That person better not come near me again. Why do people eat garlic like that? I can hardly breathe.

I hear Dani in the distance. "Dominic! You'll never guess who's here." I turn my head and see her pointing to me as her brother looks on. I'll die if he's the one who reeks like garlic.

I wander off to a dim hallway that leads to the bathroom. "Natalie, where are you? I'm at the Golden Harp like you told me. Wait! What? You told me the wrong place? You're so dead. What's it called? The Silver Tulip? You're buying me drinks tonight. Yes, I know exactly where it is. You're lucky there's a Halloween party here too. I would've looked like a total idiot. I'll text you when I'm on my way."

It's time to freshen up my red cherry-flavored lipstick. My friends always push me to use color-stay lipstick that doesn't come off for hours. They don't understand that I like to leave my mark. Everywhere.

As I rub my lips together, I turn side to side in front of the mirror with a smile on my face. This costume fits like a glove. There's not much breathing space, but it looks good. I inspect my teeth to make sure I have no lipstick on them. Nope. Good to go.

I head back down the darkened hallway. Around the corner comes Kent. Lucky me. He stops in his tracks and focuses to the side, as if searching for a way out.

I strut toward him. "Hey, Suppy. I'm on my way out. I'd like to say how pleasant it was to see you twice in such a short amount of time." My voice drips with sarcasm.

No response. He provokes me with his silence and death stares. I want to scream in his face to see if he'll even twitch. He tries to pass me, but I block him with my arm.

"What's your problem? Is it so hard to be friendly with someone who is obviously trying to be nice to you? Especially someone who gave you her favorite éclairs."

He spears me with his glare. "I threw them out. Please move. Is that polite enough for you?"

"What you need is for someone to pull that huge fucking stick out of your ass."

I'm so glad I wore high heels, because I'm almost the same height as he is.

"Oh, yeah. Are you volunteering?" He inches closer. "Give it your best shot, Prom Queen."

I happen to love challenges. On instinct, I grab fistfuls of his shirt and pull his lips to mine. We fall back against the wall. I think someone walks past us, but it doesn't matter, because my brain turns to mush. His hands squeeze my upper arms. I wait for him to shove me away, but instead, he pulls me closer. Then his hands wander down my backside, setting off a hormonal frenzy inside me. What a delightful surprise, and I want more. A lot more.

His soft lips and tongue sync with mine, but his are needier. Every single molecule in my body, even ones I didn't know I have, urge me to keep going. But reality interferes. I need to have the upper hand.

After enjoying it for one more millisecond and giving his lower lip a last nip, I push away, leaving us both breathless. I stare into his dreamy mochaccino eyes to guess what he's thinking. I'm better off not knowing because I'll just attack him again. Or he'll turn back into a beast.

I slap my hand on his chest. "See ya around." I walk away and refuse to look back. "Good luck with that stick." I wave my hand in the air.

Once I'm out of sight, I take a deep breath. That was the most amazing, blood-bubbling, ovary-squealing tongue tango I've ever experienced. I hope his soapy scent stays on my body all night.

The exit is in front of me, so I can make my quiet escape. But I still need to pay for my drink. I scan the bar and see Dani and the guys. No sign of Superman. I scurry over to them.

"I hate to leave, but I need to meet my friend at another bar. Here's some money for my drink." I toss some bills onto the bar.

Dani grabs my elbow and pulls me to the side. "Is everything okay?" Her stare circles my face, and then she bursts out laughing.

"Yeah. Why? I need to go."

"It's just that your lipstick is smeared all around your mouth and chin. What in the world were you doing?" She giggles.

"Shit, really?" I drag my fingers around my mouth to wipe it off. "Oh. I just rubbed my mouth with a tissue. I forgot I put fresh lipstick on." *Liar.*

I snag a clean napkin from a table and wipe around my mouth. "Is that better?"

"Yes. It's all gone." She giggles again.

Why won't she stop? It's not that funny. Okay, it is.

"Please don't go. My brother wants to talk to you."

Dani practically begs me, so I give in. "Only for a minute, because I seriously need to go. My friend is waiting for me." *Kent will be back any second unless he's still leaning against the wall back there.*

She taps her brother on the shoulder. "Alexa's here."

He stops talking to a blonde on his right and turns in my direction. His smile spreads from ear to ear as his fake blue eyes scan every inch of my body. Most of the time it doesn't faze me when guys do this, but I feel naked in this room. He creeps me out.

"Alexa." He extends his hand.

A wave of garlic blows in my face. I hesitate to shake his hand but do it anyway. He lifts my hand to his lips. I pull it away from him harder than I intended to. I think he just tickled my hand with his tongue. Who does that? Now I'm going to smell like garlic. Atrocious.

My cheeks sizzle, but not because of him. I feel another set of eyes branding my skin. My gaze travels to my left and meets stern eyes. Kent is back, and he's not pleased. Maybe I could cheer him up by continuing what I started before. It would be my pleasure.

Focus! Time to make my escape.

"Sorry, everyone, but I really need to leave. Nice to meet you guys." I nudge Dani's arm. "Give me a call. We can meet up for drinks soon."

Dominic advances to retake my hand, but I raise it instead. "Take care, Dominic." *Shove your garlic tongue and blue contacts where the sun doesn't shine.*

I glance at Kent and give a little nod. He stands there and drills me with his stare, but before I turn away, I notice he has lipstick all over his mouth. Oh shit. I beeline for the door as I hold back my laughter. As I find my way to the other bar, I replay our kiss in my mind. I'd typically tell a guy like him to fuck off, but there's something behind the facade, and I want to be the one who figures it out.

Chapter 6

Kent

The wall prevents me from falling over. How can a woman get under my thick skin so easily and with such confidence...twice? I caved and kissed her back. I never lose control. She tasted of red berries with a hint of gin. Damn if it wasn't the best thing I've tasted in years. I adjust my pants. My brain is in the clouds.

She makes me feel alive again. My blood poured through my veins after years of living like the dead. If I'm Superman, then she's my kryptonite. Since my mom's death, no one has ever weakened my barrier. Prom Queen has loosened some bricks in my wall, and I don't like it.

Mom always said I'd meet a woman who'd change everything one day. She might have been right. But I wrote off women a long time ago. I'm not about to change because of one kiss from *her*.

"Kent! What the hell are you doing in the hallway? I need you at the bar," Joe barks.

I scan the room and see Alexa standing next to Dani. Dominic is there too. I don't like the guy, and he knows it. He treats women like shit and thinks he's the best thing that's ever happened to them just because he can add some numbers. Dani has told me stories about him that make me want to punch him in the face. His gig with women isn't illegal though. Or numbers. If they were, I'd have thrown him in jail. I don't know why she tells Vince and me stuff about him.

Dominic kisses Alexa's hand. She yanks her hand away and wipes it off on her hip. A clear sign she isn't impressed with him. If anything, she looks disgusted.

Her eyes connect with mine, and she nods slightly. She says her goodbyes to everyone and is out the door.

"I'm back. Need another round?" I shout over the loud crowd.

They observe me with peculiar faces. Vince circles his mouth with his finger. "Dude, what's all around your mouth? Did you eat something red? Or is this a new costume?"

I grab a napkin and wipe my mouth. Shit. Her damn red lipstick. Just like on my uniform the other day. *Come up with an excuse quickly.*

"I ate some fries with ketchup on my break. No one told me I had some on my face."

"How much ketchup did you eat? You look like a kid who played in it." He laughs.

Dani glowers at me. "It looks like lipstick to me. Funny, Alexa had some around her mouth just now too. She was in quite a rush to leave when you came back."

Vince laughs. "Yeah, right. He hasn't touched a woman in years."

Now I glower at Vince.

He scratches his chin. "Sorry, bro."

"Going through a dry spell?" Dominic snarks.

Dani tugs on his lavender shirt.

"What are you dressed as, Dominic? A tulip?" I spit back.

He looks down and adjusts his starched collar.

"I wonder if Alexa remembers me. I look a lot better than I did in high school. She's just as hot as she was back then. Too bad she left." He smooths back his over-gelled hair. "I think she's interested in me. Did you see how she checked me out? What do you think, Dani?"

I laugh out loud. *Is he for real?* What did he see that I didn't?

Dominic whips his head in my direction. "What's so funny, Kent? Jealous she's not interested in you?"

I chuckle again. "You might want to change those colored contacts of yours."

He clenches his jaw because he knows I got him on that one. He always denies that he wears them. Even the time when the lens got lodged in the corner of his eye, openly exposing the brown eyes he has. It's so fucking obvious.

"Alexa gave me her phone number. Maybe we can all meet up," Dani suggests, trying to cut the tension.

I shake my head. "Negative. Don't include me in the *all*."

"I wasn't, ya big ogre." She sticks her tongue out at me.

She elbows Dominic. "Maybe I can set up a date between you and Alexa, or we could go on a double date. Don't worry, Dom. I'll work it for you."

The hell she will. Dominic doesn't stand a chance. I doubt Alexa takes shit from anybody.

Including me.

Chapter 7

Alexa

Lisa's dogs bark madly inside the house. I hear some mumbling from Lisa, and then it's quiet. I bend at my knees when the door opens, and Felicia jumps in my arms. My heavy handbag falls off my shoulder. Damn quarters.

"Hi, Aunt Lexa!" She squeezes me tight around the neck.

"I have a lot of money for your piggy bank, young lady. I tried not to swear, but it slipped out too many times. I'm sorry."

We rub noses.

"Felicia, let her get in the door, you little stinker. It's chilly," Lisa says as she takes her daughter from my arms and moves to the side so I can walk through the door.

"I was just telling her that I'm going to make her rich sooner than she thought." I pick up my bag and lift it up and down. "You should feel how heavy my bag is."

Lisa grins as she closes the door. "Why am I not surprised?"

I slip out of my jacket and hang it on the coat rack. Lisa insists guests take off their shoes when they come in. She doesn't want people to track dirt and germs through the house. It doesn't make sense, because she has two dogs. They're worse than people. But I place my shoes to the side in the hallway.

I follow them into the kitchen. "I've had a crazy few weeks, and yesterday was just plain outer limits. I couldn't help it."

"Felicia, why don't you go play with your dolls while I chat with Aunt Alexa." Lisa puts my niece down and pats her lightly on the butt.

"Okay, Mommy," she says as she runs off to the living room.

I pull out a large Ziploc full of quarters. Maybe I should wash my mouth out with soap. I should be embarrassed.

"Here you go. I have no idea how much is in there."

She inspects the bag. "I guess you did have a tough week. I'm going to have to buy Felicia a bigger piggy bank." She chuckles as she lays it on the kitchen counter.

"Is James here? I ran into two people last night he might know from high school. But then again, he was two years ahead of them. I don't remember them myself."

I wish I had my yearbook. It's probably somewhere in a box in the attic at my parents' house. Or maybe in my old room. I haven't looked at it in years.

Lisa plants her arms on the counter. "No," she says with irritation. "He got called in last minute again. They are short on staff in the ER this weekend. I'm all yours."

I sit on one of the kitchen chairs. "Good. We can have girl talk."

Her face brightens. "Anything juicy?" She sets an overflowing laundry basket on one of the kitchen table chairs.

"Want me to help you?"

Lisa places a folded towel on the table. "Not unless you want to fold James's underwear, or mine."

I crinkle my nose. "I'll pass."

"That's what I thought." She smiles.

"Let's get down to it. Is there a new flavor of the month?" She wiggles her eyebrows.

"Kind of. This week was bizarre. Like off-the-charts bizarre, and a new flavor was part of it."

"When is your life not like that? You have the most entertaining social life out of all of us. Not that I'd ever want to go back to being single."

She searches through the basket, and some of the clothes fall out. One of Felicia's lacy pink socks lies there. I pick it up and admire it. Her little clothes are so damn cute. I toss the sock back in the basket.

While trying not to laugh, I tell Lisa everything from the black cat to the bar last night. She has to press her lips together to prevent herself from interrupting or laughing.

"I got a bad vibe from Dominic. I'm going to call him Tongue Boy because he licked my hand and reeked of garlic. And he shook my hand like a girl. Limp like a noodle."

She cracks up. "You and your nicknames for men. And your garlic issues."

"He's not included in *my men*. He is only a man I know. Dr. Wanker isn't someone I went out with, and he has a nickname."

"Okay, okay." She searches for a sock that fell on the floor. She stands back up and throws it on top of the folded clothes.

"I think he also wears blue contacts. It wasn't very bright, but the way the light reflected off them made him look possessed."

"Wait. Who are we talking about? Dominic?"

"Yes. But never mind. You're the psychologist. What's your analysis of Superman?"

She scratches her chin. "Did he really have lipstick all over his face?" she asks with complete seriousness.

I drop my hand on the table. "That's all you have to say? That's your focus?"

"What do you expect when you wear lipstick even when you sleep? How many times do Tina and I and even your mom have to tell you to get the stuff that doesn't come off when you're making out with a guy? Haven't you seen the commercials the last ten years?"

I throw a washcloth at her. "I don't wear lipstick when I sleep, wiseass."

"Okay, I'll admit it's pretty crazy that you ended up at the wrong bar and he was the bartender." She braces herself on the laundry basket. "The part I want to focus on is your ovaries twitching. Are you finally thinking about settling down?"

"How can I settle down when there's no one special in my life? I don't want to date anymore. They all have shit for brains."

Lisa covers her mouth with her finger. There goes another quarter. I mouth *Sorry* and check to see if Felicia is nearby.

"Even when I break things off, they keep coming back for more. Joker the Poker is the latest one, and we only went on one date. He'll probably be another one I have to block on my phone. Thankfully, he doesn't know where I live.

"I don't have the energy anymore for the petty crap that comes with relationships. Yes, kissing Superman was off the charts, but it's beyond obvious he has some major issues. He kind of reminds me of James before he met you. Mr. 'I hate the world and then some.'" I make air quotes.

"I need some water." I push away from the table, walk to the cabinet, and take a glass. "Anyway, forget about him. Halloween got the best of me. But that witch was scary. It's like she looked right through me. She knew something I didn't. Oh, and her cackle was just like the witch on *Wizard of Oz*. It was like nails scraping on a chalkboard." I down the water and lean against the countertop.

Lisa's blond Labradors run into the kitchen, and one sniffs my hand, then licks it. I'd rather a stinky dog lick my hand than Tongue Boy. Lisa opens the door to the garden, and they run out.

"So when are Tina and Gerry coming back from Germany anyway? I miss them," I say.

"Funny that you ask. Tina called me this morning and said she's booked their plane tickets to come for Thanksgiving. They're staying until the New Year." She rubs her hands together in excitement. "I think she's going to tell us she's pregnant."

My eyes bug out. "No way! Really? Don't you think she would've told you already, being her only sister and all?"

"Just a hunch. She has textbook symptoms, but she claims she's working long hours. I'm not stupid." She crosses her arms and leans against the counter. "It'd be so much fun to have a baby around. But

Tina lives in Germany most of the year, so we won't be able to see them often. That means the pressure is on you."

"Well, don't count on me getting pregnant anytime soon. I'm going to be living in the library for the next few months. Not the best place to find my future husband."

I pour out the quarters onto the counter and divide them into piles of four.

"Speaking of the library, I love this new challenge with work. I'm bored with cardiovascular drugs. Cancer therapies are entirely different and so broad in spectrum. The research stimulates my brain. It'll be good for my résumé too.

"That woman, Dani, I just told you about, works at the cancer institute. She offered to help me out and show me around. But not only is she Tongue Boy's sister, she's also friends with Superman. I'm not sure I want to socialize with her if I'll possibly run into them again. I've had enough torture."

"Oh, really." Lisa laughs. "I think you want to be tortured by Superman. You wouldn't have kissed him if you didn't. I know you too well. You like it that he gives you a challenge. Men always fall at your feet, and finally one hasn't."

This is a no-parking zone, but I'm going to take a chance and park anyway. I'm in major need of a Starbucks triple-shot café latte. I left Lisa and James's house early because some of their friends popped over. They're all couples and lovey-dovey. Made me want to vomit. Am I jealous or just getting old?

Maybe Lisa is right. Guys usually fall at my feet and keep coming back for more even if I cut them loose. Superman acts like he hates me, a rare event. But our kiss proved otherwise.

As I get out of my car, I survey both sides of the street for cops. They're cracking down about the parking here. I don't need a ticket. The coast seems clear, so I walk quickly to the Starbucks entrance. It should only take five minutes.

I guess not. There's a line of at least seven people. I've been standing here for ten excruciating minutes as I sway side to side. The barista made a mistake with the person before me, so now I have to wait for that drink to be made again.

Once my name is called, I swipe mine off the counter. I dump some sugar in it and put the lid back on.

"Alexa, baby," I hear from behind me.

I freeze up because it's Poker. A cloud of putrid alcohol breath blows over my shoulder as he coils his arms around my waist from behind. His third leg presses against me. Why does he think he can touch me? How is he hard all the time?

I break out of his embrace. "Don't touch me, Darren," I warn. "Are you drunk? You certainly smell like it. It's the middle of the afternoon."

"Come on, baby. Don't I get a hello? I tried to call you a few times. Didn't you get my messages?" He opens his arms to hug me again. Definitely drunk and clueless.

I press my hand against his chest. "Don't come any closer. I told you I'm not interested." My voice rises, and others can hear me. "Please stop calling me."

"You don't mean that." He puts his arm around me, almost knocking the coffee out of my hand.

I shrug out of his embrace. "What don't you understand? Don't touch me again. I said, leave me alone." The other customers watch as if it's reality TV. No one tries to intervene. Typical.

"Get out of my way, or I'm going to call the police."

"Is everything okay over here?" asks a tall, bulky barista.

"It's fine. I told him to get out of my face. I suggest he does it."

Darren's nostrils flare so fast, he could fly off like a bird.

"Please leave. You're disturbing the customers," the barista says to him.

"No. Don't worry. I'm leaving. He can stay."

I point at Darren's heaving chest. "Do not follow me either."

"You'll regret this," he whispers before I can get away. He's not laughing now.

I escape out the door with my head down as I search for my keys in my pockets. Before I realize what happened, my brand-new coat is covered in coffee and some droplets land on my face and hands. A jogger just whipped by me and hit my hand with the coffee cup in it. Now the Starbucks cup is open on the ground. "Watch where you're going, ass..." I yell, knowing he can't hear me because he's too far away.

Well, isn't this great! I can't win. First Poker, and now this. I shake the warm liquid off my hand. I turn to go back into Starbucks for some napkins and a new coffee, but I refrain because of Poker. More money thrown down the drain. Maybe I have tissues in my car.

As I get closer to my vehicle, my blood boils even more. My head is going to shoot off. A cop stands next to my car, and it looks like he's writing a ticket. I'm convinced I was cursed the other day, and it's continuing into today.

"Hey, hey, hey, Officer," I call out as I rush over. "I'm moving my car now. No need for a ticket."

The cop pushes back his shoulders and turns in my direction. I slow my steps. This has got to be a joke. Superman *is* a real cop.

His eyes flicker when he registers it's me. Those damn chocolatey eyes and uniform. I swear I feel a breeze from his eyelashes every time he blinks. Quivering ovaries disco dance.

"Unbelievable." He shakes his head. "This is your car? Then again, a red Volkswagen Beetle fits you. This is a no-parking zone." He points at the large sign on the sidewalk.

I cock my hip. "Why didn't you tell me you were really a policeman? You made me look like a fool in front of your friends. Aren't you the gentleman."

He stands there with a wide stance. "It's none of your business what I do for a living."

I roll my eyes. "I see the stick is even farther up your ass. I'm surprised it's not coming out your mouth."

"Your pathetic kiss seems to have made it worse."

I take one step forward to invade his space. "You didn't seem to mind it at the time."

"I didn't want to embarrass you," he fires back.

"That's enough!" I don't know if I want to punch him in the face or go at it with him on the hood of my car. "I'm done with this conversation." I stomp to the driver's-side door and hope that a passing car doesn't clip my ass. I probably sound like a horse with the boots I'm wearing. "I've had enough of the psycho in Starbucks and now you. As you can see, I have coffee all over me. A jogger ran into me when I came out of Starbucks," I yell over the roof.

His face softens a tad. "What psycho? Did someone hurt you?"

"Why do you care?" I huff as someone honks his horn. I pull my car door as close to me as possible.

"Because I'm a police officer and should make sure you're okay."

I tilt my head. "And if you weren't one, you probably wouldn't give a shit."

"Bingo," he says with childish enthusiasm.

I smack my hand on the hood. "I feel so sorry for you. Your mother must be so proud. How can anyone stand to be around you? How are you allowed to have a gun in your possession? You should look into some anger-management classes or buy a blow-up doll. I'm outta here."

I get in the car and slam the door.

His knuckles bang on the passenger-side window.

I start the car, shift into drive, and open the window a crack. "This is getting really boring." I lean over the armrest.

His nasty glare makes me want to burst out laughing. He rests his fat fingers on the window glass. Okay, he doesn't have fat fingers, but I'm pissed off and am trying to hate him.

"Please lower your window more."

I growl and do it. "So you do know how to use the word *please*. Can I go home now? As I said, I'm soaked with coffee. Or are you going to pull your gun on me?"

"First of all, *never, ever* talk about my mother. Second, put out your hand."

Aha, hit a sore spot. Good to know for next time. If there will be a next time.

"What? Why? I don't have the time for this." With one hand resting on the steering wheel, I look through the windshield and then back at him. The urge to press the gas pedal and drive off increases by the second.

"Do you always challenge police officers this way? If you do, I'm surprised you aren't in jail. Or let me guess—you bat your long eyelashes and show off your dazzling green eyes so they won't give you a ticket."

He acts it out perfectly, and he's right.

"Now you're harassing me just like the asshole in Starbucks. Or is that what raging cops do nowadays? Please let me go, or I'll report you," I threaten through gritted teeth.

"Well, do as I say. Hold out your hand, or I'll take you to the station and have your car towed. Coffee stains and handcuffs."

I wouldn't mind him using handcuffs on me.

Seriously, Alexa? But Kent plus handcuffs equals enticing. Focus!

"Fine." I extend my arm with the palm up.

He places a folded white piece of paper in it.

"Are you giving me your phone number? Are you crazy? Why would I ever go out with you?" I throw it on the passenger-side floor like I touched a spider. "Adios." I close the window and take off, almost snagging his hand.

Once I park my car in the garage at my apartment building, I open the white piece of paper. My face burns up. It's not his phone number. It's a ticket. Little fucker. Now the score is tied.

Chapter 8

Kent

I fidget in my seat as I drag my hands up and down my thighs. My cheeseburger sits there getting cold.

"Bro, what's up?" Vince asks with fries sticking out his mouth. "You're unusually quiet and stewing over something."

I rest my chest against the table and fold my hands under it. "I ran into that chick Alexa yesterday. I gave her a parking ticket, and man was she pissed."

"No shit," he says as he dumps a huge pile of ketchup onto his burger.

"Three times now, to be exact."

"When are you going to admit you kissed her? That whole ketchup excuse was a load of shit, but I didn't want to get into it in front of Dani and her brother. She tried to get info from me, but I claimed you denied having anything to do with Alexa."

I point my thumb at my chest. "She kissed me, and it pissed me off because I liked it and kissed her back. I don't know the last time I even got laid, let alone kissed a woman. She backed away first and just walked off. She's nuts. Every time we've been together, we're at each other's throats. We can't say one nice thing to each other. The tension and heat between us could melt a glacier. She seems to hate me even more now that she knows I'm a cop."

"That sounds like your normal self. So what's the problem?"

I sit back and cross my arms. "She doesn't take my shit and gives it right back. Not something I'd expect from a woman like her. She seems to like the challenge as much as I do."

He freezes just as he goes to bite his burger. "A woman like her? What's that supposed to mean?"

"Someone who gets whatever she wants, has luck on her side, who knows nothing about suffering, or has a lot of money. Get my drift? She's my exact opposite."

"Maybe that's what you need. Do you really want to hang out with someone just as miserable as you?"

I shrug and shove a cold, soggy french fry into my mouth.

"Not that this is a news flash, but you can be a big downer more often than not. You need someone to show you the brighter side of things. Maybe someone who can bring back the old you."

"You know me, Vince. I can figure people out quickly. She's tough as nails, to the point it's almost attractive."

Most of the time I read people well. When I graduated from the police academy, my main goal was to become a detective. I love gathering facts and collecting evidence to solve a case. I'm good at connecting the dots. I've had the opportunity to assist in a couple of cases with other detectives. I put that plan on hold when my sister was diagnosed with breast cancer. Now she's close to finishing her treatments, and once she's healthier and I'm convinced she can make it on her own, I'll focus on my future again.

"Dude, you've only seen her a couple of times. You don't know her at all, but something tells me you want to get to know her better. Opposites do attract."

I run my hand through my hair. "I have no idea what's going on with me. Ever since I met Alexa, I feel like something has changed in me. It's like her positivity was injected into my blood. She sucks you into her realm of charm. It's infectious. I'm fighting it."

"What the hell for? You've got to stop making yourself miserable. Do you ever think about how you bring your sister down with you when you're always thinking she's going to die any second?" He takes a deep breath. "I know why you do it. But everybody deserves to know what it's like to be happy."

"I never said I was happy," I grumble.

Vince shimmies out of the diner booth. "Hey, babe," he says to Dani as he kisses her.

"You guys ate already?" She pouts, then flicks her hair.

It's annoying how she flicks her hair all the time. One time a chunk of it got stuck in Vince's mouth.

"You're a half an hour late. You know that, right?" Vince laughs.

She scoots over and sits across from me. "Kent told me to meet you guys here at twelve thirty."

"Did I? My fault. Sorry." I'm not really, because I did say twelve thirty. I wanted to talk to Vince alone, as I haven't seen him since Friday night. I don't want to talk about Alexa or any woman in front of Dani. She has a big mouth, and she thinks she knows everything. If I say anything of interest, I'm sure it will go directly to Alexa.

Dani rests her chin in her hand. "Vince, I was thinking."

"Oh no. That's always bad when your head spins like a Ferris wheel." He massages his forehead but cracks a smile.

She elbows him playfully. "Dominic thinks it's his big chance to finally go out with Alexa. He thinks it's fate. Maybe we can set up a double date, or I could go out to dinner with her and then you and Dominic show up unexpectedly."

Vince drapes his arm over the back of the booth. "Do you think Alexa would like him? Dominic's a bit of a womanizer," Vince mentions lightly. "And he and I don't hang out, so I'm not going to pretend like we do."

She doesn't like it when we talk badly about Dominic. Little does she know that Vince and I hate to be around him.

"I don't know. It's not like I'm best friends with her. That's for her to decide. But I'd do it for Dom. Alexa said we should get together soon anyway."

"Speaking of Alexa, Kent ran into her again yesterday. He gave her a ticket."

She shoves my arm. "No way. Was she speeding?"

I shake my head. "She parked in a no-parking zone. I was in the middle of preparing the ticket when she came back. She didn't take it too well."

"Who would? I'm sure you weren't the friendliest cop either. Thank God you didn't know she works for Quadro. You would've probably thrown her into jail."

I hate pharmaceutical companies and the healthcare system. I'm convinced there's a cure for cancer out there, but since the big pharmas would lose a lot of money, they don't tell anyone. So the price of healthcare is sky high.

My mom died of breast cancer three years ago. All the chemo and radiation she went through did absolutely nothing. It made her last months of life utterly miserable. She didn't look or act like the strong, beautiful woman I knew. Cancer sucked every living cell out of her, and I had to watch knowing I couldn't do anything about it.

Now I'm watching my sister go through the same thing. Her breast cancer was caught much earlier though. The doctors say she'll survive, but I won't believe it until I see it. It's hard for me to see the two most important women in my life suffer.

"When did you find this out?" I snap.

"At the bar on Friday night. When you took a break, I believe. I mentioned where I worked. One thing led to another, and she told me about her job."

"What does she do there?"

"She's a sales rep and might be moved to oncology. She's studying oncology for work. I offered to help her out, to get some info from the medical side of things. Maybe I should suggest she talk to Abby."

"Hell no. Don't go there, Dani. You know how much I despise everything about the pharma industry." *Now I have a good reason to despise Alexa too.* "I won't allow a sales rep to convince Abby to try new drugs or interventions. They only want her to be their guinea pig. She has one chemo treatment left. Just leave it."

"I know you hate them, but that doesn't mean Alexa is a bad person. If I want to help her, I will."

"Do what you want, but keep her away from Abby."

And me.

Chapter 9

Alexa

It's been one week without anything out of the ordinary happening. No black cats, witches, or parking tickets. I think my curse is over. I just had two successful sales meetings, so it's time to treat myself to some éclairs. My last visit to Matt's café, Belle Vie, was when I gave my éclairs to the beast. I catch myself looking for him every time I see a police car. But he hasn't been popping up anywhere. It's too bad, because I'm craving some eye candy.

As usual, it's packed in the café. The smell of freshly baked éclairs and other treats tease my nose. I'm in seventh heaven every time I walk in here. Matt recently moved his bakery from New York City to Hoboken, New Jersey. The space is large enough to not only be a bakery but a traditional French café too. Unfortunately, it's located a couple of blocks from my apartment. Now I'm always tempted. The size of my waist is going to double if I don't stop coming here so often.

I inspect my newly manicured fingernails while waiting in the long line to the counter. On a typical day, I would head right to the back, but I don't see Matt or his wife, Kayla, anywhere.

"Hey, Alexa! Back again?" Matt greets me as he walks out of the kitchen. "Come on back and take your pick. You know the routine. I just made a batch of your favorite éclairs."

Matt isn't technically family, but he's close enough. He's been James's best friend since they were kids. I'm the little sister Matt never had. They tortured me when we were young.

I do as he says with a smile on my face and watch him approach a young woman sitting at a table facing the window. She turns in his direction and smiles. No way. It's her. The woman from the hospital. She wears her cherry-colored head scarf like it's a fashion statement. Love it! I've got to meet her.

Matt walks back toward me and tugs my arm to follow him. I peek over my shoulder at the woman. She watches him and then looks at me. She smiles so bright that it lights up the room. I think I have a girl crush.

As we get farther in the back, I ask him, "Who was that girl? The one with the red—" I swirl my hand around my head.

"Oh, that's Abby. She's one of our regulars. Kayla loves her." His face loses its usual sparkle. "I don't know every detail, but she told Kayla she has breast cancer. Her appetite comes back ferociously once she gets over a round of chemo."

"How sad. She looks so young." I look toward the window again. "I thought maybe that was why."

"I'll introduce you. Just give me a second," he says while washing his hands. "From what Kayla has told me, she seems pretty open about her health and what she's been through. Maybe it would be helpful for you to talk to someone who has cancer."

I hand him some paper towels.

"So where's Kayla today?"

His eyes focus on a massive bag of flour instead of me. "She didn't feel well when she woke up this morning. I told her to stay home. For sanitary reasons, she shouldn't be here. I don't want to hear a customer got sick because of the food I made."

I don't question him, but I wonder if she's pregnant. That would be awesome if both Tina and Kayla were pregnant at the same time. There would be more babies to spoil rotten.

"Before I get back to work, let me introduce you to Abby. Then come back and take what you want." He fills a sparkling silver bowl with flour.

I wave away the flour swirling around in the air.

We squeeze through the tables, banging into some chairs. Abby turns in our direction. Her face brightens as she stands up.

"Hi, Abby. Sorry to interrupt again. I want to introduce you to someone."

She approaches me with ease and extends her hand.

"Alexa, this is Abby. She's one of our regulars and loves to come here to eat some sweet treats and do crossword puzzles. Now Kayla and I are doing them with her in our spare time. It's become a new obsession of ours."

I shake her hand and grin at her like she's my idol. Why? "Hi. I saw you at the hospital. Do...do you remember me?" Since when am I nervous around someone? Especially a woman.

"Yes, I remember you. Are you a regular also?"

"She's my best friend's sister," Matt chimes in. "I've known her since she wore pigtails. And if you want to get a little more complicated, Kayla's cousin, Gerry, is married to Alexa's sister-in-law's sister, Tina. We are quite the twisted bunch." Matt elbows me while Abby chuckles.

"Alexa, do you want your usual? One mini salted caramel éclair, one double-chocolate mousse, and a large cappuccino?"

"Yes. I'm starving. I'll go get it."

"My brother loves those too," Abby adds.

Matt pulls out a chair. "Sit and talk to Abby. I'll be right back."

"Thanks, but I can do it."

He holds up his hand. "I know, but I'd like to do it. Abby, do you need anything else?"

She shakes her head.

He clears some dirty dishes off a few tables along the way and greets some customers.

I hang my coat and handbag over the back of the chair.

"Abby, I have to say, that head scarf looks gorgeous on you. You have such a beautiful face. That color red is my favorite. My car is that color. My lipstick. My nails." I wiggle my fingers.

"Thank you." She giggles and touches it with her hand. "That just made my day. I'm so used to wearing them. I've made them in every color. But yellow is my favorite. The bright yellow with a hint of orange that brightens everything like the sun. I need it when I'm having a bad day. I have my last chemo treatment right before Thanksgiving. Hopefully, my hair will start to grow back quickly after that."

"You make them yourself? How cool."

She stuffs her hands under her legs. "Before I got diagnosed with breast cancer, I worked for a small clothes designer. I went to school for design. Since I stopped working, I make these in my spare time. It keeps me busy. I don't have the money to buy a good wig."

"I'm sorry you're sick. I didn't mean to bring it up. I was hoping your scarf was just for fashion. You surely can pull it off. You should sell them."

"I don't have a problem talking about it. It is what it is. I'm just lucky it was caught in time."

"Do you mind me asking how old you are?"

"Not at all. Twenty-nine."

My hand goes straight to my heart. "Wow, you're so young. I can't even imagine. I'm so sorry. I've been researching cancer treatments. It's a huge amount of information. Each cancer case is handled differently depending on the person. I'm beyond overwhelmed."

She grabs my hand. "Please don't tell me you have cancer too?"

"No, no, no. It's for my job. I'm a pharmaceutical sales rep."

Her face crinkles.

"What's the matter?"

"Don't let my brother hear that. He hates pharma companies and the healthcare system in general. Oh, and hospitals. No, wait. He pretty much hates everything. Well, except me and a couple of his friends." She chuckles. "He thinks they're all out to screw us. Conspiracy theory. He was just here, but he had to leave for work."

Her phone rings on the table. "Speak of the devil." She lifts up her finger. "Excuse me for a second."

"No problem." I relax in my chair and pick up one of the crossword puzzle books. I scan it to see if I know any of the answers. Almost the entire book is finished.

Abby leans away from me and covers her ear. "What's up, big brother? You forgot your wallet again? That's like three times now. Let me check, but I doubt I have it. Why would you give it to me in the first place? Hold on a sec." She lays her phone on the table and searches through her enormous bag. Out come two other crossword puzzle books with crinkled edges, several pens and pencils, a mini crossword puzzle dictionary, sunglasses, package of tissues, lip gloss, hand cream, and another head scarf.

"Wow. It is in my bag." She smiles at me and picks up her phone.

"I got it. Okay. See you in a few." She stuffs everything back in her bag.

"Sorry about that. I don't know how I ended up with his wallet. If I knew I had it, I would've gone shopping. He'll be here in a few minutes. I can introduce you, but leave out the part about working for a pharma company." She pretends to slit her throat.

I swivel in my chair. "I'm going to find Matt. He never came back with my éclairs, and I'm ready to faint from starvation. I'll be right back."

I walk around the counter and notice he's on the phone. I wait a few minutes to see if he gets off. I finally give up and go back out front but stop in my tracks. Oh man. There's Dr. Wanker standing in line and Superman standing at the door, putting his sunglasses on. I swear Dr. Wanker is following me. But then again, maybe Superman is too.

I'm in clear view from both sides. I have nowhere to run without making a total ass out of myself. Too late. Dr. Wanker sees me and flashes me that sleazy smile that makes me lose my appetite. Oh no, he's coming this way. What do I do next? I know what to do, but this might totally backfire. I never thought I'd be so excited to see Superman again. Well, maybe I did. He's looking mighty fine in that sexy uniform.

Chapter 10

Kent

My eyes are screwing with me. It's so damn bright in here. I put my sunglasses back on.

"Kent! Lovebug. I'm over here. I just ordered your favorite éclairs."

Lovebug? It can't be. Why do I keep running into her? I want to hate her, but when I see her glowing face, it's impossible not to be sucked in deeper.

She swerves through the chairs and runs up to me. Her arms wrap around my neck like a soft scarf, and her glossy lips connect with my cheek. It tingles just like every time she touches me, but this time I don't want the sensation to stop.

"Just follow my lead, Superman. I need your help," she whispers. A waft of her sweet, fruity perfume teases my nose, making me high like a cat playing with catnip. *Ignore it.*

I take off my sunglasses. I'm sure this will be entertaining.

"Hi, Dr. Walker. Funny seeing you here. Let me introduce you to my boyfriend, Kent. He's a police officer here in Hoboken." She wraps her arms around my waist and snuggles into my side. My entire body is inflamed, and it feels better than I want to admit. Thankfully, my pants are thick, and I have a lot of things hanging from my belt.

Boyfriend?

Dr. Walker hesitates. "Your boyfriend?" He steps closer and shakes my hand. "Nice to meet you, Officer. Good for you. Alexa's quite the catch."

Is this man for real? He's got to be at least twenty-five years older than her. He licks his lips and eyes her like a piece of raw steak. Now I understand.

"She is, isn't she?"

She looks up at me in surprise, but I hesitate to kiss her on her red, hot lips. I aim for her cheek instead. I can't ignore the euphoric pleasure clouding my brain though. I'm supposed to hate her.

"Good to see you, Alexa. I'm going to get back in line."

"Bye," she says with fake interest.

Once he's back in line, she tugs on my jacket and whispers, "I'm so sorry. I have this weird feeling he's following me. I needed to do that to scare him. You came in at the perfect time. Thank you."

Following her? First the guy at Starbucks and now this old man. Does she attract assholes? I guess so, because I'm one of them.

"Excuuuuse me. Alexa, are you dating my brother?" Abby's voice hits a high octave. "Kent, you never told me you have a girlfriend." She crosses her arms, and her eyes narrow. "How long has this been going on?"

My head whips to Alexa, and I let go of her. "No, she most definitely is *not* my girlfriend," I spit out and take a step away from her.

Alexa slaps my arm. "Be quiet and stop treating me like I have a venereal disease."

"Do you?"

Her face turns blood red from anger. Wax could melt off of it. *Good. But I have no idea why I like to piss her off so much. She makes it so easy.*

"Can we please go outside to talk about this? We're making a scene," Alexa suggests with a firm, low voice. "Kayla and Matt wouldn't like it, and I don't want anyone to hear us."

"You know Matt and Kayla?"

"Yes. Is that a problem for you too?" she snidely responds over her shoulder.

They grab their jackets as Alexa urges us out the door.

"But I don't understand. How do you two know each other?" Abby questions us from behind as we step out of the café. I turn around and see the hint of a smirk while she buttons her coat. She's getting the wrong idea.

"We..."

Alexa pinches my arm like a little girl on a playground would.

"What the hell was that for?"

"Excuse me. I'll answer this." She turns her back on me as she tells Abby the entire story about us, with her arms flying around in animation. Abby's face lights up with amusement. Well, she left out the kiss. I still replay it in my mind, but I'll never admit it.

I glance at my watch. "Am I needed for this conversation? I just want my wallet. My shift starts in thirty minutes."

"So that's why you've been so distracted lately," Abby presses me.

"Isn't he always distracted? Oh, wait. I mean pissed off." Alexa chuckles.

Why is that funny?

"Yes, that too. But he's distracted more than usual. He's been forgetting his wallet, as you have witnessed. He doesn't remember what he's talking about, goes to the gym more often, and stares into space." She giggles. "That's cool that you know Vince and Dani. And Matt and Kayla. Small world."

They change the subject of conversation every two seconds. Nice to see Abby is enjoying this. They talk like two old ladies. Maybe I can escape without them noticing. At this point, I'm willing to forget about my wallet.

"Can I interrupt your boring conversation? I wouldn't get your hopes up that my forgetfulness is because of her. She's a sales rep for a fucking pharma company."

Alexa's head whips toward mine, and Abby's eyes turn into saucers.

"How do you know that? Did you do a background check on me or something? If you did, I'm going to kick your ass."

"Pipe down there, Rocky. Dani told me."

She holds her hand up. "Wait a second. Why were you even talking about me? And don't you dare tell me to pipe down."

"Anyone who supports the pharma industry is an enemy, in my book. I should've known just by your personality. Are you always so chipper and friendly, or is that an act for your job? You don't care what you're selling as long as you make a buck. You probably have no idea what misery is."

I just went too far.

Abby barges in between us. "That's enough, Kent."

Alexa steps around Abby. "Oh. Don't you worry. I can handle this."

She stabs me in the chest with her finger. I think it's a good idea I'm wearing a bulletproof vest. "Now you listen here, pig with a gun. I may have a pretty face, but you can bet your ass that's not why I'm good at my damn job. Just like any other guy, you don't look past it. Oh, she's blond...she's just stupid and flirts her way through life."

She pokes me again in the chest, making me step backward.

"Every single thing I have is because I worked my ass off for it. No one gave it to me. If I wanted to marry a rich guy and live off his money, I could have. But I have respect for myself. So don't you dare judge me and try to bring me down because you're fucking miserable. I'm proud of what I do, and I don't have to explain myself to idiots like you." Alexa steps back but then forward again. "And you aren't the only one in this world that has seen family members suffer, so take your pity party somewhere else." She storms back to the café.

Crack. I press my stinging cheek. Abby just smacked me across the face.

"Go and apologize to her right now. I can't believe you just did that. I've been putting up with your bullshit attitude for way too long. I know why you're like this, and I try to be sympathetic, but to see you verbally attack Alexa is beyond forgivable. It's like you're blaming her for all that has happened to Mom and me. I'm not six feet under, and I don't plan to be for a long time. So wake up and join the living."

I'm speechless. This is fucking crazy. I glance behind me and see Alexa talking to Matt in front of the café. He scowls like a dad would when trying to protect his child, then they both walk back in.

"I love you, but you scare me, Kent. You have severe issues that you need to deal with. If you don't, you will eventually lose everything and everyone."

She bumps my shoulder with hers as she rushes past me. I turn to look at her. Before she goes back inside, she glances my way. "I don't know how I know this, but you finally met your match. Don't screw it up."

I remain frozen in my spot, trying to digest what just happened and what I said to Alexa. I have never spoken to someone like that ever in my life. I just hit rock bottom.

"And by the way, you have a lipstick mark on your cheek." She snickers.

Son of a bitch. I rub my fingers down my cheeks and examine them. Sure enough, bright-red lipstick. Third time's the charm.

"I'll see you tomorrow." With my head down, I walk away filled with regret. Abby's right. I need to get my head out of the sand, and I need to apologize to Alexa. But not now. We both need time to cool off.

I stop at the end of the block. I still don't have my wallet.

Chapter 11

Alexa

My heart pounds in my ears. The nerve of him. I swear I'd love to ram a stick up his ass, but he already has so many up there, I'm not sure it would fit.

"Alexa, trouble in paradise?" Dr. Wanker snickers. "I saw you fighting with your boyfriend. If he really is your boyfriend." He meddles like a slimeball, then coughs up a lung into a napkin. So foul.

"Of course he's my boyfriend, but that's none of your business."

A flash of enjoyment dances in his eyes. "If you need someone to talk to, give me a call." He reaches his hand out with a business card.

I step back. "I'm fine. Please leave me alone."

"As you wish," he says as he bows, then leaves the café.

He's wigging me out. I don't like it that I've seen him a couple of times within a few weeks.

I massage my eyebrows. Why can't I be on a deserted island by myself? Now I know I'm cursed. I've never had such a fiery conflict with someone like I do with Kent. I either want to kill him or rip his clothes off. I'd rather the second, but either could cause bodily harm. I chuckle to myself.

Abby darts toward me. "Alexa, I'm so sorry about my brother. There's no excuse for him to treat you like that. I'm mortified."

She speed talks without taking a breather. It's hard to keep up with her. I place my hands gently on her shoulders. "Slow down. Deep breaths. In and out. In and out." I mimic her movements.

After one big exhale, she composes herself and adjusts her outfit.

"Are you okay now? You shouldn't apologize for him. It's not your fault. He just needs a severe beating. He's not the only person who hates the pharma industry. I've heard it all before."

Her eyes droop with sadness. They have the same eyes.

"I hate getting personal since we've just met, and I know it's absolutely none of my business, but what happened to him that makes him act like that? Is it because you have cancer, or is there something else?"

Abby motions to our chairs and we sit down.

Two mini éclairs wait for me on the table, but I can't stomach them right now. My cappuccino is probably too cold to drink. Caffeine is a major no-go right now with the overdose of adrenaline pumping through my veins.

"My dad ran off with some bimbo when I was six. Kent was twelve. Dad moved to Las Vegas, and we never heard from him again. Even today I still don't understand how he could do that to my mom or his kids. Mom was the happiest, sweetest, most selfless person you'd ever meet. She was beyond beautiful. Three years ago, she died of breast cancer. It was caught too late. She rarely went for checkups. After being diagnosed, she had a double mastectomy, hysterectomy, chemo, and radiation. Nothing worked because it was too aggressive and spread quickly to her lymph nodes and the rest of her body." Her eyes are focused on something over my shoulder.

"We watched her change into a completely different person. It sucked out her beauty and replaced it with emptiness. We hardly recognized her at the end." Her eyes fill with tears, and her attention switches to me.

I squeeze her hand. "I'm sorry. You don't have to say anything else."

"I try to remember what she was like before she was diagnosed. She was a strong, independent woman. Even at six years old, I knew she was heartbroken, but she kept it hidden from us as much as possible. She was always there for us. She was our sunrise. Always bright and gave us a home filled with love. But as I said, cancer changed everything. Darkness set in."

"Did you get tested for the BRCA1 or 2 gene mutation? Did your mom have it?"

"By surprise, I don't have the genes, and neither did my mom. It was pure coincidence that I was diagnosed with breast cancer too. Once Mom was diagnosed, I was diligent with my annual breast exams."

I'm so glad I had my last checkup during the summer.

I let out a long sigh and sit up in my chair. "I'm really sorry that you've both suffered so much. Now I can see why Kent is the way he is. I'm not saying it's okay how he just went off on me, but it helps me understand him better. It's amazing how people handle situations differently."

She nods gently as she applies lip balm to her lips.

"How are you so cheerful? Not many people would be like you."

"I can't waste my life being miserable and always wondering why me, why my family. That seems to be Kent's job. I'm a breast cancer survivor. Granted, I'm not out of the woods until I'm at least five years cancer-free, but I'm going to claim it now. Chemo is beyond horrible, and there are days I have no energy to get out of bed. The fatigue is unlike anything I've ever felt. I don't even want to talk about losing my hair and having a double mastectomy, but if being positive is what it takes for me to survive, I'll do it. I want to live every day like it's my last. Cancer has opened my eyes to what's truly important. My mom suffered so much more than me. I don't deserve to complain."

She points to the salted caramel éclair in front of us. "Now éclairs are important. They make my day a little bit sweeter."

She chuckles as I break off a piece and offer it to her. She puts it in her mouth, and I take a big bite of my piece too.

I slowly chew and savor the sweet-salty combination. I try to enjoy it as if it were the last one I'd eat.

"Enough about me. What's going on with you and my brother?" she asks with a naughty grin.

I inhale a crumb. "What do you mean? We can't stand each other," I reply between coughs.

"Let me be the judge of that." She perks up in her chair and looks behind me.

"Kent?" she says with surprise.

I hunch down in my seat and pretend to work on a crossword puzzle. I don't want to give him any attention, but it takes everything in me not to make a peep. Even though he's a total ass, I can't help but enjoy our banter. It's fun to have someone challenge me. It sounds ridiculous, but it is. The tension between us is just warming up. Soon it will boil over. I look forward to when that happens.

"I forgot to take my wallet from you. Can I have it please?" he says with a softer tone than before.

Abby searches through her bag again. She finally finds it and hands it to him.

"Thanks."

He stands so close to me that his thigh almost touches my shoulder. But I still don't acknowledge his presence. Even though I have goosebumps under my long sleeves. *Do not react!*

"Number four across." His thigh slightly brushes against my shoulder.

I look up at him. "Huh?" *You suck at this.*

"Number four across on the puzzle. Try *regretful*." His eyes droop like a puppy dog's.

Is this his way of saying he's sorry? Because it's kind of working for him.

His gaze flickers to Abby. "See you. Call me if you need anything." He's out the door in seconds.

Abby and I study each other without words to see if we agree on what just happened. I check what the clue for four across is and am not surprised it has nothing to do with the word *regretful*. We both nod with silent agreement.

The next minutes are spent munching on éclairs and laughing like we're old friends. I like her. It's amazing how positive and courageous she is. I picture her fitting in with Lisa and Tina. She's already friends with Kayla and Matt.

"I love it that you called him Superman. And lovebug. That was hysterical. You should've seen his face when you called him that. Like a deer in headlights."

"I feel bad that I did that, but I had to. The man I introduced Kent to is someone I don't want near me." I explain why I'm uncomfortable around Wanker. "Kent swooped in at the perfect time with his uniform on. It also helps that he's drop-dead gorgeous." My voice drifts off.

Abby stands up. "We're having so much fun that I forgot I was meeting someone here."

"Dani." She waves. "Over here."

I swivel in my chair.

Dani smiles, but then her forehead creases in confusion as she walks over to us. "Alexa, what are you doing here?"

"It's weird, right?" Abby says as she hugs Dani.

"Alexa, how do you know Abby?"

We sit together, and I tell her everything that's happened since I saw her on Halloween. She can't stop laughing. Abby fills her in on my fight with Kent.

Dani glances at me and says, "Wow. You must have wanted to punch him."

I lean back in my chair. "I walked away before it got to that point. I've heard it before, just not in such an abrupt way. Like it's my fault."

It bothered me a teeny-tiny bit. Usually, I don't care what people think of me. It's how I've always been. My life has been easier because of this one trait. Most people are controlled by what others think about them. My motto is "take it or leave it." I refuse to mold myself into someone else just to get a person's approval.

"I don't know," Abby says. "My analysis—and I could be way off base since we were only together for a few minutes—is that he was mean only to push you away. He's afraid of women because our mom died and now I have cancer just like she did. There's a fear it will happen to any woman he cares about. He doesn't interact with any women unless he has to. Well, Dani, you're the only female he talks to, but he looks at you like a sister."

"You think he likes Alexa?" Dani asks in shock. "Like really likes her? It sounds like he acted the way he always does with women."

"I think Kent likes Alexa and her sassiness. She stuck up for herself quite nicely. It was badass. I was in awe. It's too bad you missed it."

"No offense, Alexa, but I don't think he'll ever be interested in any woman. Not even a woman like you."

I lean forward. "A woman like me? What exactly is that supposed to mean?"

She tosses her frizzy long brown hair over her shoulder. "It's not an insult. You're too beautiful for him. Different class, too." She waves a hand at me. "Look at you. You like fancy clothes, name-brand handbags, and you drive your cutesy red Beetle." She flicks my hair. "Blond hair and red lipstick."

Dani's pissing me off. She doesn't have a clue who I am or what I'm like. Just because we went to the same high school years ago doesn't mean she knows me now. I didn't interact with her then. But then again, I shouldn't care.

"How do you know what kind of car I drive?"

"I had lunch with Kent the other day. He told me he gave you a ticket. And how much you pissed him off."

"Oh, and he's a real angel? I'm not a fan of the whole angry-cop act he's got going on. Don't even get me started."

Dani claps her hands with a mischievous grin. "Forget about Kent. Let's talk about my brother, Dom. He's a whiz in finance and works in Manhattan."

A.k.a....boring.

"He wants to see you again since he didn't have time to talk to you on Halloween."

Just enough time to lick me though.

I glance at Abby, and she's eyeing Dani in surprise, but not in a good way. "What's up, Abby?" *This should be good.*

"I don't know, Dani. Dominic doesn't have the best track record when it comes to women. From what you've told me anyway. Do you really think it's a good idea?"

"Of course. He's my twin brother. She's all he talks about. They went to the same high school, so it's not like they're complete strangers. It only takes one woman to change a man." She nudges me playfully.

I shake my head. "I'm not here to change anybody, so no thanks. I've written off men for a while. Freaks are coming out of the cracks left and right."

Dani gasps.

"Not that Dominic is a freak. I just need a break."

"Are you at least attracted to him? Most women are."

"Let's throw him a party then. If he has such a long line of women waiting for him, he can pick one of them. Even if I found him attractive, I find a lot of guys attractive. Even Kent is. But that doesn't mean I want to go out with them."

She's annoying me, so I threw that out to piss her off. No one forces someone on me—I don't care how good he looks.

Dani's face brightens, and she says, "Let's go out one night. How about next week?"

"Only if it's you and me. I'm not interested in being fixed up with anyone."

Chapter 12

Kent

Like homemade cookies, the smell of bacon always draws me to the kitchen. Abby's making breakfast, her favorite meal of the day. She takes advantage of eating between treatments. Only one left. She's been a powerhouse through this entire situation. Unlike me, who's been a mess and only shows it by being an asshole to innocent people.

I haven't had the chance to speak to Abby about what happened the other day with Alexa. I also needed to process what they'd said to me.

"Good morning. I hope there's enough bacon for me."

"There sure is. I made two packages this time. Any leftovers can be for BLTs." She opens a cabinet and takes out two plates. "Please set the table and put some bread in the toaster."

I place the plates on the small kitchen table Mom bought years ago. We need a new one, but we don't have the heart to get rid of this one. Refinishing it is on my to-do list. I drop four pieces of wheat bread into the toaster.

"How are you feeling today?" I drape my arm over her shoulders and squeeze her to my side. "You're not too cold without something on your head?" I kiss her temple.

It took me a while to get used to Abby losing her hair. It was the same with Mom. They both had thick, wavy hair like mine. You read about how people who suffer from cancer lose their hair, but it doesn't sink in until you see it with your own eyes. I hope I never have to see it again.

"I'm good. I had enough energy to do yoga when I woke up. The countdown has begun. You know I can't stand this yo-yo effect. I just want my life to go back to normal. Whatever normal means."

She flips a sizzling strip. "So where have you been? Hiding or adding more shifts?"

"Both, I guess." I grab forks and knives from a drawer and set them next to the plates. "I arrested two drunk people last night. One female driver who crashed into a parked car. Her blood alcohol level was over 0.10 percent. Thankfully, no one was injured. Then I arrested a man pissing on his neighbor's front lawn."

She giggles while cracking an egg on the side of the frying pan, and then another. "I'd rather you deal with situations like that than crazy people shooting their guns."

"Me too."

I love my job, but it does scare me that one day I'll be in a position where I have to shoot someone. I've had to pull out my gun to threaten someone, but I've never had to pull the trigger. I've seen an increase in violence lately, but situations were diffused quickly with little force from the police. I don't tell Abby everything, because I don't want to scare her, but deep down inside she knows what my job entails.

"Sunny-side up like usual?"

"Do you even have to ask?" I tap her hip with mine.

We chuckle as I reach for the coffeepot. While I pour some in my favorite old gray mug that was waiting for me, she places her empty lemon-yellow cup next to mine and refills it with steaming green tea.

As I'm about to drink my first sip, she asks, "Did you conclude that you were completely out of line with Alexa and you want her to have your babies?"

I slouch like a little kid getting reprimanded by his parents. "Yes," I confess. My head shoots up. "Wait. What? You're crazy. I meant yes to being out of line." I knew she'd have us married off with kids already.

"Ha. Gotcha on that one. Here's the bacon. Go sit down."

I place a couple of strips on my plate and drop into my chair. "Why do I have the feeling that isn't all you're going to say?"

She slides an egg onto my plate like a pro. "Because you know me so well." She laughs.

That I do. We balance each other. Even though she's going through hell, she stays grounded and has a positive outlook. She's calm when I'm agitated, she's nice when I'm mean, and she's pleasant when I'm pissed off.

Deep down inside, I'm petrified of losing my sister. She's the only family I have left. My parents had no siblings, and our grandparents passed away years ago. My dad is as good as dead since he never makes contact with us. He didn't even come to Mom's funeral. I want nothing to do with him anyway. For all I know, he could be dead too.

"I like Alexa. We ended up hanging out at the café for two hours or so. She's not a sleazy sales rep like you think she is...or who you're trying to convince yourself she is. Dani was there too. It was nice to have girl time."

"How does Alexa know Kayla and Matt anyway? Just through the café?" I calmly ask as I eat a large forkful of eggs.

She places her fork on her plate. "Matt is best friends with Alexa's brother. They've known each other since they were kids. Kayla's cousin is married to Alexa's sister-in-law's sister."

That's a brainteaser. I drink more coffee so I don't have to talk.

"You're quiet, so I guess I'll keep talking. After Dani and Alexa left, I stayed a few minutes longer and hung out with Matt. He told me a little bit about Alexa. She's protective of her family and friends, generous, and extremely confident but not a show-off. It's more that she's an intelligent, independent woman, which can be intimidating."

"And you forgot to add she hates the police."

"I don't think she hates the police. Just you." She covers her mouth to hide her obvious smirk.

I sneer at her.

"She didn't talk about it much. Maybe it's something you should talk about with her. You have the wrong picture of her and she of you. But..."

I wag my finger. "Nuh-uh. No buts."

"She sure gives you a challenge," she says anyway. She peeks at me over her cup while she drinks her tea.

"And what's your point? What did they tell you?"

She puts down her cup. "I knew you'd talk now. Dani asked Alexa a question about you two, and it made me wonder. Alexa denied it."

"Are you going to tell me or not?" I huff.

She giggles. "Dani asked if you and Alexa had kissed at Joe's bar."

I lean away from the table and cross my arms. "Why would she ask Alexa that?"

I shouldn't sit with my arms crossed, because it gives off the wrong body language. In my profession, it's important to understand the meaning of body language to judge what a person is feeling or going to do. With my arms crossed, I'm on the defense.

She laughs again. "Dani said you both looked like identical clowns that night. There were lipstick marks on your faces after you were both away from the bar at the same time. Maybe something similar to the lipstick mark on your cheek the other day." She grins.

I don't know if I should tell her. She'll make it out to be more than it is, and then it'll be blown out of proportion. She'll have us married next week. And she'll end up being right.

"Well, did you? It'd be so unlike you, but I'd love it if you did." Her smile grows wide, with a bacon bit stuck to the corner of her mouth. I motion with my finger to alert her that it's there.

Do I tell her the truth? She deserves nothing but the truth about everything I do.

I purge a long breath and brush my hand through my damp hair. "Fine. In all honesty, she kissed me. Right after she told me I had a giant stick up my ass." I point my finger at her. "And don't tell Dani that. It's none of her business."

She wriggles in her chair and squeals. "You have several. I love Alexa even more now."

I rub my face and groan.

"I've only seen her a couple of times. I've never known someone with so much confidence and attitude. It drives me nuts. But it makes her even more attractive."

"Matt described her perfectly then. Did you kiss her back, or did you stop her?"

I push my plate away. "I really don't want to talk to my sister about kissing a woman."

"Who cares. Give me some juicy stuff to think about during my last chemo treatment."

"That's not funny. But yes, I kissed her back. I almost shoved her away, but I couldn't help myself."

It's been an eternity since I've kissed a woman. Women flirt with me, but I don't react. Nothing clicks. But it's for the better.

My mom once told me that one day, a woman will knock me blind and my life will never be the same. Our souls will collide, binding us together for the rest of our lives. I didn't believe her at the time because if she had that with my dad, they would've stayed together. How could she tell me these things when she never experienced it herself? It makes me both sad and angry. She deserved so much better.

But is Alexa the one she spoke of? She gives off this energy beam that lights me up. Every time she's around, her aura swallows me whole, and I don't want to let go. And that is annoying as shit to admit.

I find myself looking for her blond hair when I'm patrolling the streets. Hoping to get one glimpse of her light to get me through the day. My very own energy shot.

I realize Abby's still looking at me, waiting for something. I guess I wasn't finished.

"She stopped first and walked away," I growl.

"Now I understand why you went off on her. You like her, but you don't like it that you like her. The whole pharma thing is just an excuse to push her away. The question is, why?"

"Think what you want."

The guilt still eats at me for the way I treated her. I was wrong and fully admit it. I do plan to apologize when I see her next. But will she accept the apology? She definitely won't melt in my arms and kiss me again.

Abby stands up and grabs two napkins. She hands me one. "Anyway, what happened once you got back from your break?"

"Dominic was there flirting with her. She didn't stay long and didn't seem interested in him."

Abby lays her latest crossword puzzle and a pencil next to her empty plate, then sits down again. "Dani's pushing to set her up with him. Supposedly he liked her in high school. Not sure that's a good idea, but something tells me Alexa wouldn't put up with his crap anyway."

"Did she agree to go out with him?" My voice cracks.

"Why? Jealous?"

"Hell no. I wouldn't trust that guy with any woman. Even someone I don't like."

"Like Alexa?"

I clear my throat, but I can't look at her straight in the eye. "Right."

She studies her crossword with crinkled eyebrows. "Hmm. This is a tough one."

I take my dish to the sink and dump the rest of my coffee down the drain. "What's today's challenge?"

She taps her cheek with the end of the pencil. "Five-letter word for something you hate so much that you love it. First and last letters are *A*."

I open my mouth to say something but stop short. Abby's sly grin grows.

Alexa.

Chapter 13

Alexa

I kick off my black pumps as soon as I walk through the apartment door. What a waste of money. I have bloody, stinging blisters on the backs of my heels.

I have only thirty minutes to get ready. Dani begged me to go out tonight to a new bar in Weehawken called Kaleidoscope. I've been busy this week with nonstop sales meetings all over the place. I've put over two hundred miles on my car. Today, I had an all-day cardiology conference in New York City. I'd give anything just to chill tonight.

For the first time in a while, I don't have one ounce of desire to go out. The bar scene is losing my interest. Maybe it's because of the men I'm meeting or because I'm looking for decent men in the wrong places. All the good ones are taken or married. Or it's all the socializing I've had to do to save my job. Natalie asked me to stay in the city for some drinks, but I'd rather stay near my apartment.

I look forward to crashing at my parents' or James's Thanksgiving weekend. I haven't discussed it with anyone yet. Maybe do a spa day with Lisa and Tina. I need a break. Or maybe I won't wait until then and go before.

My closet is full of clothes I hardly wear. What a waste. Maybe tomorrow I'll go through it and see which pieces I can donate somewhere. I remove a maroon fitted V-neck cashmere sweater off a hanger. Tonight, my favorite skinny jeans are coming out with me. A couple of months ago, I found deep-red Adidas sneakers with white stripes. They match my sweater perfectly. A stylish outfit with comfort. My feet can't take any more punishment. It's not my usual attire when I go out on a Friday night, but I don't care. I think about it again. Nope. I really don't care.

There are no signs saying I can't park here. No need for another ticket or having my car towed. One more check in the mirror. I've decided to keep my hair down and added loose curls to it.

To the left of the bar entrance is a group of young guys smoking. "Hey there, beautiful," flirts one of them.

I crack a smile as I walk through their cloud of smoke. Instead of feeling flattered, I'm annoyed. What's wrong with me?

The crowd is thick and suffocating. A prism of color decorates the bar. No wonder it's called Kaleidoscope. I wander around until I spot Dani, then I stop in my tracks. Tongue Boy is with her. I'm going to kill her. There was no mention of Dominic coming. He better not lick me or smell like he ate a garlic bulb, but then again maybe he should. Then I'd have more reasons to avoid him.

I approach them at the bar bench where they're standing. Dominic moves away to whisper something into a blonde's ear, which makes me more than delighted. I tap Dani on the shoulder.

"Alexa," she squeals. "You're finally here." She reeks of alcohol already.

"What do you mean, finally? It's exactly eight."

"Oh. I thought it was later than that. We've been here since seven." She giggles, then hiccups. "Let's get you a drink."

She yanks me by the wrist, not gently, to the bar that has nonstop shelves of liquor behind it. Vibrant colors light up the bottles. It's too colorful here. When she lets go of my wrist, I massage it. What's her deal?

"Do you want another drink? Or just some water?"

She downs the rest of the one she has. "Hell yeah. A vodka cranberry would be great."

I order her drink along with a glass of water and a Blue Moon beer for me. The thought of drinking hard liquor right now makes my stomach turn since I'm starving. I inspect the bar counter for a menu. "Can we order food here?"

"No. Just drinks."

My stomach rumbles. "I wish I'd known that. I haven't eaten, so I can't drink a lot since I have to drive home. Did you drive tonight?"

"No. Dom. We came in his brand-new Beamer. You should check it out later."

Like I care!

"I thought you said it's a girls' night out. Why is he here?"

"He's always wanted to check out this bar, and he knew you'd be here." She clicks her tongue.

I want to hang myself. "I told you I'm not looking to date anyone right now. Don't feed him false ideas."

Our drinks are placed on the bar. Before she picks hers up, I notice her hands are shaking. How much has she drunk so far?

"He knows, but he can be quite persuasive when he wants something." She wiggles her eyebrows.

He'd be barking up the wrong tree.

"Let's stay here for a few minutes," I urge.

She shrugs and leans against the bar. I ask the bartender for some water for Dani. She needs it.

"Did you get highlights?"

She fluffs her hair while chomping on gum. "Yeah. I wanted a change from my boring dark-brown hair. I thought about going blond like you to see if blondes have more fun, but I chickened out."

"What are you talking about? You have great hair with or without highlights." *When it's not frizzy.*

"Do you bleach your hair?"

I snap my head back. "Absolutely not."

She rolls her eyes. "It must be nice."

Bad mood much, or is it the alcohol? This is going to be a fun night. I'll be playing babysitter.

"So where's Vince tonight? Working?"

She shrugs with indifference. "He should be off duty by now. He might stop by, but he's tired. Is that okay, since you're against policemen?"

"I don't have a problem with Vince. I don't even know him. He seemed like a nice guy when I met him on Halloween. Are you two serious?"

I tilt my head to see her face. She doesn't respond right away and stares into her glass. "We've only been together for a little while. We have fun and are exclusive, but we do our own thing. Things might change in a couple weeks." Her voice perks up with a mischievous tone.

"I don't get it? What do you mean, things might change?"

She waves her hand in front of her and chuckles. "Never mind. Don't listen to me. I have to slow down." But she chugs her drink anyway.

I hand her the glass of water. "Drink this."

"Alexa," Tongue Boy calls as he approaches us.

My body deflates. Now there are two people I loathe when they say my name. I'm so not in the mood. Someone please rescue me from this nightmare.

With a forced smile, I say, "Hey. How's it going?"

"You look gorgeous." He leans in close to my face, as if he's going to kiss me.

I put my beer glass between our faces. "Cheers." I take a long swig.

He clears his throat and steps back. I feel the heat from his flaming cheeks, or is it from the hot lights in the bar? No. It's his cheeks.

I step away from the bar. "Will you excuse me for a minute? I need to use the bathroom."

"Do you want me to come with you?"

It wasn't Dani who asked, but Dominic.

Now he's tracing his finger down my arm. I swear I'm going to punch him in the face. Did he think it was an invitation to go at it in a corner?

I slap his hand away. "I can find it myself," I retort while walking away. If this is his version of persuasion, no wonder he's still single. Jackass.

I don't really need the bathroom. I just want some space, and I've only been here for ten minutes. People move out of my way as I search for a spot to hide for a few minutes. I lean against a wall as my phone vibrates in my leather jacket. I pull it out and look at the number. It says, *No Caller ID*. That's the third or fourth time today. Whoever they are never leaves a message.

I press my phone to my ear and plug my other ear to hear better. "Hello," I shout.

Pure silence, but then I hear something. I push the phone harder against my ear. It sounds like someone's breathing heavy.

"Hey, perv, stop calling me. You obviously have the wrong number."

"No, I don't. You forgot your beer at the bar," the male muffled voice whispers.

I stiffen and then the line goes dead. I stare at it for a few seconds. I inspect the space around me and shove the phone into my pocket as I walk back to Dani. Now I'm relieved to be with people I know.

As I get closer, I notice the smile on Dominic's face when he catches my eye. My stomach turns. Why do so many men nauseate me right now? But I'm glad to see Vince showed up. I don't see Superman lurking about. I want to smack myself because I'm disappointed.

Kent is arrogant, mean, and he carries a gun. I shouldn't like him. But I can't help the spike in my pulse when he's near me. Now that I know why he's so miserable, I can sympathize with him. Since Abby's his sister, I can't imagine he doesn't have a soft interior.

"Hey, Vince. It's good to see you," I say as I rejoin the group. "Man, you're big. I didn't notice the first time I met you. You sat the entire time." He has to be at least six three, and from the way his shirt fits him, I'd say he's built. I think Superman is a little shorter.

"Hey, Alexa," Vince responds.

Dani wraps her arms around his waist and kisses his neck.

"Here's your beer, beautiful." Tongue Boy hands it to me.

I'll hold it, but I won't drink it. He's the type who would slip a roofie into it. Granted, Dani is right next to him.

"Arrest anybody today?" I giggle because I'm sure Vince hears that a lot.

"Nope. Not today. It was pretty quiet." He takes a sip from his beer bottle.

Dominic tugs me to his side, but I pull away and give him a dirty look. He has the nerve to wink at me. He is completely insane.

"So he's the next victim on your list," mocks a guy nearby.

All eyes focus on someone behind me. I turn around and find a drunk Joker the Poker. He's no joker tonight, just like at Starbucks.

"She'll chew you up and spit you out. She flaunts her shit, making you want her, and then she walks away before putting out," he yells, alcohol thick on his breath.

Maybe he has an alcohol problem. But I think everyone has a problem lately.

"We went on one date, asshole. I told you to leave me alone. Now get the hell away from us."

"Truth hurts, doesn't it."

"Not your version of the truth. Go stalk another girl." I turn my back to him.

"Don't turn away when I'm talking to you, bitch!"

Dominic doesn't defend me. Vince does. He grabs Poker by the shirt and pulls him far away from us. He's practically airborne. We stare with our mouths wide open. This is when I love that he's a cop. Vince is in his face, probably warning him that he's a police officer.

Poker's friends come to his rescue and talk to Vince. They all nod and pull him away to the other side of the bar.

"I'll stay here to make sure you're okay," Dominic declares and then puts his arm around my shoulder.

Oh my God. I ball my hands at my side and shove him away. "Stop touching me!"

He regains his balance. "Sorry. But I thought..." He fumbles while straightening his perfectly pressed pastel-pink button-down shirt. He eyes Dani, as if questioning my actions.

"You thought what exactly?" I ask, but my eyes focus on Dani. *What did she tell him?*

"Alexa," Dani pleads.

"Look, Dani. I agreed to come here to meet you alone. Not to be pawed by your brother or harassed by a guy I went out with once. I'm done here."

Dominic opens his mouth to say something, but I cut him off.

"Alone," I snarl.

"Alexa, I'm sorry. Please don't go," Dani yells as I walk toward the exit, never looking back.

I ignore her and keep going. First Dominic's here, then the phone call, and now Poker. I want to go home and eat a massive bowl of Lucky Charms. I wish Tina still lived with me.

"Alexa, are you okay?" Vince asks with concern as we meet by the exit.

I shrug because I don't know if I'm okay. Ever since Halloween, my life feels like someone else's. Nothing seems to be the same. Like there was a glitch in time that shifted everything.

"I need to go home. This is all a bunch of bullshit."

"You need to be careful with that lunatic." He aims his thumb to the crowd.

"Which one? Dominic or the drunk?"

He chuckles. "Both, but the drunk guy seems to be a loose cannon. As for Dominic, I'd stay away from him, but I think you know that already."

"When I first met the drunk guy, he was more of a goofball than anything. I never saw him like this until I told him I didn't want to go out with him again. Tonight's not the first time I ran into him. I saw him the other day, and he embarrassed me in public there too."

"You need to watch yourself. Do you want me to walk you to your car?"

"You don't have to do that. It's parked not too far from the entrance. Thanks though."

Dani hollers for Vince in the background.

He opens the door for me. I step out and freeze. There's Superman strolling toward us. He stops as well. My mental wall shoots straight up in defense because I don't know what mood he's in this time. But I can't ignore the butterflies in my stomach and the instant heat on my cheeks when I see nothing but genuine concern on his face.

Chapter 14

Kent

Why does Alexa look so livid? And why is Vince with her? Vince lifts his chin in Alexa's direction and then goes back in. We know each other's gestures, so something happened, and it doesn't look good.

Alexa and I stay where we are and remain silent. I don't know if I should let her speak first or if I should.

She shakes her head and stomps to her car, making the sensor safety lights flash on like a strobe light on a theater stage. I follow her but have to pick up speed because she's walking so fast. She faces her car while searching for her keys in her bag. I walk around her, so I can view her from the side. If she only knew what her scent does to me.

"Alexa, what happened? And don't tell me nothing."

She stops and deadpans me, killing me with her icy-green eyes. "Like you really care? If I recall, you made it very clear how much you despise me. Even though I never did anything to you."

Her car chirps and lights flash. Before she can open the door, I block it with my arm. She jumps back.

"I don't hate you," I say softly and slowly. "I'm trying very hard to"—I take a deep breath—"but you make it so damn impossible."

Her stare circles my face like she's examining my brain. I twitch when she throws her hands in the air and yells, "You men. I can't handle any of you tonight. Men say women are crazy, but tonight proves men are complete whack jobs."

I ease forward. "Why? Is that why Vince called me?"

Her eyebrows squeeze together. "Vince called you?"

"Yes. We don't like Dominic. Dani mentioned how she's trying to fix you up with him and that he'd be here tonight. Vince called me to stop by."

She backs away from me. "It's none of your business who I date. I don't need a babysitter or a bodyguard. I'm not a weak little girl who can't take care of herself."

I cross my arms over my chest. "Who are you then?"

She massages her temples with her eyes closed. "I'm someone who's tired of assholes harassing me. I'm starving and want to go home and eat a bowl of Lucky Fucking Charms," she confesses. "In peace." Her voice drifts off as if she has no energy left.

Lucky Charms? Now that was unexpected. That's Abby's favorite cereal. Again, Alexa shocks the hell out of me. I don't want her to leave, but I'm not sure she'd come home with me if I asked her to.

"You really want Lucky Charms?" The sensor light turns off.

"Why are you asking? Is that something else that pisses you off about me? Please let me go home." She reaches to open the car door. The damn sensor light blinds me again.

"Don't be so stubborn. Just answer the question."

She looks up at the stars and pinches the bridge of her nose. "Yes. It's been my favorite cereal since I was little. I don't care that it's pure sugar and completely unhealthy. I just want some."

She licks her lips, and all I can think of is how they tasted when they were pressed against mine.

"Want to come to my house?"

She laughs in my face. "Why would I want to go with you? You're probably just as psycho as the guys inside that bar."

I pull my phone out of my pocket and call my sister. While it's ringing, I watch Alexa. She's beautiful no matter what she wears, how she styles her hair, or what mood she's in. Her lips look even more kissable without cherry-red lipstick.

"Hey, Abby. I hope you weren't sleeping. I'm here with Alexa. Do you still have a good stash of Lucky Charms?" I roll my eyes. "Just answer the question." Alexa's tension seems to be decreasing. She's almost smiling.

"Good. There's enough. I asked Alexa to come over. She's craving Lucky Charms." I pull the phone away from my ear as she screams in excitement into the phone. Abby's been talking about Alexa for days, pushing me to apologize and ask her out. It just might happen tonight.

"Are you done screaming?" I say to Abby.

Alexa chuckles.

"She thinks I'm psycho, so I'd like you to give her your word that I'm not. Good. Hold on." I hand Alexa the phone.

She's hesitant to take it but has a sweet, faint smile on her face. "Hi, Abby?" she says as she plays with one of the buttons on her coat. "So what do you think I should do? Did he take his bipolar meds tonight?"

She glances at me from the side, then looks away.

"Mmm-hmm. Promise? It's your fault if he acts up. Okay. Okay. See you soon."

She gives me my phone back. "Abby wants to talk to you again."

I press the phone to my ear, afraid to hear what Abby's going to say. "What's up? I promise I'll be on my best behavior. If I'm not, I'll do the dishes for a month. See you soon." I hang up and stuff my phone into my pocket.

"So what will it be? I can drive and then bring you back here. It's good to see you parked legally tonight."

She cracks up. "You just made a joke." She stops, and her face twists. "At least I think it was one anyway."

I laugh along with her. It's been a while since I've genuinely laughed.

"Abby says I'm safe with you, so I'll take her word for it. Where's your car, Superman?"

We head to my truck. "Superman? That's the last name I'd think you'd call me tonight."

"Instead of psycho, prickly pear, beast, or Mr. Angry?"

"You forgot to add asshole to that list. But I'll take Superman, even though I don't deserve it."

She stops in front of my truck. "No car...but a black Ford pickup. It fits your rough edges."

I open the passenger-side door for her.

"Wow. What treatment," she jokes. "You must really hate doing the dishes. Being a gentleman must be hard for you."

I'm going to ignore the digs she throws at me, because I deserve every one of them. "Do you need me to help you up? It's a little high."

She scopes out how high it is and then hauls herself up with no problem. "Nope. I'm good."

She flashes me her killer smile, which renders me breathless.

"I call you Superman because of the conversation we had when you told me your name was Kent. Clark Kent. Superman. Suppy. Get it?" she says as she fastens her seat belt.

I walk to the other side of the truck and get in. "Yes. I'm glad my last name is Hayes. But I don't deserve to be called Superman. At least not yet."

The light is still on inside because I haven't closed my door. I gaze at her and smile. A genuine smile.

She stares right through me, but I turn away to close the door. "Everything okay?"

In the darkness, she says, "You have the most beautiful smile. It's the first time I've seen it. You should do it more often. It lights up your face."

That's because I'm looking at you.

"Abby says the same thing. I'm sure anything is better than my typical scowl."

We drive in silence during the short trip to my house, but my body is alert to every movement she makes and every breath she takes. I have this urge to enclose her tiny left hand with mine. But why? I don't deserve to. I'm a jerk. Why would she want to be with a guy like me? I should say *I'm sorry* now, but I just pulled into the driveway.

Abby waits for us at the door. Maybe I should be worried to have both of them in the same room. Two against one.

I'm up for it.

Chapter 15

Alexa

He pulls into a narrow one-car driveway that his truck barely fits into. What an adorable house, at least from what I can see in the dark. There's only the front porch light providing me a sneak peek. It's white with black shutters, like my parents' house. White wooden stairs climb up to a decent-sized front porch. What a great view of the New York City skyline from here.

I'm a bit surprised he lives in this section of Weehawken. It's expensive. I unhook my seat belt and open my door. Superman is already at my side and reaches his hand out to help me down.

I slip my hand in his and enjoy the normality of it. Like this is the way it'll always be from now on. It reminds me of when our bodies wrapped around each other when we kissed. A connection I would do anything to replay.

"Such a gentleman. Sorry if I'm a little scared that your alter ego might pay a visit."

Before he can respond, Abby trots down the front steps. "Hi, Alexa. I'm ecstatic you're here. It makes my Friday much more exciting," she says, faster than the roadrunner on speed. She hugs me as if we've known each other forever.

"I was watching the Hallmark Channel and doing my crossword puzzles. I don't need to see those sappy movies, thinking someday a guy will come and sweep me off my feet. Eating Lucky Charms is so much more fun." She intertwines her arm with mine and drags me to the front door.

"You never know. It can find you when you least expect it." I turn and look at Kent. Our eyes connect, as if what I said hits us in the heart at the same time.

"Come on inside. I've set up the kitchen table. Bowls of Lucky Charms await."

"Sounds good. I had no desire to go out tonight, but now I'm glad I did. This is far better than a stuffy bar."

I enter the house and am surprised by what I see. It isn't fancy, but it's well kept. Not a bachelor pad at all. Shiny hardwood floors travel into the living room to the left. A beige recliner and sofa face the TV that's mounted to the wall. There's a fireplace in the corner. Colorful pillows are scattered around to add life to the room. I'm sure a touch from Abby. The old floor probably creaks in special places, just like the porch steps did. To the right is the dining room, which looks like it hasn't been used in years. Which it probably hasn't. The furniture looks ancient.

"Should I take my sneakers off?"

"You don't have to. We never do," Abby answers as she walks down the hallway.

"Let me take your coat." Kent holds out his hands.

I wiggle my shoulders to let it slide off my arms. "Thanks."

He winks at me. Seriously, he has to be bipolar. And I don't do bipolar. Don't get me wrong—I like this side of him, but I want him to stay like this.

I trail behind Kent as he leads me to the kitchen. Abby babbles away, but all I can focus on is how broad his shoulders look in his white button-down shirt. The sleeves are cuffed at his elbows, showing off his solid forearms. I'm sure he's cut since he's a cop. Was this really a good idea to come here? *Hell yeah.*

"And here's the kitchen." Abby's movements remind me of the models on *The Price Is Right* showcasing the prize sets.

It has dated oak cabinets and a cream-colored Formica countertop. A sweet, tiny wooden table for four stands in the middle of the narrow U-shaped kitchen. The floor is white-and-black-checkered linoleum. It's outdated, but it's still charming. What a difference in tastes between my kitchen and this one though. It's a bit depressing without color.

"May I use your bathroom?" A laugh escapes, catching us both by surprise.

"What's so funny?"

"To get away from Dominic tonight, I said I had to go to the bathroom, but I lied and hid in a corner. Now I really need to go."

"The bathroom is right across the hall." Kent points to a door behind me. "Be careful. The toilet overflows sometimes."

I crinkle my nose. "No. Really?"

Abby smacks him in the gut. "No. Kent's just trying to find his sense of humor again. He lost it a long time ago." She playfully pushes him.

They're just like James and me. It makes me miss my brother.

I giggle and walk away. When I return to the kitchen, Abby and Kent are waiting for me at the table.

I sit in the seat across from him. Kent eats Captain Crunch instead of Lucky Charms. I used to eat that too when I was little. He eats politely. I'm surprised he's not slurping the milk or sucking it through his teeth. I compare us to Beauty and the Beast. He's not physically unattractive like a beast, but his pent-up anger and rudeness make him ugly. My gut tells me if he opens up, I'll find a beautiful soul inside. Tonight I'm seeing another side of him...one I might not be able to resist.

I pat my lower abdomen. Damn ovaries. Whose side are they on?

We're interrupted when my phone rings. "Sorry. Let me see who it is." *Please don't be the guy who called at the bar*. I see that it's Dani. Why am I hesitant to tell her I'm with Kent and Abby?

"Hey, Dani. Yes, I'm fine. I'm hanging out with Kent and Abby at their house. I ran into him when I left," I say as I drape my hair over one shoulder. "Don't worry. He's being nice and is in a good mood tonight."

Abby smirks at me.

"I left my car in the parking lot, and he drove. I'll call you in a couple days. Have a good weekend."

I place my phone on the table. "I guess Dani was worried after I left. Vince didn't seem to mention to her that he saw you in the parking lot."

I pick up a lone pink heart marshmallow and toss it into my mouth. It melts on my tongue. No matter how many times I eat Lucky Charms, it still takes me back to when James and I were little, sitting at the kitchen table, eating our breakfast in our flannel-feet pajamas. A sweet taste of the past.

"What did Vince say to you when he asked you to go to the bar?"

Kent finishes chewing. "He told me you and Dominic were there."

"He said we were there *together*? I told Dani that I'd meet *her* at the bar. I'm not sure I would've gone if I'd have known he was going to be there. I relaxed a little when I saw Vince."

"Don't worry. He just said you were both there with Dani."

"Did you go there because of Dominic or me?" I'm curious now. Why is he being so nice to me tonight? Does he feel bad about our little fight? I want him to apologize. Or is it possible he's jealous?

"For both. I wanted to warn you about Dominic. Dani has told me some stories. Not sure why she tells Vince and me how badly he treats women, when we're cops."

"Does he do things that can put him in jail?"

He shakes his head. "Not that bad, but I wouldn't be surprised if he does. He treats women like they owe him something. Stringing them along while others wait in the shadows. He thinks he's hot shit since he works in the financial district in Manhattan and has a penthouse overlooking the Hudson."

"Who cares. Dominic does nothing for me, especially after tonight. Do you want to know what he did to me when I saw him at the bar on Halloween?"

Abby waves her hand in excitement, like she's in a classroom. "Oh. Oh. Me."

Kent nods as he laughs at Abby.

"Now remember—Dani and Dominic went to the same high school as me but graduated one year later. I don't remember them. But that was years ago."

"Do I want to know this? Because it will probably make me hate him even more," Kent says.

"He licked me."

"Eww. Gross." Abby shivers.

Kent's face turns to stone. "Where did he lick you?" He says through gritted teeth.

"Relax. Only on the top of my hand." I chuckle.

"It's not funny," he comments.

"It wasn't at the time, but I can only laugh now because it's so disgusting. Anyway, he went to kiss my hand, and when he did, he tickled the skin with his tongue. I call him Tongue Boy now. Don't even get me started about how much he reeked of garlic."

Kent chokes on his water.

"My nicknames are code so people don't know who I'm talking about. Only my friends know. There are ears everywhere."

"Well, I'm glad you call me Superman...and I'm glad I didn't eat any garlic tonight."

"Dominic kept touching me like I was his girlfriend tonight. What made him feel like he could touch me like that? Who knows what Dani told him before I got there. I had no desire to be there in the first place, and then I saw him when I arrived. Then the other guy went off on me."

Kent stiffens and leans over the table. "What other guy?"

"I went out with a guy once about a month ago. Once," I emphasize. "I told him I didn't want to go out with him again. He didn't believe me. I ran into him at the Starbucks the day you gave me a parking ticket." I squint my eyes at him. "Thank you for that, by the way."

His eyes flicker with amusement.

"He tried to put his arms around me. When I told him not to touch me, he turned like a switch, acted like a completely different person. He was drunk then too. He was at the bar tonight. He tried to embarrass me. Little do people know, I'm not easily embarrassed. Vince dragged him away from us."

"What's his secret nickname?" Abby asks as she clears the table and puts the dishes in the sink.

I clasp my hands under the table. I'm not sure I should tell them. But why do I care? Kent will probably hate me tomorrow anyway.

"Joker the Poker."

Kent laughs out loud. "Do we even want to know why?"

"I'll give you some advice. Never rub your third leg against a woman you hardly know. Especially on the first date. He came up behind me and poked me in the back more than once. He did it at the Starbucks also. I guarantee he stuffs a banana in his pants when he goes out."

Abby howls as she puts the milk away. "That's the funniest thing I've ever heard."

"Thanks for the advice." He stands up from the table. "Why Joker though?"

"He thought he was a comedian, and it was annoying as hell. That's why he shocked me with his change in behavior. I guess he's an angry drunk."

Kent rubs his chin. "Any more I should know about before I do the dishes as promised?"

"Do you really want to know?"

"Yes," Abby chimes in.

Kent waves his hand toward himself, encouraging me to keep going.

"Remember that doctor I introduced you to before you had your tantrum at the café? I call him Dr. Wanker. No big reason other than I think he's a wanker."

"You went on a date with him?" he asks in shock.

"No way! He's twice my age. He's a proctologist I know from a clinic in Manhattan. He wasn't one of my clients, but he was always there. Get this—he has an obsession with my knees."

Kent's eyebrows shoot up while Abby shakes her head in disbelief.

"I'm not going to get into it. I saw him at the hospital the day I ran into you. And then at the café. I don't know if he lives around here. It doesn't sit well with me. That's why I asked you to act like my big bad cop boyfriend."

"Why didn't you want to go out tonight?" Kent says as he opens the dishwasher.

"Just tired of the bar scene, I guess. I've had a long week with work, and it continues tomorrow."

The air thickens as I explain my job situation and how Dani and Abby offered to help me gain some experience. I wait for Kent to explode, but he doesn't.

"Alexa, let me show you the head scarves I've made. You've only seen a couple. They're upstairs."

I glance at Kent.

"Go on up. Abby loves showing them off when she finds someone who's interested. I'll be in the living room when you come back down."

We walk upstairs and enter the first room on the right. The walls are a friendly light canary yellow with white crown molding. The hardwood floor is hidden under a circular white area rug with a yellow floral design. A large modern sewing machine stands in the middle of the room. A pin cushion sits like a giant porcupine next to it.

I wander around and stop at a table with an assortment of thread spools, buttons, clips, gemstones, and various vibrantly colored fabrics.

Abby twirls in a circle. "This is my sewing room, if you haven't guessed already. Kent renovated it so I could occupy myself when I hide in the house. He's pretty handy that way. That's why this house is still in good condition. I decorate it with some of the things I make, like pillowcases and curtains."

"What do you mean, hide?"

"I guess *hide* isn't the right word. When I get close to another chemo treatment, I stay close to home and hardly go out. I'm afraid that someone will get me sick, and then chemo could be delayed. It happened once." She sits down on a chair in front of the sewing machine.

"It's also for when I have bad days after a treatment. I know I seem happy all the time, but there are days I don't want to get out of bed. The fatigue is awful. Most people don't see that. I look at my naked self in the mirror and think about how ugly I am. I know people stare at me and what they say behind my back. I hate to be pitied. Today was one of those days."

I trace my fingers lightly across a beautiful bright-purple paisley fabric that Tina would love.

"You hide it well, since you seem pretty cheerful right now."

"That's because you're here. You have a way of lifting people's spirits when you're around. No one's ever told you that before?"

"Yeah right." I huff. "Or I make them turn into psychotic assholes."

She taps my arm. "I'm serious. Even Matt said so the other day."

"I pay Matt and Kayla to say things like that."

"It's nice to have another female around the house."

"I thought Dani was around a lot?" I say nonchalantly as I twirl a sky-blue ribbon around my finger.

"She comes and goes, mostly with Vince lately, but she has a different personality. We like her because she's been good to me whenever I needed help, but she's closed off in a way. She only lets people in so far. Maybe it's because she needs to cut off her emotions in the hospital. It seems to stay like that outside the hospital too. You're the first woman Kent has brought home in years."

Just hearing that makes my insides glow. I don't understand why he suddenly wants to be around me tonight if he can't stand my profession. It's my job, and it's not going to change. Even if I get laid off, I will look for a job at another pharma company. I'm not a fan of his occupation either, but that's out of fear.

I notice a stand with several hooks, almost like a coat hanger. It has several head scarves hanging off it. "Are these all the ones you've made?"

"No. I have a drawerful. A nurse approached me a little while ago about displaying some at the children's Christmas party they throw every year. Maybe let the kids try them on. She thinks I could sell some. It's amazing how much attention I've gotten because of these. I would've never thought about it."

"Are you going to do it?"

"I told them no because it would be too stressful after my treatment. But I offered to do something for Valentine's Day or some other holiday. If it can make a child feel better somehow, I'd love it. It would be more authentic to come from someone like me, who understands what they're going through."

"That's true. I love the idea. Do you ever think about what you want to do once you've fully recovered? Do you want to go back to your old job if you can? Maybe you can sell your scarves for a living."

I remove a maroon-colored scarf from one of the hooks. "I love this one with the crystal beads. They look like Swarovski crystals. You could wear this to a party with a matching colored dress."

"Ya think so? Let me try it on again. I couldn't tell you the last time I dressed up for something."

She walks up to me and removes her daffodil-yellow head scarf and grabs the one from my hand. I'm speechless but try not to show it. I've never seen a woman completely bald. Now that the colorful scarf is off her head, her face is pale with gray patches under her eyes. My heart weeps for her. I'm suddenly bashful, as if she were standing there naked. My eyes dart in every direction to avoid staring at her. I turn away and pretend to search through her scarves again.

"It's okay, Alexa."

Without looking at her, I say, "What's okay?"

"I know it's weird to see me like this. You can look at me."

I turn in her direction. "I'm sorry. All the studying I've been doing and all the pictures I've seen...they didn't prepare me for this. Pictures aren't personal, so you don't become attached. Us standing here *is* personal, and I'm already attached."

"This is the real me, just without hair. It's rare that I let anyone see me without my head covered. At least I still have eyebrows. But one day you'll see me with beautiful hair again and color in my face. Hopefully, back to my wavy dark-brown hair."

"Like Kent's."

She snaps her fingers. "Exactly, just like my brother's. But it's kind of nice not having to fuss with my hair in the morning. Just put on the scarf and go.

"I should show you a picture of me before I was diagnosed. But that can wait, since I have a gut feeling this won't be your last visit here."

Me too.

"Kent wanted to shave his hair off to support me, but I made him promise not to. Why have us both without hair? It wouldn't change my diagnosis."

"But he's your brother and he loves you. It's his way to show it."

I dip my finger in the container of gems and stir them around. "Anyway, you amaze me. You truly do. Kent must be so proud of you."

"He doesn't show it all the time, but I know he is. Everything about me scares him. He's so afraid to lose me and questions why I have to suffer too. Because I'm sick, he thinks he's not allowed to enjoy life either. Tonight was the first night in a long time I've seen him relaxed and laughing. Again, you have something to do with that."

She yawns into her hand. "Sorry, Alexa. I'm super tired. I need to go to bed. It hits me out of nowhere sometimes. If you don't mind, I'll say good night up here." She pulls me in for a hug. "Please come back. It's nice to have life back in this house again."

"I promise I'll come back." I stroke her arm gently. "Can I bring you something? A glass of water at least?"

She shakes her head. "No. Thanks though. I should be fine. All I want is my pillow."

We walk out of the room together. I have this intense urge to coddle her like she's my little sister. She deserves all the love and support she can get. It makes my heart weep, knowing she has no mother or father to comfort her.

I don't know what's happening to me. Why do I feel so much for this family when I hardly know them? Eating cereal for dinner with them was the best night I've had in a long time. Am I getting older, is my biological clock ticking, or do I need to reevaluate which direction my life is going in? Maybe all of the above.

She leans against the bathroom doorframe, as if she has no more energy to stand. "Bye, Alexa. Please tell Kent I went to bed and he doesn't need to check up on me."

"I will. Sweet dreams. Don't let the bed bugs bite."

She flashes me a sweet, tired smile, then closes the bathroom door.

I have been blessed all my life, but I've never fully appreciated the important things. Things that aren't superficial. I've always been healthy and always assumed it would stay that way. But so do many others who have fallen ill. Having a nice car, money, and a spacious, modern apartment won't mean shit once I'm six feet under.

I've been happily gliding along in my life because it's been good to me. Bad things happen to people I know, but it's like I've been in a protective bubble. Ever since I saw that cat, I think the bubble has burst.

Exposing me to the negative world around me.

Chapter 16

Kent

The old staircase creaks, alerting me they're coming back down. I walk around the corner and only see Alexa step off the last stair.

"I was wondering if you two fell asleep up there. Where's Abby?" I rest my hand on the post and glance up the stairs.

"She suddenly became very tired and went to bed. Will she be okay?" she asks, eyes filled with worry.

"That happens a lot. When her body tells her it's tired, she listens."

I teeter back and forth on my feet with my hands in my pockets. "Do you want to stay for a little while longer? Have a beer or something else to drink? Do you even drink beer?"

She doesn't move away from the stairs. I stand still as her eyes search my face. I wipe around my mouth. Maybe there's a piece of Captain Crunch on it. I know I don't have lipstick on my face, because I haven't had the pleasure of her lips on mine and am not sure I ever will again.

"Is there something on my face?"

She giggles. "No. I'm just trying to figure you out. You're still being nice to me."

"Does that translate to, you want to hang out for a while?" I turn around and head for the kitchen. I hear her soft footsteps behind me.

"Yes, I'd like to stay. What kind of beer do you have?"

I hold open the refrigerator door with my arm like a V. She comes around and rests her chin in the crevice. I prevent my body from moving even though it wants to quiver from her touch. It doesn't help that she's so damn cute, putting her head there to begin with.

"I have Heineken or Corona Light. Abby treats herself to a Corona Light every once in a while. If you want wine or a martini or something like that, I don't have that type of alcohol in the house."

"No worries. I'll have a Corona Light." She removes her head from my arm. "I ordered a beer at Kaleidoscope but left it on the bar when I walked away for a few minutes. Normally I never leave my drink alone. When I came back, Dominic handed it to me. I instantly thought he could've slipped something into it."

"I wouldn't be surprised. Follow your instincts. If you feel uncomfortable around him, stay away. I would if I were you. I wonder why Dani's forcing him on you. Is it a twin thing?"

"I don't care. Let's not talk about them anymore."

I place a Heineken and Corona Light on the counter. "Do you drink your Corona with lemon or lime?" I push items around in the fridge in search of either one. "A lemon is all I can find."

"Then lemon it is."

I prepare the lemon and hand her the bottle. "Too bad it's cold out. I would've suggested we go outside. There's a great view of the city from the front porch."

"It's not too cold. Let's go."

We put our coats on as we wander out to the front porch. I remove a box of matches from my pocket and light the large lanterns Abby had bought. I place them closer to us so we can see each other. The porch light blinds people.

We plop down on the top step and face each other as we lean against the white pillars. Our legs extend flat, with our feet in between each other's. Perfect fit.

She takes a deep breath and sighs. "This is nice. Thanks for bringing me here, for rescuing me from that nightmare tonight."

"You're welcome. It makes me happy to see Abby excited about something." My voice drifts off. I want to tell her I'm glad she's here, but I don't know how to say it. Why would she want to be here with me after I was such a dick? Maybe she only came because of Abby.

"She's amazing. I've never met such a strong woman. When I saw her for the first time, she stood out, but in a good way. I was amazed how beautiful she looked with her head scarf. Not everyone can pull that off like she can."

"That's what I always say. I know it doesn't help when I'm in a constant shitty mood. She tries to be upbeat for the both of us."

"Can I say something?" She hesitates. "I'm sorry for being so direct, but don't you think it should be the other way around? I can't even comprehend the hell you've both gone through with your mom and now her. Well, I can to an extent. But Abby needs someone positive in her life. Someone to look up to, a Superman of her own. I don't think she wants to see her only family member pissed off all the time because of her. It just makes her feel guilty and like a burden."

My body stiffens as anger tries to seep in. I take a couple of swigs of beer and lean my head back against the post. "You're right."

"What did you just say?" She chuckles while sitting up straight, her face aglow with amazement. "I don't think I heard that right. Say it again."

"You. Are. Right, Lady Alexa." I hug one of her feet with mine.

She glances at our feet and grins, but it disappears. "I'm sorry about your mom and Abby. My brother, James, was once engaged to a woman named Jessica. She was pregnant with their baby. She got severely ill one day when she was near the end of the pregnancy. It hit so fast that both she and the baby died before she could get to the hospital. James is an ER doctor. He blamed himself for months for their deaths, that he should've noticed the symptoms. He was a complete mess and just as angry as you are. I forced him to move in with me to get his life back to normal. My parents and I had to be the positive and supportive ones for him when everyone else deserted him.

"Jessica was like a sister to me. And their baby was going to be my nephew. Our families went through hell and back. But time healed us. James met Lisa, now his wife. They have a beautiful daughter, Felicia. There's a lot more to their awesome story, but I'll save that for another day."

She places her bottle on the lower step. "You and I have experienced some horrible things. You think that I walk around without a care in the world and get everything handed to me. I choose to live my life differently. Life is too short to be miserable all the time."

I hold up my hand. "Alexa, stop before you say anything else."

"Nope. Just let me finish."

I nod.

"I like my job and being around people. The thought of being stuck in an office all day long makes me want to pull my hair out. I'm a social and positive person by nature, and I have a brain. My major in college and grad school was science and public health. One thing led to another, and I started in sales at a pharma company and realized I was good at it. I believe in what I do. Just because you hate the system doesn't mean I *am* the system. I hate guns, but I don't hate you." She wiggles her feet between mine.

"If you have such a problem with my job, maybe I shouldn't be here right now. If you're going to judge me for something I don't have control of, then we have a real problem. I don't want to be ridiculed for what I do for a living."

"Is it guns you hate or the police?"

"Guns scare me. I don't hate the police, but the profession scares me. I hear horrific stories every day how officers are shot while on duty. Or that one story where a policeman was on his way home with his uniform on. He stopped to help someone and got shot simply because he was a cop. I can't imagine what his family went through. If I were married to a cop, I'd worry that when he walked out the door, he wouldn't walk back through it at the end of the day. I'm not sure I could do it."

I snap my fingers. "Damn. I was going to propose to you tonight, but I guess I'm going to have to return the ring I found at the bottom of the Captain Crunch box. But I hope to become a detective. Would that make you change your mind?"

"Abby was right. You did find your sense of humor. You're cute as hell, but be serious now."

"What you fear comes with the profession. We sign up knowing that there's danger involved, but we want to help people. We risk our lives to protect others. We wear bulletproof vests at all times and carry our guns, hoping we never have to use them."

"But then there are stories about cops killing people when it wasn't necessary. If someone's doing something illegal, why can't you just shoot them in the knee instead of killing them? I know this is a controversial topic, but you know what I mean. Right?"

"Well, yes. But I can give you an example about the pharma industry too. Why is it so difficult to get medical marijuana? There are so many restrictions that it's near impossible to get approval for a patient. Maybe if my mom were able to use medical marijuana when she was sick, it would've made the end a lot more comfortable. But if it's not fully legalized and stays restricted, pharma companies don't lose money."

Seconds of silence pass between us. "We both have our issues, so what do we do about it?"

"Let me start with this." I take a deep breath. "I owe you a huge apology. The way I treated you the other day was unforgivable. I cringe every time I think about it. You didn't deserve that. I walked away with my heart in my throat. Your job gave me an excuse to stay away from you, even though I didn't want to. The guilt has been eating at me ever since. I have never treated a woman like that before. I promise you I'll *never* do that to you again."

"You better not. I really don't want to cut your balls off and feed them to the million sewer rats around here."

My hand instantly covers my balls as I cringe at the thought. "I'm surprised we're sitting here together since we have such different views on things. But you have never disrespected me like I did you. I don't deserve to be here with you, but I'm glad you're here. I've been waiting for the right time to apologize."

She cocks her head. "You don't deserve it, but I forgive you. I understand why you are the way you are. There's no place I'd rather be tonight. But how did you know you'd ever see me again?"

"Ever since we met, we keep running into each other. Abby talks about you nonstop. I think you're her idol. I don't believe this is all a coincidence." I'm mesmerized by her beauty as a breeze blows wisps of hair to the side. I wish I had a camera to capture her this way. "Do you?"

She whisks her hair away from her face. "No," she says softly, then shivers.

"Are you cold? We can go back in."

She shakes her head.

I walk into the house and grab a blanket off the couch. Once I'm back outside, I kneel next to her. "Lean forward a little bit." I wrap the pink fleece blanket around her shoulders and pull the ends closed in front. "How's that? It's not red, but pink is close enough."

"It's perfect." She teases me with her sexy smile, which I don't think I can go another day without seeing again.

I brush her cheek gently with the back of my hand as I close my eyes.

"What's the matter now?"

"Absolutely nothing. I was thinking how damn soft your skin is. Another reason to like you." I tap her nose.

"Stop it now before you give me a reason to like you." She winks at me.

I rub my thighs. "Do you want another beer?"

She hands me her empty bottle. "I'll stick to water now. I shouldn't stay too much longer. I need to drive home, and I have a long day tomorrow."

One day she won't need to leave, because my heart is telling me, with or without our differences, this will become *our* home.

Chapter 17

Alexa

I don't really need to leave, especially when his backside looks luscious in those black jeans he's wearing. Beast or not, every time I see him, he gets yummier and yummier. My hands ache to touch his gorgeous unruly mop of hair. Him caressing my face was the sweetest gesture. Something is happening between us, but what is it exactly? How can we be anything when we both have strong opposing opinions?

The front door opens, and I hear my phone ringing. Kent walks out of the house with it in his hand.

"Someone's calling you."

It's so late. I take it from his hand and look at the number. *No Caller ID* again. I groan as I cut the call.

"Hey. What's wrong?"

"I'm not sure. It could be something, or it could be nothing." I swivel my legs forward onto the lower step.

He sits down next to me. Close enough that our arms touch. Neither one of us moves away.

"Someone has been calling me nonstop, but the number comes up as *No Caller ID*. It was another thing that pissed me off at the bar, because this person called there too."

I explain to him what the man said to me. He sits erect on the stairs.

"Now I'm assuming it was him again."

"Did you recognize the voice, or do you have any idea who it could be? Did you look around the bar for any familiar faces?" he says with a direct tone.

A police officer's voice, like when he gave me a ticket. It's kinda hot.

"Not really, but the background noise of the bar muffled his voice. When I went back to Dani, within a few minutes, Poker was there harassing me. For a split-second I thought maybe it was him, but he was too drunk and didn't see me there until then. At least I don't think so. And when he calls me, his number shows up."

"I don't like it. There are a couple of things to think about. All the caller has to do is type in star sixty-seven before your phone number to prevent you from seeing his number. There are a couple of apps out there that can reveal the real phone number. I can check for the best one and install it for you if you'd like."

"Did you just switch to cop mode?" I flirt.

"Be serious now." He bumps shoulders with me. "Be careful and let me know if you get any more calls. Or will you agree to let me install an app?"

"I'm sure I can load an app by myself, but I'll let you do it. It gives me a reason to see you again." I bump him back and then continue to lean against him.

"Alexa, I've seen some crazy shit. Before Abby got sick, I was training to become a detective. I helped out with some cases. What about that doctor you said might be following you? The one at the café. It seems odd. Don't you think?"

I crinkle my face. "Dr. Wanker? I can't imagine he'd have the backbone to do something like that. He did question if you were really my boyfriend after he saw us fighting though. But how would he know my phone number?"

He takes my hand in his. It's so unexpected, but wow, do my hormones and specific body parts do a happy dance.

"I don't like it. Please be careful." He lists all the things I should and shouldn't do.

I can't take him seriously, because his protective mode is such a turn on. I need to go home before I beg him to use his handcuffs on me. I guess there could be some positives if I date a cop.

I pull my hand away even though I don't want to. "I can't believe how late it is. I should go home. Can you please drive me back to Kaleidoscope so I can get my car?"

"Sure. Let's go."

Some cars still linger in the parking lot, but mine is by itself. Kent pulls up to my car so his truck lights shine on the driver's side. The truck is close enough that I quickly notice something on my car door.

"What the hell is that?" I shove the truck door open and jump out. I hear Kent do the same.

I stomp to my car and bend over to examine the paint. Someone has keyed my car. Kent traces the line with his fingers. The key line is almost as long as the door, and deep.

"Son of a bitch." I kick the gravel. "Why would someone do this? That's going to cost a fortune to fix."

"Maybe it was the drunk asshole."

"I have no clue at this point. I met him at a restaurant when we went out on the one date. He could've seen me get out of it. I don't think we discussed what kind of car I had."

"Let's go inside and ask the manager if they have cameras installed outside. Then maybe we can see who did it."

I like it that he said *let's*, because there's no way in hell I'm standing out here alone. I don't have a good feeling about any of this.

A while later we walk out of the bar with no answers. Since they just opened, they haven't installed security cameras yet.

"Well, Officer, what do we do now? Or what should I do now?"

He stops, turns to me, and places his hands on my shoulders. "Unfortunately, there's nothing we can do if there are no witnesses."

It's so tempting to wrap my arms around him. I could perfectly lay my head on his chest.

"Maybe I'm worrying over nothing. Maybe it was just a random jerk."

"You could be right, Alexa, but maybe not. That's a pretty long mark. Let's see how the next days go. Will you please call me if anything else happens?"

"Are you going to give me your phone number? Maybe I'll start cranking you to give you a real reason to hate me." I walk toward my car but glance back at him with a smirk. "Don't think that I forgot about what you said when you first showed up here tonight. Something about trying to hate me but can't."

"Alexa," he says softly behind me.

"No worries, Suppy. Once you hate me, you'll never let me go." I flash him a sexy smile over my shoulder.

"That doesn't even make sense." He inches closer to me.

I imagine his arms caging me in while he nips at my neck. Damn, I wish *he* was a poker.

"Ha. I know. Just sounded good at the moment." I giggle, then catch my reflection in the window. Horrible. I ruffle my hair. "I need to go."

He reaches around me and opens my door for me. "Can I have your phone so I can add my number to it?"

I type in my password and hand it to him. He types away and rings his phone. "Now I have yours." He hands it back with a delicious grin. "Will you send me a message when you get home, so I know you got there safely?"

"Yes, Dad," I say as I get in.

He leans in close. "I hope you never look at me like your dad."

"What would you like me to see you as?" I say under my eyelashes.

"Your Uber," he mumbles.

Huh? "Wait. What did you say? Your Uber?"

He cocks his head and shakes it ever so slightly. "Try again. Just think about it." He kisses me lightly on the cheek, then closes the door. He goes straight to his truck and jumps in. He motions for me to go first with a big-ass smirk that I'd love to see every day.

Then it hits me, and I melt in my seat like a snowman in Arizona. My smile grows ear to ear just like his.

He wants to be my *future*.

All the way home, my mind spins on what Kent said. His future. I'm thinking nothing can wipe this smile off my face...and then I see my apartment building.

I park in the damp, grim garage, and I'm slammed into full alert. What if someone *is* stalking me? The hair on my arms springs high. My eyes dart in every direction. I inhale deeply to calm myself. I'm never afraid of anything. Well, there is one thing I'm deathly afraid of, but I'll tuck that back into the mini compartment in my brain, where it will stay.

With my purse in hand, I step out of my car and head to the stairway, my feet moving faster than my usual strut. I analyze my surroundings. My ears feel like they have grown to the size of megaphones. I look over both shoulders, then jump out of my skin when I hear a clattering noise. It had better be a rat.

After several long strides, I run through the door and up the stairs to my second-floor apartment. Wearing sneakers tonight was a godsend. The apartment key is in the door despite my shaking hand. I've never been so ecstatic to be in my apartment before. I quickly lock the door, wishing I had ten locks to secure it. With my back against the door, I drop my bag on the floor and take my phone out of my pocket.

My heart explodes when my phone rings. I yelp. It slips out of my hand like a bar of soap, but I catch it before it smashes on the ground. Fear prevents me from turning it over, but I'm too curious. Maybe it's Kent.

No Caller ID.

I cut the line and call Kent.

He picks up after one ring. "Kent, the person just called again. I'm wigging out over here. It's as if he knew I just walked into my apartment."

"Calm down, Sunshine. It'll be okay. You're safe in your place. Make sure the door is locked. What street do you live on?"

"Crescent."

"That's a safer area. I have to work until five tomorrow. Can I stop by after to install the app on your phone? Or we can meet somewhere. Your choice."

The thought of him coming over here tomorrow makes me feel safer—and excited. I wish he were here right now. "Sure. Come over. Bring Abby with you. I can make you both dinner." I hold my breath because all I hear are crickets. "Never mind. It was a stupid suggestion."

"Sunshine, I'd love to stay for dinner, and I'm sure Abby will be thrilled."

Sunshine? I kind of like that nickname. I'll take it.

"Well, okay." I toss my coat on the couch. "Great. I'll make something simple, like pasta. Sound good?"

"Perfect. Just chill out with the garlic. I know someone who hates the smell of it. She's like Dracula."

"You do have a funny side to you. Please, please, please stay this way."

"I thought it was long gone. I think I'll have him stick around for a while. So about tomorrow. I'll go home to shower and pick up Abby. We can be there at six thirty on the dot."

"That works. I have a meeting tomorrow in the city until three in the afternoon. Why they would have it on a Saturday is beyond me." I stifle another yawn. "Thank you, Kent," I say with complete sincerity.

"Wow. I think that was the first time you said my real name. Or the second time. You must be serious right now. I like how it sounds coming off your tongue. But I still want to earn that nickname Superman, so you're not allowed to say it again."

He makes me think about his tongue, how delicious it was and how I wanted more. And still do. Will it ever happen again?

"Listen. You'll be fine tonight. It's late, and I need to be at the station early."

"Oh. I'm sorry for keeping you up."

"I wouldn't have it any other way. I'd stay up all night for you. Good night, Sunshine. Sweet dreams."

"See you tomorrow. Good night." We both stay on the line.

"Hang up, Sunshine."

"No, you first."

"Is this high school now?" He chuckles.

"Maybe. On the count of three, we both hang up. Okay? One, two, three..." He laughs again and then the line is cut.

What's happening between us? He shocked me all night with his sweetness, but I hate it that I'm on full alert that he'll go off on me again.

Differences or not, whatever is going on, I can't wait to see what happens next. What a bizarre concept. So unlike me.

Chapter 18

Kent

I lock my truck and walk into the station with a smile on my face. For the first time in I don't know how long, I'm happy. At least that's what I think this is. Or maybe I'm hopeful for the future. These are emotions that have been hidden in my closet for years; I hardly recognize them. I called Alexa *Sunshine* last night. It poured out as if I've always called her that and have known her for more than a couple of weeks. How can someone barge into my life and disrupt it in such an unexpected, amazing way?

Sunshine is exactly what she is. She exudes warm, soothing energy that lifts my thick layer of anger and replaces it with peace. Just like she did the first time we met.

I've been trying to ignore how she makes me feel, because guilt washes through me. Abby is sick, and my focus should be on her. Good things shouldn't happen to me when my mom and Abby have been delivered hell in a handbasket. Or am I trying to deny that a relationship with any woman could ruin me again? I've lost and almost lost the two most important women in my life. What if my *like* for Alexa turns to *love*? And what if something happens to her?

Alexa is right though. How am I helping Abby by being a depressive asshole all the time? I'm not like that with Abby, but I am around other people.

A hand slaps me on my shoulder just as I finish pouring myself a cup of coffee. "Hey, Kent."

"Good morning, Vince."

He stumbles back and almost drops his everything bagel. If Alexa were here, she wouldn't come near him after he eats that. You eat one of those bagels, and the garlic stays with you the entire day.

"Did you just say *good morning*? What happened to the morning growl instead? Have you been sniffing paint chips?" he jokes. "Or did you spray your pillow with Alexa's perfume? Dani told me she was at your house last night. I'm surprised you're still alive"—he inspects my face—"or don't have a black eye after the way you treated her."

I punch his arm but smile anyway.

I rip open some sugar packets and shake them over the cup. I crumple them, then toss them into the trash. "She told me what happened in the bar. It seems Dominic was his normal self. And that other asshole is lucky I wasn't there to see him treat Alexa like that." The hot coffee slides down smoothly. I was restless after I hung up with Alexa last night. I can't keep her out of my mind, but I'm not complaining.

We walk over to my desk. Vince sits in front of it and props his boots on top.

"I warned the other one to stay away from her and slipped it in that I'm a cop. Even after she left, he stayed on the other side of the bar. He was plastered."

I shuffle through some forms I need to fill out for court on Monday. "Did Dominic say anything about Alexa after she left? She wants nothing to do with him. What's the deal with Dani forcing him on her, anyway?"

"I have no clue. I asked her a couple of times, but she gets defensive. Maybe it's a mission of his to score with Alexa because she wouldn't give him the time of day in high school. He needs to get rid of that chip on his shoulder. Alexa handled herself pretty well. She's tough but underestimates how many psychos are out there."

"I think she got a taste of that last night. Someone keyed her car in the parking lot too. I'm wondering if it was that guy. I can't imagine Dominic would do it. He probably doesn't have the muscle to key it so deep." I rest my elbows on the desk.

"Dominic? With his pink shirt and manicured nails? He would worry more about getting dirty from her car than actually keying it." His eyebrows crinkle. "He didn't do it. When the drunk one was making a scene, I was the one who defended Alexa, not him. He's an asshat."

I scratch my cheek to keep my blood pressure down. The more I hear about Dominic, the more I want nothing to do with him or Dani. Dani has been great with Abby, but other than that, I don't have a relationship with her.

"Maybe it was some random guy who keyed her car. But she's also getting crank calls from someone. She had one at the bar and was pretty upset about it. The guy made it seem like he was watching her inside the bar."

Vince pulls his feet off the desk and leans forward. "I know the way you analyze everything. You're already trying to figure out if she's being stalked. Try not to get ahead of yourself, and don't creep her out."

"She's already creeped out. She got a phone call at my house and another one when she walked through her door when she got home last night. Maybe this person keyed her car and is following her."

"I'm assuming the caller is smart and blocks the number."

"Yup. I'm going to Alexa's apartment later to load an app that will reveal the number. I need to ask Detective Griggs which one I should use."

"Going to her apartment…just to install an app," he says. "Can't she load it herself?"

"Sorry to interrupt, Kent. Here are the papers you requested for that drunk driver case," a clerk says as he hands them to me.

"Thanks." I place them in an orderly stack on the side of my desk.

"This could be nothing, but I want to make sure. I can't ignore it."

106

"Especially when you have feelings for her."

I nod, and a smile grows on my face. But then I force it away. "I never said I had feelings for her." I avoid eye contact with him, knowing I'm full of shit.

Vince bends over in laughter, bagel crumbs shooting off his shirt onto my desk. "I call bull. You didn't have to say anything. I see you've finally found someone who won't put up with your array of shit. I love it." He breaks out laughing again. Other officers in the precinct turn their heads.

"What's so funny?" asks the nosey dispatcher, Pamela.

"Attention, everyone. I think Kent found his future wife."

Can he yell any louder? He's like a girl.

"Tell her to stand in line. I know a million women who would love to be his wife."

Whistles break out through the room.

"Shut up. Don't you have paperwork or something else to do before we go on patrol?"

"Yes, but I enjoy embarrassing you more."

Chapter 19

Alexa

I push through the twirling golden doors of the newly renovated Marriott near Central Park. My eyes spring open at the exquisite elegance. The lobby screams luxury. A massive glass table greets me with a gorgeous red, orange, and yellow floral arrangement that would fill up my living room. Flowers do nothing for me, but these are eye-catching.

Two staircases with mahogany railings and cream-colored oriental-style runners gracefully curve up and meet at the first floor. A massive chandelier dangles from the ceiling, throwing off soft spectrums of light. Of course, I love the lobby even more because everything is accented with scarlet red.

Ahead of me, the Vault sign dazzles. Natalie told me to meet her and some others there before the meeting starts. I make my way in and search for familiar faces. The bar is full, so I have to squeeze my way through. My head almost gets stuck between two people's shoulders. I greet a couple of coworkers and ask them where Natalie is. They point to a little corner, but what I see makes me almost lose my balance. Natalie's whispering into Joker the Poker's ear. My stomach drops. Darren works for this company. This is bad. Really bad.

He must be from the company that was bought out by Quadro, a salesman. My competition. And now he's talking to my boss and flirting with her.

Before I can turn around, Natalie sees me and waves me over. Darren glances in my direction and his eyes bulge but quickly turn to slits. I'm stuck because I don't know if I should admit I know him or pretend that I'm meeting him for the first time. I don't think he would cause a scene because that could cost him his job. So that means he's probably going to play it cool, like he's the good guy.

I plaster a smile on my face and have no problem playing the same game. "Hey, Natalie. Tell me again why we're here on a Saturday."

She laughs, but as if to impress Darren. "Hi, Alexa. Let me introduce you to Darren Whitehead."

Whitehead? He told me his last name was Whiteman. Interesting that he lied. Don't even get me started on names for him now. I don't know which is worse, Whitehead or Poker. He should be in sales for dermatology products.

"He's from the other company and works the same territory as you, but in oncology. He's ranked as one of the best in sales.

"Darren, this is Alexa Kramer. She's one of my top reps in the cardiovascular division."

His upper lip is sweating. He wipes his hand on his shirt in front of everybody, then extends it out to me. I don't want to touch him, but I have to. I shake it for a millisecond and drop it because it's sweaty and sticky. What the hell was I thinking when I agreed to go on a date with him? His bloodshot eyes never leave mine. *Hungover much?* The glass he's holding probably has vodka in the orange juice. He'd better keep our personal issues outside the office.

"Darren, do you have experience in cardiovascular? Or just oncology?" I ask.

"Just oncology, but *several* years of it."

Nice emphasis on *several*, buddy.

"Everyone's filtering out. It's time to go to the conference room," Natalie says.

Darren urges her to go first but cuts in front of me. He clings to Natalie's side and has her laughing with one of his stupid jokes. I'm sure he's worried I'll tell her what an asshole he is. Or he'll kiss her ass because I'm his competition and she's the district manager. I'll let her figure that out for herself. Unfortunately, she always complains about how she's still single at thirty-eight years old. He's a good-looking guy, so I'm sure she'll fall for his flirty bullshit. It worked with me at first. To a degree, anyway.

A couple of hours pass by painstakingly slow. We did some team-building exercises in different rooms. Darren was never in my group, but I saw him a couple of times with Natalie. Now we're all gathered together again in a conference room for one final speech. I can hardly keep my eyes open. I wish I had one of Abby's crossword puzzles. Not that I could use it here. I cover my mouth to hide my yawn.

Natalie nudges me and whispers, "If you want to keep your job, don't fall asleep while the head of sales is talking."

I roll my eyes. *Whatever.*

After I spoke to Kent last night, I tossed and turned for hours, trying to convince myself that I'm overreacting. No one is following me. The key mark was random. But then the voice from the guy on my phone replays in my head. He told me he didn't have the wrong number. That's what spooks the shit out of me.

I lean over to scratch my ankle and turn my head to the left. Darren's suspicious eyes are pinned on me. What's his problem now? I do everything in my power not to move one facial muscle or blink my eyes. He crosses his arms, but his cocky smirk remains. I sit back up in my chair, fold my hands, and pretend his presence doesn't bother me. Hopefully, he can't see through the facade.

"Have a good weekend, Natalie." I wave to her and provide my ticket to the coat check.

As I put one arm in my coat, it becomes lighter. I glance over my shoulder and pull my jacket out of Darren's hands. "What do you think you're doing?" I snap as I walk away from him.

"I'm being a gentleman," he says with a sly tone as he follows me.

I turn abruptly, quickly scanning to see if there's anyone around us. "We both know you're nothing close to a gentleman, especially after last night. Oh, and your last name is really Whitehead? It sucks to be you, doesn't it? How convenient you never told me where you worked. Why is that? Worried about competition?" I snap as I vigorously button my coat.

"I didn't even know you worked here until I saw you today."

"You're so full of shit. I told you where I worked—oh, but you were probably drunk then too."

"You wish. I have pull in my company, so I'm not worried about your measly sales."

"Measly sales, huh. You should do some research when you get home." I chuckle. "I saw how you were already snuggling up to Natalie during the meetings. To have *pull* with her too. Let me guess—you played the comedian card to get on her good side. I'm curious what she'll think when your bipolar personality makes its appearance the first time you don't get your way."

He clenches his jaw. "You'd better keep your mouth shut."

"Is that a threat? Because your eyes surely reflect it. Or maybe it's insecurity. Oh wait. I guess you have one hell of a hangover." I cross my arms. "Will there be a repeat performance like last night at Kaleidoscope? I bet you're the one who keyed my car in the parking lot and who keeps calling my phone," I hint slyly.

He leans in closer, and I step away from him. "Key your car? I don't know what the hell you're talking about. I don't even know what kind of car you drive."

"Funny how you don't remember anything. Stay away from me at work and outside of work." Now I step closer. "Just remember— I've been with Quadro for years. I also have *pull*. So don't screw with me."

I pivot and walk away while I try to simmer down. He pushed my buttons. I'm never unprofessional, but right now this means war.

Chapter 20

Kent

The entrance door to Alexa's apartment building is propped open. Anybody could walk in here. I search the area for a camera. Nothing. Great security for a nice apartment building like this one.

Abby slaps my hand away from my hair. "You're very annoying right now. You look great."

I glance at my watch.

"And no, we aren't late," she answers before I can ask.

"Should we have brought flowers or wine since she's cooking dinner for us?" I don't know why, but I have a weird feeling she's not a flower kind of woman. Something I'll have to find out.

"You bought her favorite éclairs, so I think this will win her over. It's funny how you both like the same ones."

Alexa's blazing smile welcomes us at the door. "Howdy! Come on in." She gives Abby a hug.

I close the door and secretly inspect it. It has a cheap knob that wiggles when I touch it. No deadbolt.

When Abby steps away, she hands Alexa the box and says, "These éclairs are for you. They're from Kent, but he's acting all weird right now."

She's going to embarrass me all night. But isn't that what little sisters do—annoy their big brothers?

Alexa places the box on the table, walks over to me, and kisses my cheek. She places her hand on my chest and caresses it. "Thank you. That was very sweet."

I reach for her hand and squeeze it gently. "Sunshine," I say softly.

She wipes her lipstick off my cheek. This time I wish she'd keep it there.

"Thanks for inviting us for dinner." Abby distracts us. "It's been a while since Kent and I have had a meal cooked for us."

"No problem. I love to entertain." Alexa hangs our coats and then ushers us to the shiny red kitchen. "Dinner is almost ready. I decided to make homemade mac and cheese."

"With breadcrumbs on the top?" Abby asks, almost drooling.

"Of course. Nothing but the best for my guests." Alexa transfers the éclairs from the table and places the box on the kitchen counter next to the fancy coffeemaker.

It smells delicious in the kitchen, but I could've sworn I smelled lilies when I walked through the door. I can't stand the smell because it reminds me of funerals. I don't think it was her perfume. Lilies for me is like garlic for Alexa.

She opens up a cabinet with several types of glasses. "What would you like to drink? I didn't know what you'd want, so I have a little of everything. Beer, wine, juice. Help yourself, if you don't mind, while I finish up here."

I open the sparkling stainless steel refrigerator. "Let's see what kind of beer you have. I'm not much of a wine drinker."

She barely brushes against me while she slides a red apron over her head, then ties it around her slim waist. The image of her wearing it with nothing underneath runs through my head. The cold air from the fridge hits my hot skin just in time.

"I bought Heinies because that's what you drank last night." She glances over her shoulder. "Abby, Corona Light or a glass of white wine?"

"I'll pass. Liquor's a no-go until I have my next chemo, so water is fine," she explains as she sits down at the dinner table.

We get our drinks and toast to the evening. Instead of sitting down, I lean against the counter across from the stove and cross my arms. Alexa bends over to look into the oven. I can't help to enjoy the perfect view. I inspect her as if I'm searching for clues. Her tight black pants accentuate her voluptuous curves. Her confidence and charm make her even sexier. She is the definition of a real woman. I take a long, slow swig of my beer.

Abby clears her throat. I look at her, and she raises an eyebrow. Caught red handed.

"Alexa, your apartment is beautiful. It's so lively," Abby says. "Red, red, red. It's nice to see color. I had to add some color to Kent's house when he wasn't looking. It was a typical bachelor pad when I moved back in. It definitely needed a girl's touch. At least Kent is a clean bachelor."

"Thanks. Not everyone likes red kitchen cabinets, but it blends with the living room décor. I'm sure you've noticed I love the color red. I wear it almost every day. It's fun and is my signature color." She smiles at Abby as she tosses salad in a bowl.

On the counter next to the refrigerator is a clear jar with a bunch of quarters in it. "Saving up for the laundromat?" I pick it up and shake it. "You can always come over to our house to use the washing machine."

She snickers. "Funny enough, that jar is for my four-year-old niece. I told her I'd give her a quarter every time I swore. It worked for a couple of days, but ever since the day I met you, I've been swearing like a truck driver again. I know it's unattractive, but this is me. If someone doesn't like it, there's the door." She flashes me her sexy smile.

"It's a part of your attitude I like. I can't say I'd love it if that were your entire vocabulary, but it adds to your tough Jersey Girl outer shell. I've never met a woman as intimidating as you."

She throws a dish towel at me. "This is coming from a cop. I think you've dealt with much worse."

"I wish I had an aunt that promised me something like that, but with ten-dollar bills. But that's wishful thinking since we don't have any aunts or uncles," Abby points out. "Neither of our parents had siblings."

"Kent, your house is in good shape. How old is it? It looks like it was built in the late sixties. Am I right? I couldn't see the outside so well since it was dark," Alexa says while chopping tomatoes.

"You're good. Are you an expert on houses too?"

"I'm an expert on a lot of things." She winks at me over her shoulder. "But with regards to houses, not me. My dad has his own real estate business. My brother and I learned from him throughout the years."

I edge closer to her so I can observe her face. "Our mom's parents built that house when the prices for land were dirt cheap. When my father left us, we moved in with them. My grandfather taught me everything about repairing and renovating houses. After they died, the house transferred to my mom and then to me."

She points her knife at me. "You could make a fortune if you sold it. Especially with that view from the front porch. It's ridiculous how expensive the houses are in Weehawken. Who am I kidding—New Jersey in general. Sometimes I wonder why I rent this place for the price I do. But I like living in a busy city. I'm not sure I could ever live near my parents or brother in Morris County. It's too quiet. It's great for a long weekend or a break, but that's about all I can handle."

I gesture toward Abby. "Abby and I have discussed selling the house, but it'd be hard for us. It's the only thing we have left from our family. It keeps us close to Mom and our grandparents. There's no mortgage, so it's affordable even with the ridiculous taxes. It's a perfect size for a small family."

"We thought we were going to have to sell the house when Mom was sick. The medical bills piled up fast," Abby says as she massages lotion into her dry hands. "But our neighbors loved our family, so they started a fundraiser in her name. We were able to pay off most of the bills with that money. She had a small life insurance plan that helped too.

"Now that I have cancer too, we wouldn't dare let them help us again. I'm too stubborn. I don't want help. But we do have a healthcare administrator this time around. He guides us on how to get monetary assistance for the expenses that won't be covered by my insurance. Healthcare has changed since Mom died. I can't say it's better, but we know a lot more compared to then."

Alexa hands me the salad bowl. "Please set this on the table and sit your cute butt down. The mac and cheese is ready." She pulls the hot pan out of the oven and places it in the middle of the table. "Let's dig in." She pulls off the apron and tosses it on the counter.

She bends over the table, and her perfect cleavage peeks out of her shirt. I wish she were for dessert, not the éclairs.

I need to remember that Abby is here.

"I hope you had a good day, because mine was pretty shitty. Want to know why?" she asks while she scoops each of us healthy portions of the steaming macaroni.

Abby raises her hand. "Another quarter in the jar. You swore," she taunts. "Sorry. You said *shitty*."

"I think I have a quarter." I lean to the side and pull some loose coins from my pocket. I hold one up. "Here's my donation to... What's your niece's name?"

"Felicia."

I get up from the table and toss the quarter into the jar. *Clang.* "Here's my donation to Felicia's college fund. Maybe I should toss a couple more in since college is so expensive." *Clang, clang.*

"Nice. My sister-in-law, Lisa, will love you both." Alexa chuckles while she fills up her plate.

"Your day couldn't have been that bad—you're still chipper," I point out.

She bobs her head back and forth. "That's because you two are the highlight of my day. I've been looking forward to it the entire afternoon."

"So was I." Abby mimics what I'm thinking. "I had no plans this weekend. You are so much more fun. So give us the scoop about your shitty day."

Alexa gives her the evil eye.

"I'm allowed to swear." Abby smiles, then puts a big forkful of cheesy macaroni into her mouth. "This is so good, Alexa."

It's been a relief to see her eating so well these past few days. I can't wait until she gains back some weight, gets some color in her cheeks, and her hair grows back. She doesn't realize I watch everything she does. I know when she's exhausted, when she's emotional, how much she eats, and if she's lost more weight.

"I ran into Poker again. His real name is Darren, by the way. He was at the meeting I went to today. Get this—he's an oncology sales rep for the company that was bought by my company. And his territory is the same as mine. I was beyond shocked when I saw him."

I put my fork down before I bite it in half. "Did he harass you?"

She reaches over and lays her hand on mine. "Relax," she says softly.

I loosen my clenched jaw.

"He was a perfect gentleman in front of everyone. We didn't acknowledge that we knew each other. We had a heated discussion after the meeting was finished, but I held my own. I'm his competition, and he doesn't like it. I saw him kissing my boss's ass. Not sure why, since she's not his boss, unless they know something I don't. Layoffs are coming. I have to watch his every move. I trust him even less now."

I need to simmer down. I don't like how this sounds. It seems too coincidental with the phone calls, his outbursts, and now working at the same company. The more she tells me, I'm convinced she's being stalked.

"He lied to me about his last name. It's Whitehead." She smacks her hand on the table. "How funny is that?"

Abby bursts out laughing.

"You could come up with some interesting new names for him," I say after I drink the last drop of my beer.

"Hell yeah, I can. But I won't. I must remain professional." Alexa rolls her eyes.

She points to my empty beer. "Do you want another one?"

I hold my hand up. "I'll have another later."

"Kent told me about your car. Did you ask Mr. Pimple...what's his name again?" Abby chuckles.

"Darren," Alexa and I say in unison.

"As for keying my car, I threw it in the conversation to see his reaction. He looked clueless. My gut tells me he didn't do it. I also mentioned the phone calls, but he never responded. He focused on my car."

I lean back in my chair to pace myself. She's even an excellent cook. Is there anything she can't do? How is it that she hasn't been snatched up by some other guy? I mentally smack myself in the face because I'm already in too deep.

"Vince said Darren was wasted last night. Did he look hungover?"

"His eyes were bloodshot, but that was about it. I'm not sure others would even notice. He must have a secret potion to cure hangovers. Or he's an alcoholic and has vodka with orange juice for breakfast."

Alexa props her head on her folded hands. "I wasn't going to say anything because I wanted to forget about it. But I'll tell you anyway." She gets up from her chair and removes a piece of paper from a paper bin. "After I got home this afternoon, a bouquet of white lilies was delivered here." She hands me a tiny card.

Lilies. I was right. I flip the card and read it out loud, "Thinking of you." It's signed with a *D*. "So *D* for Dominic or Darren."

Abby scopes out the kitchen and living room. "Where are the lilies? I don't smell anything."

"I did when we first arrived."

"I put them in my office and closed the door. It sounds like a bitchy thing to do, but within seconds it reeked like a funeral home in here. I had to open all the windows to get rid of the smell. I was too lazy to throw them in the dumpster outside."

"So who do you think sent them?" I ask while trying to keep calm. My emotions are screwed up when I'm around her. Am I jealous, worried, or angry?

"It wasn't Darren after our confrontation today. Only other person would be Dominic."

Abby takes the card from my hand. "I guess he thinks you're still interested."

"I was *never* interested. He wasted his money on the wrong woman. Flowers do nothing for me. Who knows what Dani is telling him."

"Kent told me about the phone calls you're getting," Abby says. "Did you get any today?"

Alexa shakes her head and sits back down. "So far nothing. It's the first day without a single call. Maybe it was just a spoof."

Negative.

"I'm still going to load the app on your phone. I spoke to a detective, and he told me which one to use. The only problem we have is when a burner phone was used. This app will tell you the number, but if it's a burner phone, we won't find out who it is right away. Also, if the person is smart and used one, we could hit a dead end. They could use it once and throw it away."

"But again, this could be us worrying about nothing," Alexa stresses, then sips her wine.

"Maybe so, but I'd feel better if we knew for sure."

Chapter 21

Alexa

We all lean back in our chairs. I pat my belly. "I guess we enjoyed our meals. Our dishes are practically licked clean. Why don't you two digest in the living room. We still have those éclairs to eat."

Abby stretches her arms over her head. "I'm ready to pop. You're an awesome cook. My body thanks you. I haven't eaten like that in a long time."

We all stand up at the same time and take our dishes to the sink. "Wow. Thanks for the help. I have my own system when I clean, so I'll do the rest." I shoo them away. "Go and relax."

I wipe down the counter one final time. It's so quiet. Did they leave? I walk to the living room, and my heart erupts like a volcano. Abby's fast asleep on the couch. Her head rests on Kent's thigh; his arm drapes over her shoulder. His other hand clasps his chin, as if deep in thought. I suddenly realize how much they need each other. They have no family. She looks up to him as a brother, father, and a friend. I'm almost jealous. No, I am jealous, because I want to be like a sister to her too. Not to him of course. It's so absurd to feel this way when I've only met her a couple of times. Even though she's twenty-nine, she seems younger because of her frailty.

Kent looks up and smiles softly. It's incredible how a genuine smile can make someone glow. He's beautiful once he lets his true self shine through. My hormones kick up a notch when I see him like this.

He points to a red satin pillow on the other corner of the black sectional and then points to Abby. I nod in understanding. I hand it to him and watch him sidle his way out from underneath her. He swiftly but smoothly places the pillow under her head. She stirs but remains asleep as he lays a blanket over her.

"Sorry. She needs power naps," he whispers.

"It's no problem. I'm glad she feels comfortable enough to sleep here. I can't help but want to take care of her. Should we lay her on my bed?"

"No. She'll be okay there. Since she's been sick, she's learned to sleep anywhere."

He walks to a table covered with picture frames. I explain who everyone is. I point to one frame. "This pretty little girl is Felicia. Now you know who you donated money to."

"You have a big family. You're lucky. I wish we had that. Especially now. It's hard to take care of her after her treatments. I only have so much vacation time. Abby refuses to have a nurse come to the house because she thinks she can do it alone. I think she's also embarrassed, but she never says it. She won't let me see her when she's sick. I make sure I'm in the house when she gets home, just in case she needs something. Dani tries to help out when she's not working. I hope I can take off when Abby has her treatment next Friday. I've been trying to rearrange shifts to keep a couple of days open. It doesn't look good."

"I can take care of myself," Abby grumbles.

Kent's eyes dart in her direction, and I cover my mouth to stifle my laugh. She wasn't asleep after all.

"What did you hear?" Kent asks.

"Everything." She grins with her eyes closed.

My phone rings on the counter. Kent motions for me to get it, and he follows me.

I pick it up after the third ring and release the breath I was holding. "It's just Dani," I say.

"Hey, Dani. How's it going?"

I cover the phone with my hand. "She's with Vince and wants to know if I want to go out. Should I tell them to come here for a drink? Abby, is that okay?"

She gives me a thumbs-up above the couch.

"Check that Dominic isn't with them," Kent suggests.

Good point.

"If it's just you and Vince, why don't you come here for some drinks?"

I take small plates out of the cabinet and place them on the table while she talks to Vince. "Great. Come whenever."

"Can I play with your phone now?" Kent asks as he reaches out his hand before I put it back on the counter.

I hand it to him and then open the box of éclairs. "If either one of you wants an éclair, please help yourself. Thanks for bringing more than enough. Now Vince and Dani can have one if they want."

Abby's power nap seems to have helped. She comes to the table and sits down. Kent follows behind while fidgeting with my phone.

"Can you please type in your password?"

I type it while he holds the phone because I have an éclair in the other hand. I'm so full from dinner, but I don't care. They are too hard to pass up.

"Alexa, I totally forgot to show you something." From her bag, Abby pulls out a tiny periwinkle head scarf with a bitsy blue butterfly on it, similar to a small broach.

"Remember last night when I told you about possibly making head scarves for children at the hospital? I played around today to come up with some ideas. Here's the first one I made." She hands it to me. "I thought about making plain scarves and then creating little accessories the kids can attach to it. Maybe a bow or flower. This one has a butterfly. I still need to think of ideas for boys. They're not as easy. I'm not sure they want to stick a car or football on their head. Maybe I should find some fabric with cars or trucks on them. Or maybe even superheroes. Then again, boys probably don't want to wear anything on their heads other than baseball caps."

I'm in awe that she's so creative. "This is amazing. You really have the talent for design."

She blushes. "Thank you. I enjoy it. I think I'll talk to the nurses and show them samples before I agree to sell them. You should come with me since you have sales experience. I need a cheerleader. Maybe show me what to do or say."

Kent looks up from my phone. "Abby, don't bother her with this stuff. She has enough going on."

"Actually, I think it's cool. I have a flexible schedule, so if we can work something out, I'd love to go with you. Granted, this is not my area of expertise, but I might be looking for a new job soon anyway."

What if I am out of a job soon and have no money to pay for my lifestyle? Maybe I should live in a cheaper apartment. I shiver. I don't want to think about it. There are sales jobs everywhere.

"I'll get the door," Abby offers when the doorbell rings.

I finish the last bite of my éclair and wipe my mouth.

I lean over Kent's shoulder. "Everything okay with loading the app?"

"Yeah, but it's more complicated than I thought. I need to play around with it a little bit more." He taps on his own phone.

"Abby? What are you doing here?" Dani asks as she steps through the door and gives her a big hug.

"Alexa made us dinner."

She crinkles her face, then sees Kent at the table. "Us?" She pouts as I walk up to them. "And we weren't invited?"

"Vince knew I was coming over tonight," Kent hollers from behind me.

Dani eyes Vince. He shrugs his shoulders. "What's the big deal? I didn't think he'd still be here since he only had to do something with her phone," Vince explains to Dani.

"Sorry, Dani. It was a last-minute thing." I hug her.

"Hey, Kent?" She walks over to him while her eyes inspect the layout of the apartment. "I guess Alexa likes guys who yell at her." She ruffles his hair.

He ducks away from her. "Cut it out, Dani."

She punches him on the arm. "I'm just kidding. Lighten up."

I focus on Vince and try to ignore her comment. "Hey, big guy. I'm glad you both came. It's nice to hang here instead of going out. I had enough action last night."

"I'm sure you did." He turns toward the kitchen. "This is a great place. Is there a garage for this apartment building? Parking's a bitch."

"Yes. It's below the building. But it's only for people who live here. I'd never be able to have a car here if there wasn't one. It's too expensive to park, and I don't like to use public transportation."

"I'm not a big fan of it either. I pass this building all the time. I always wondered what the apartments looked like inside."

I toss their jackets over the back of the sofa.

Dani twirls around in the middle of the kitchen. "Nice digs, Alexa. Your modern kitchen is so colorful. The cabinets and refrigerator sparkle. Do you wash them every day? If this is your style, you'd love Dom's apartment...but I guess it's mine too, since I live with him. Thankfully, it's double the size of this one. I don't hear when he brings his next conquest home. Maybe you'll be the one he brings home but doesn't make leave before sunrise."

I could hear a pin drop, as everyone freezes and looks at her with big eyes. Kent's face could shatter a window. Does she ever listen to what comes out of her mouth?

"Filter, Dani," Vince says.

"What? I just meant that maybe she's the one he'll settle down with. I'm not trying to be mean. He's always dated girls that looked like you, Alexa. Now that he's found you again, maybe it's fate."

"I don't care what you think it is. I'm not interested, so back off," I say firmly, then walk over to the refrigerator. "So now that that's settled, what would you like to drink?"

Dani sits next to Abby on the couch. "Abby, I was thinking."

"Oh no, not again. Watch out," Vince yells from the kitchen.

I laugh, but Dani ignores him. "Why don't we throw a party at your house to celebrate your final chemo treatment? You deserve it." She grabs Abby's hand and shakes it in the air.

Abby's face lights up. "Really? I haven't been to a party in so long. Forget about a party for me. I still have some doctor's appointments to go to before I can truly celebrate. How about a Christmas party? We can decorate a big tree and hang mistletoe."

It's too funny how she talks when she's excited.

She jumps up from the couch and runs over to Kent. "What do you say? Can we have a party?" She wiggles his shoulders.

He puts the phone down and looks over his shoulder at her. "Sounds like a great idea. We have something to celebrate this Christmas."

"Alexa, do you want to help us plan it? You love red, perfect for Christmas decorating," Abby exclaims as she sits back down on the couch.

"I'd love to, if that's okay with you, Dani. I go a little overboard when it comes to decorating because my mom goes crazy every year. I've learned from the best. The tree is usually up the weekend before Thanksgiving."

Dani shrugs. "Definitely. The more the merrier. Decorating is not my strong point."

We look through our calendars and pick the best weekend for it.

"Yay! It looks like the second weekend of December works for everyone. First Alexa agrees to help me with my scarves, and now a party. I could jump out of my skin with excitement. Thanks for suggesting it, Dani." She prances through the room and hugs everyone.

While Kent and Vince get back to my phone, we discuss the party and selling Abby's scarves. I peek at the men every few minutes. Their faces are serious. How can it be so complicated?

"You know what, Abby? I can ask Matt and Kayla to cater the party. I'm sure he'd give us a good deal. Kayla's cousin is a famous German chef and will be here at that time. I'll ask him to cook something. What do you both think?"

"A famous chef? Hell yes." Dani beams. "Did I mention I'm not good at cooking either?" She lifts her beer in the air, then chugs it. "I'm just good at drinking the alcohol."

I nod because most of the times I've seen her, she had been drinking a lot.

Abby bounces on the couch. "That would be so cool. They should all be invited."

"Alexa, sorry to interrupt the excitement, but we're good to go with your phone," Kent says from the kitchen.

"What are you doing with her phone anyway?" Dani asks as she stands up with me. "You guys look too serious for a Saturday night."

"Kent's loading an app to track a phone number," I respond as I carry empty glasses to the sink.

"Why? Gotta stalker?" she teases as she wraps her arms around Vince's shoulders.

"Actually, she might," Kent responds.

Her eyebrows rise so high they almost meet the hairline. "Really? I was only joking. Alexa, you don't have much luck with men right now, do you? After last night with the drunk and your fights with Kent."

"Don't forget your brother. He didn't help things either," Vince adds.

She pulls away from Vince, then looks at me dumbfounded. "What? He just really likes you, Alexa."

"How exactly does he like me? He doesn't even know me. If he did, he would've known that I don't like flowers. He wasted his money sending me lilies today."

"Lilies? Interesting choice. He mentioned he wanted to send you flowers, but I didn't think he would do it." She looks around. "Where are they?"

"They're in my office because the scent was overpowering. Maybe his conquests enjoy flowers like them, but I don't."

Dani twirls her hair around one finger. "You remind me of Mary in the movie *There's Something about Mary*. You know, the one with Cameron Diaz and Ben Stiller? Just like Mary in high school. You were so nice and beautiful. All the guys gravitated to you, but you didn't realize it half the time. They all wanted a chance, but you never showed any interest. And if you did, you lost interest fast. Tearing their hearts in two." She mimics ripping a heart apart and then starts laughing.

"Are you saying Dominic is a stalker like the guys in the movie?" Kent inquires with a snippy tone.

Dani shoots daggers at him. "No. Dom would never stalk a woman. He might be a bit too forward, but he'd never stalk someone. He's better than that. He has too much pride." She cocks her hip. "I know you don't like him for some reason, but I hope you aren't implying he's the one calling Alexa."

"No, that isn't what he's saying. I got the calls before I even spoke to Dominic. But again, we can be overreacting about the situation. So let's all chill out."

Who am I trying to convince? Everyone else or myself?

"Let's get back to the phone tracking. Do you think you can do it?" Dani asks Kent.

He explains why it's hard to track a burner phone. "Why do you think terrorists use them?"

She nods, then puts her arm around me. "I'm sorry I made a joke. I hope it turns out to be nothing. But I'm sure it's scary. Why don't you change your phone number?"

"That was going to be the next thing to suggest," Kent says.

"It's not that easy. I use my phone for work too. It would be complicated, and I don't want to get my work involved unless I need to."

"This is your work phone?" Kent says in shock. "Then it could be someone you work with or one of your clients."

"I've never had a problem before. We're overthinking everything. I haven't gotten any calls today, so let's not talk about it anymore. Kent, please show me how it works before you leave. But for now, it's Saturday. Let's have some fun."

Chapter 22

Kent

Abby flashes me the look that means she's exhausted and needs to go home. Vince and Dani left a while ago to go for a drink somewhere.

"Alexa, we should get going. Abby's ready to drop."

"I've had so much fun," Abby mumbles as she yawns, "but my body wants to collapse. I don't know how long it's been since I've stayed up this late."

Alexa hands us our jackets. "Don't say another word—you need your rest for Friday. I'm glad you both came. You're so fun to be around. Come back anytime."

She embraces Abby. "Please let me know if you need anything this week. Call me if you want to talk about your scarves or the Christmas party."

"You're the best. I'm not sure I can do it on my own."

Abby motions to the door. "Kent, I'll wait in the hallway."

"I'll be there in a second."

Alexa takes my hand and inches closer. "I hope you enjoyed yourself even though you were sort of working."

I push a strand of hair behind her ear. "More than you know. I've had a great weekend because of you. The first in a very long time." I lean in and kiss her cheek. When I move away, her eyes roam to my lips. Her expression speaks a million words. We want to see each other again, but we don't know how to say it.

I tug my jacket over my shoulders. "My week is busy, but we'll talk somehow. You know what to do if something else happens. Call me right away regardless of the time."

I turn to leave, but she grabs my hand again. "Kent, I know I hardly know you and Abby, and tell me to mind my own business if I'm overstepping, but please call me if you need help on Friday. I heard Dani tell Abby she won't be able to help. If you have to work, I'm here if you need me. But I don't know if Abby would want me to."

I brush the back of my hand gently across her cheek. "That's very thoughtful."

"Kent?" Abby interrupts outside the door.

Alexa bites her lip and steps back.

"Good night, Sunshine. I'll talk to Abby about Friday. Don't forget to lock your door."

She nods and waves to us before she closes it. I wait to hear the lock click.

I tap Abby's arm to go in a different direction than the way we came. "I know you're tired, but I overheard Alexa say there's a garage. I want to check it out. It'll only take a few minutes. Is that okay?"

She nods and closes her jacket tight. We find the garage, and it's hardly lit. About thirty to forty cars can park in here. Alexa's car is in a secluded dark corner. The car exit is not too far away, but the security gate isn't closed. I walk over to it, and a sign says it's out of order. Anyone can get in here. This is an expensive apartment building, but it doesn't have the type of security one would expect. There are no security cameras here either. It doesn't make sense.

"Can we please go home?" She shivers. "I'm exhausted and freezing."

I put my arm around her. "Sorry, sis. Let's go."

Chapter 23

Alexa

I happily whip out my credit card and give it to the saleswoman behind the counter. "I don't know why I get excited over black skinny pants. I have several pairs at home, but these will look fabulous with my high-heeled black boots."

She smiles while packing them in a bag. "I have two pairs too, but don't tell anyone," she murmurs with a grin.

I glance to my left and see a quick movement over my shoulder. Someone wearing a baseball cap stands behind a rack, facing away from me. He's practically in between the clothes, as if hiding.

"Here you go." She hands me the bag as she walks around the counter.

"Thanks." I step to the side and place the bag on the floor between my feet to put my wallet away. The man is still behind the rack. Something doesn't sit well with me. Maybe he's waiting for his wife or girlfriend though.

The saleswoman approaches him and asks if he needs help. He shakes his head, and she walks away. I pick the bag up, but my eyes roam in his direction again just as he removes his cap. I gasp. It's like a train wreck. It's hard to look away. His scalp is partially shaven and there's a red swollen scar running down the side behind his ear. Large chunks of hair on the other side are gone, with patches of gray and brown hair remaining. My stomach is in my throat as he scratches near the scar. I'm convinced I'm stuck in a horror film. Now I wish I'd never come to this store. That image will never be erased from my memory.

The screeching of hangers across a rack drags me back to reality. I cover my ears even though I have a plastic bag in one hand and my purse in the other. I'm sure I look like an idiot. Get me the hell out of here.

And again, Matt's café is packed. No matter what time I come here, it's busy. I'm surprised to see two empty seats by the window. That will be nice for Abby. The sunshine will give her an extra dose of vitamin D.

She asked me to meet her here so we could ask Matt and Kayla about baking something for the party. Even though she likes to stay away from crowds when she's close to a treatment, she insisted we meet today.

I came prepared though. My hand rummages around my bag to find the antibacterial wipes I bought. Once I find the package, I wipe down the table. It's not that I think the café is dirty—you just never know who's touched the table. I sanitize the chairs as well.

"Looking for a job?" Matt chuckles behind me.

"Don't joke. I might be unemployed soon." I ball the dirty wipes up and place them on the edge of the table. "Abby's meeting me here. I want to make sure everything is extra clean for her."

"I understand. She told me about Friday. Kayla and I are thrilled that it's almost over for her."

"Abby," I exclaim.

She spins in our direction and beams. Again, she's wearing a pretty new head scarf. A turquoise color, similar to my eyes. She's even wearing colored lip gloss.

"Hey there." She greets us with air kisses.

We chitchat until Kayla joins us.

"Now that you're both here, I have a favor to ask you," Abby says to Matt and Kayla with a contagious smile.

Her excitement oozes out of her. She can hardly sit still. I remain quiet as she asks them to help out with the party.

"Abby, it would be an honor to prepare something for your Christmas party. You and Kent have so much to celebrate," Kayla says with enthusiasm.

I readjust myself on the wooden chair. "I thought we could also ask Gerry to help out with the food. You can bake the sweet delights, and he can make the savory dishes."

"We'll see him at Lisa's during Thanksgiving weekend. We can ask him then. I'm sure he'll be all for it. He's good like that," Kayla assures Abby.

"Is it too last minute to plan a party during the holidays?" Abby asks.

"Not when Matt and Gerry are involved. We're going to throw the best bash ever. Right, Alexa?" Kayla nudges me.

"You betcha. I can't wait!"

"I can't thank you all enough. I'm so glad Dani suggested this." She covers her mouth. "Oops. Damn. I should've asked her to come today."

"No worries," I assure her. "I spoke to her yesterday. She's working today anyway. I told her we'd ask Kayla and Matt. She can't wait for this party."

"Okay. We need to get back to work. We'll talk soon."

Matt and Kayla wish her good luck for Friday and walk away hand in hand. They are so damn cute. For the first time, I'm envious of their marriage.

We turn in our seats to enjoy the sun shining in. As my eyes adjust to the glare, I see a man wearing a baseball cap and sunglasses across the street. Is he taking pictures of the café? Could it be? I jump up. My hand hits my empty coffee cup, and the spoon falls onto the floor. I bolt for the door. A bus slows in front of the café, so I can't see across the street. Once it drives away, the person is gone. I check in both directions, but I don't see anyone.

"Alexa?"

I feel a hand on my shoulder, and I twitch.

"I'm sorry. I didn't mean to scare you. What's the matter?"

"I don't know." I scan the street again. "There was a man taking pictures of the café. He was across the street."

"So?"

"I think he was just in a store I was at. But he had a camera in front of his face and sunglasses this time." Am I imaging things, or is this paranoia?

"Maybe it was just a tourist taking a picture. You know how lovely the café looks from outside."

"Sure. You're probably right." *I don't think so, but I'm not going to tell her that.* I shiver because I have no coat, and neither does Abby. "Abby, let's get back inside and finish our food. You'll get sick without a coat on."

I keep repeating that it's just a coincidence, but haven't I been saying this all along? How many will there be before I admit they're not coincidences at all?

I slap a fake smile on my face as we sit back down. "So tell me what else is going on? Are you ready for Friday?"

Abby's forehead crinkles.

"What's up? You can tell me."

"I feel bad asking."

I rest my head on my hand. "Ask me what?"

"Kent has to work during the time I have chemo. He might not get out in time to pick me up at the hospital. It all depends on how I feel after chemo. I offered to take a cab home, but he refuses to let me do that."

"I have to agree with him. If you aren't feeling well, the last place you want to be is in a disgusting taxi. Around what time do you think you'll be able to go home? I'm busy until noon, but after that I'm free. I plan on driving to my parents later in the day."

"Around two or so. I can't give you an exact time."

"No problem. I can hang at the library, and a nurse can call me when you're ready. Easy peasy lemon squeezy."

"All you need to do is drive me home. That's it." She swipes her arms to her sides. "After I have chemo, I go straight to bed."

"Are you sure Kent won't mind if I drive you home? He hasn't mentioned it to me since Saturday."

"I discussed it with him, and he was fine with it as long as *I* asked you. Not him. Believe me—he'd tell me if he didn't like it. He trusts you."

"Kent surprised me last weekend. He showed me a side of him I would've never guessed he had. We've spoken almost every night since. He's laid back, funny, and beyond sweet."

"He doesn't let anyone see that side, so that's how I know you're special. Different than all the other women."

"All the other women? I'm not sure I want to hear that."

"He's handsome and wears a uniform. Women flock to him, trying to get his attention. But he never gives them the time of day. Your sitting at our kitchen table was a miracle in itself. Why do you think I was so excited? But I'm biased because I already love you."

"Aw, you're so sweet."

"I want to see him happy for once. He smiles when you're around. Vince even commented the other day. Joking around that Kent's becoming a softy."

"Is that a bad thing?"

"No way. Vince has been his best friend for years. He loves it that Kent is lightening up. He also poked fun about him finally finding *the one*."

I crack up. "Vince is crazy!"

"Alexa...I think he's right."

I stack our dirty dishes to occupy myself. "I wouldn't go that far." My heart is in a frenzy just contemplating the idea.

"You should've seen how he observed you at your apartment, as if he was sucking in every little morsel of you. I don't think he has a clue what to do about his feelings for you."

"He's not the only one," I mutter.

I'd felt his eyes roam down my body, leaving a trail of heat behind. Little did he know that I hadn't been sweating from leaning over the stove—but from him being in the room. My skin tingles just thinking about it again.

I shove Abby's leg playfully. "Since when did you become such an expert on love and romance?"

She sighs. "I'm not. I call it like I see it, and you two have it." She taps her chin. "To quote Dani, 'It only takes one woman to change a man.'"

Chapter 24

Alexa

Nurse Patty just called to tell me that Abby's ready to go home. I can't wait to tell Abby about the conversation I had with Patty about the scarves. We set up a tentative meeting after the holidays to discuss things in more detail.

I sit in the waiting room, biting my nails. I don't know what to expect when Abby comes out. Kent kept apologizing, but he has nothing to be sorry about, because I wanted to do it, for Abby and him.

My stomach drops and my eyes water when I see Abby. She's pale as a ghost and is in a wheelchair. Her head rests in her hand. Her body looks depleted of all energy. She looks even skinnier than the last time I saw her. There's a little pea-green hat on her head.

I'm asked to sign a couple of forms to record that I picked her up. Then the nurse passes me an envelope to give to Kent.

"That's all, dear. Abby's ready to go."

"This is my first time. Is there anything I should know before I take her home? Should I use the wheelchair to take her to the car?" Abby hasn't said a word. Kent told me what I needed to do, but I want to hear it from the nurse too.

"Is your car parked by the front exit?"

"Yes."

"Take her in the wheelchair. Then you can just put her in the car. She reacted badly to this treatment, so she's pretty exhausted. Just get her home so she can sleep." She hands me Abby's bag.

I'm shaking and my hands are frozen because I don't have a clue what I'm doing. But I offered to do this, so I need to suck it up. I'm usually in control, but meeting Kent and Abby has pushed me into a realm of the unknown.

A few minutes later, I buckle her in the front seat of my car. She lays her head on the headrest and is almost asleep. I rub her leg to assure her everything is okay and we're on our way back to her house. She nods and closes her eyes.

While driving, I continually look between her and the road. My body is so stiff that I'm sitting ramrod straight in my seat. My butt cheeks are firm, like two bowling balls. Sweat drips down my back. I won't relax until I know she's safe at home and in her bed. Every movement or moan startles me. All I ask is that she doesn't throw up in my car. I brought a bag with me just in case, but she's so weak that I don't think she'd be able to control it.

My phone rings, but it's not connecting to my car for some reason. I can't worry about that now.

Kent's home is only a few houses away, but it feels like a hundred. Once I pull into the driveway, I rip my fingers off the steering wheel. My hands are cramped because I held on to the wheel for dear life.

I open her door and shake her gently. She's fast asleep. I can't carry her, so I need to wake her up. But before I do that, I search through her handbag and find the house key in the last damn place I look. I could stuff their entire house in this thing.

I tug her arm. "Abby, it's time to wake up. We're in the driveway. In two minutes, you'll be in your warm bed and can sleep for as long as you want."

She groans in response and leans forward. I wrap one of her arms around my neck. I've read every patient reacts to chemo differently, but she is nearly comatose.

My phone rings again, but whoever it is will have to wait. One step at a time, that's all we can do. We finally make it to the door, and I open it with record speed even though I have only one free hand. My heart pulses in my ears.

The second we get through the door, Abby almost faints, but I catch her. As I'm holding her up with two arms, she vomits all over my shirt and then the floor. My brain goes into overdrive. I drag her to the bathroom as fast as possible to get her to the toilet before she does it again. It doesn't faze me that it's all over me.

I sit us both on the floor and position her so it's easy for her to throw up in the toilet.

"I'm so sorry," Abby sobs. "It's never been this bad before," she says with the little energy she has left.

She stiffens, and I react in time to help her lean over the toilet. Once she's finished, I search through the cabinet under the sink for towels so I can wipe her face. There are none. Maybe there are some in the kitchen.

"Abby, I need to get some towels. Are you okay to be alone for a few seconds?"

She nods and lays her forehead on her arm.

I bolt to the kitchen and search through every damn cabinet and drawer, slamming them left and right, and there's nothing. *Fuck!* I grab the paper towels off the counter. Just as I get to the bathroom, she throws up again but doesn't fully make it into the toilet. My body vibrates like a leaf because I don't know how to do this, and it's horrifying to see what she's going through. The smell alone makes me gag.

"You can do this, Alexa," I say to pump myself up.

I wipe up what I can and throw the dirty paper towels into the little garbage can. I smell atrocious, but we both do.

She shivers in my arms. Her clothes are wet, so I reach over and turn on the heater.

"Abby, I need to leave you here for a second. You need fresh clothes and more towels."

"Laundry room. Around the corner," she whimpers.

"I'm going to lay you on the little rug here. I'll be right back."

She's twitching badly.

The laundry room has two basketsful of folded clothes and two towels. I snatch them and race back.

"Abby, I need to take your shirt off. It's not healthy to be in soaked clothes, especially in your condition."

"No."

I can barely hear her weak voice.

"I'm embarrassed. No one has ever seen me naked."

"Don't be ridiculous. We're both girls."

She has no energy to fight, so she lifts up her arms to let me remove her shirt. When I do, I'm shocked to the core. She has no breasts, just indentations from the mastectomy. I'd assumed she'd had reconstructive surgery at the same time. Scars run perpendicular from the breastbone to under her arms. My chest is so tight that I'm rendered breathless. She doesn't deserve this. No one does.

Deep breaths, deep breaths. This poor girl is lying half naked on a bathroom rug, in a body that will never ever be the same. And this is someone who caught her cancer early. She had to witness her mother suffer even worse.

"Here's a warm sweatshirt. I think it's Kent's since it's huge, but it will keep you warm." I help her into it and rinse her face off with a warm towel. Her lips are chapped.

"Let me get you some water." I stand up, but she hangs on to my hand.

"I feel horrible. I'm so scared when I'm like this." She bursts into sobs.

I sit on the floor and cradle her in my arms. My eyes overflow like a waterfall because I can't explain the feeling I have in my chest. It's heavy with compassion and adoration for her. I lightly rock her back and forth. She snuggles up to me and whispers, "I miss my mom."

Our floodgates open, and we sit there crying together.

"You're the closest person to it. I'm glad you're here."

"Me too, Abby. Me too." My flowing tears drip on her cheek.

I startle when I hear Kent down the hall.

"What the fuck is this? Abby! Alexa! Where are you?"

"We're in the bathroom and need help." I want to sound calm, but deep down I'm a nervous wreck. Maybe I did something wrong and put Abby in danger. Kent will be mad at me.

In seconds he's on the floor with us. "Oh my God. Alexa, Abby, what happened?" He pulls Abby into his arms. "Let's get her to the upstairs bathtub to warm her up."

I follow him out of the bathroom, and then Dani dashes through the still-open front door. She freezes right before she steps in the vomit still on the floor. "What's going on? Kent tried to call you, but you never answered. He called me at home, worried, thinking you were still at the hospital."

I explain what happened, but they're too busy taking care of Abby to listen. Dani is like a machine and knows exactly what to do. While she's in the bathroom with Abby, Kent's in Abby's bedroom, searching for pajamas. I quietly walk downstairs, quickly clean up the floor, grab my things, and escape this nightmare.

I rush to my car in hopes that Kent won't realize I've left. As I pull out of the driveway, he runs out the front door and calls my name. I put the car in drive and speed away with my heart in my throat.

I'm such a coward.

It's pouring rain, but I can't drive fast enough to get to my parents. My nose is sore from rubbing it with tissues and then the back of my hand when they were all gone. I reek of vomit, as does my car. I could have changed my shirt in Kent's driveway, but I wanted to get out of there as fast as possible.

Should I have stayed? Yes. But I had no idea what to do, and I felt like a fly on the wall. I've never run from anything before. I can't stop thinking something is wrong with me.

The gates to the driveway open, and I'm relieved to see my mom's car. I park next to it and start to get out. The red front door opens, and Mom steps out with Felicia and Lisa. The sight of Mom makes me break down, and I run to her.

She drops her umbrella and wraps her arms around me. "What's the matter, baby? What happened? Are you hurt?"

I sob into her shoulder and hold on to her tightly. "I love you, Mom. I don't say it enough, and I'm sorry. I'm so lucky to have you." Is this what a panic attack feels like? My lungs are empty, and my heart pounds out of my chest. Even though it's freezing cold, the pouring rain feels good on my face.

She cradles my face with her hands. "I know you do. But, honey, you need to calm down. I've never seen you like this, and you're scaring me. You weren't supposed to be here until later."

Something wraps around my leg. I glance down to see Felicia's aquamarine eyes filled with tears. From under her *Frozen* umbrella, she hands me a tissue. My grasp on Mom loosens, and I kneel.

"Don't cry, Aunt Lexa," Felicia says while dabbing my wet cheeks with a tissue Mom gave her.

I must look like a clown. "Let's get you inside, Felicia."

We all step inside and shake the rain off us.

"Why are you crying?" Felicia asks with her sweet, innocent voice.

I want to pick her up but I'm disgusting. "I'm very sad. Sometimes that happens."

She hugs my leg tightly, as if she knows I need hugs like my life depends on it right now. How do kids know these things?

"Let's let Alexa take a warm shower." Mom motions for Felicia to let me go. "Then you can give her as many hugs and kisses as you want."

"Wait. My bag's in the car. I need a change of clothes, if you haven't smelled me already."

"I didn't want to say anything, but you smell like vomit. Are you sick?" Mom asks.

I shake my head. "No, but that would be easier than what I've just experienced. Just give me a second."

She nods, and I run back to the car.

As I pull my bag out, my phone vibrates in my hand. I loathe my phone. It's Kent, but I can't talk to him right now. What would I say? I hit End but see he's called five times in the last twenty minutes and left a message. Two other missed calls with a number I don't recognize. I should send the numbers to Kent, but I can't deal with it right now. I turn my phone off.

"Come on, Alexa. You're going to get sick," Mom calls out.

I don't care. A little cold would be nothing.

Voices travel through the house as I walk down the stairs. A hot shower is just what I needed. I'm not 100 percent, but I'm better than before.

I walk into the kitchen and am greeted by the comforting smell of hot chocolate. Mom and Lisa sit at the kitchen nook with their mugs and an open bag of mini white and pink marshmallows. A couple of them have trickled onto the counter. My favorite, and Felicia's too.

"Hey. Is there enough for me?"

"Of course," Lisa says as she rises, then hugs me.

I didn't say hi to her when I came home crying like a baby.

"Where were you all going when I arrived? I hope I didn't ruin your plans."

"I was going to take Lisa grocery shopping, but that will just have to wait. We want to know what happened."

Lisa eases up to me and whispers in my ear, "If you want time with Mom alone, please tell me. I'll go watch the movie with Felicia until James gets here."

I squeeze her hands. "No. I want to spend time with you too. If anybody would understand what happened to me, it would be you."

Lisa is a psychologist and deals with issues like this every day. I've never been out of control like right now. Talking to her will probably help me. I haven't updated Lisa about Kent since I saw her last. Matt and Kayla know more than anyone.

I point to an empty cup. "But first I need some of that hot choco with extra marshmallows." I crack a smile because I feel safe here. My life seems so fragile outside this house.

"Why don't you both go into the living room. I'll bring you yours," Lisa offers.

I grab the bag of marshmallows and follow Mom into the living room. I curl my legs under me on my favorite spot of the couch, covering myself with an old fleece blanket we've had since I was little.

Within seconds a steaming mug is placed in my hand. One at a time, I plunk marshmallows into it until it looks like it's only a cup of marshmallows.

Mom and Lisa sit patiently waiting for me to open up. I take a careful sip and put the cup on the coffee table.

After several minutes of telling the entire story up until I came home today, minus the stalking, my eyes are full of tears again. I can't even think about the mystery caller, and I don't want to worry them. Lisa handed me a full tissue box in the middle of the story. She and Mom snagged some too.

I pull my legs out from underneath me because my feet are numb.

"I feel so unglued. How can I have such strong feelings for two people I hardly know? It's like I fell in love with both of them. They have no family, and it breaks my heart. Kent has rough edges, but he's showing me what's hidden behind his emotional wall. Abby is strong on the outside, but all she wants is a mother to lean on. She can only do so much bonding with her brother."

Mom inches closer to me. "Honey, you're so full of compassion for others, but you don't realize it. You've always been the first to stand in line to take care of someone or to defend them. Look how you took control of James when he was at rock bottom. You always put your family and friends first. You have so much capacity to love."

"You're like Tina, in a way," Lisa adds. "She knew she was the mother hen for everyone. But you've never realized it because it was in you since birth. It's your personality."

"But am I too materialistic? Here Abby has these horrible scars across her chest and no hair, and I worry about how red my lipstick is and if I need a manicure." I wipe under my eyes. "That's what I'm talking about. My problems are minuscule compared to others. I personally don't know what it's like to suffer. I watch it from afar."

"When she said she missed her mom, I thought my heart was going to shatter. Going through such a terrible sickness and having no mother to rely on has got to be awful. Then I imagined she was you, Mom." My lip quivers when I look at her, and she tucks me to her side. I glance at Lisa. "Or you or Tina. Please promise me that you'll get annual checkups."

They both nod.

Now I understand the anger and resentment Kent carries. To see the two most important women in his life suffer and not be able to do anything to stop it.

"So now you know why I was so upset when I arrived here. I take so much for granted every single day. I go about my day without a worry in the world. Kent and Abby have opened my eyes and shown me how lucky I am to have family and friends to rely on. They rely on each other, and that's it."

Lisa moves to the edge of the couch. "I miss my mom every single day, even after all these years. I'm lucky to have my dad and Beth and your parents." She smiles at Mom sweetly. "Don't even get me started on how much I hate that Tina lives in Germany."

"I don't know what to do with these emotions. My relationships have never lasted. I've never had that zing that everyone talks about. That spark. But I think I have it with Kent. No. I know I do. From the first second I touched him, I've been drawn to him." I pull my hands through my hair and grunt.

Lisa giggles. "I can't believe he's a real cop. You have to admit, it's kind of funny how you met. But the first impression isn't always the real one. You don't know what the person is dealing with at the time. Kent is the perfect example. He misjudged you too. Think about what James was like when I first met him."

"Alexa, it's normal to be confused. You're not used to this, and it's quite fast, but sometimes that's how it goes. When I met your dad, it was a whirlwind romance. I couldn't think straight for weeks because I was knocked off my feet. It always happens when you least expect it. You need some time to catch up. Talk to Kent."

"Mommy," Felicia says as she skips into the living room, her curly hair bouncing up and down. She hugs Lisa and asks, "Can I have some marshmallows now?"

"Sure, but you have to ask Aunt Alexa because she's queen of the marshmallows today."

She climbs onto the couch and wraps her little arms around my neck. "What's the matter, Aunt Lexa? Your eyes are shiny again. Do you need more marshmallows?"

I giggle and pull her onto my lap so she's facing me. "I have a crush on a boy I call Superman, and I don't know what to do about it."

"What's a crush?" she asks innocently while playing with a strand of my hair. "You want to smoosh him like a bug?"

I burst out laughing. I wanted to do more than smoosh him when I first met him. "A crush is when you like someone a lot, but more than just a friend."

"Like Mommy and Daddy."

"How did you get so smart?" I tickle her until she slides off my lap.

We all turn our heads when we hear footsteps in the kitchen. James strolls into the living room, then turns around and leaves.

"Daddy." Felicia runs after him.

He chuckles as he walks back into the room and scoops her up. "Sorry, but when I see three women sitting together with dirty tissues everywhere, I'm not sure I want to know what's going on."

I get up and walk toward him. After he puts Felicia down, I pull him into my arms. "I love you, James. Never forget that."

"Love you too, sis."

My old bedroom always gives me a sense of safety and peace. I lie here on my bed cuddling with a throw pillow, protected in a bubble of loving memories. I'm glad Mom hasn't redecorated it. Of course there are dollops of red everywhere. A couple of my cheerleading trophies sit on shelves on one wall. A picture of me as prom queen rests on the old wooden desk. All superficial things that I'm embarrassed I cared about so much back then. I should pack everything up and store it in the attic.

How easy life was when I think back to high school and college. But then again, I always thought life wasn't so hard for me. I worked my butt off and got what I wanted. Things always fell into place for me. I have done it on my own, though, and that's what I'm most proud of.

Tina and Gerry arrive on Wednesday and will be staying at Lisa's for their entire visit. Tina is obsessed with Black Friday, so I'm sure Lisa and I will tag along. I need a major distraction from my life. I suggested we go for manicures or pedicures.

Lisa and James are hosting a big party on the Saturday after Thanksgiving. That's when my family and Lisa's family will get together. Matt and Kayla will be there, as well as Kayla's brother, Tyler. Apparently, he's tired of California so he's moving back to New Jersey or New York. Tyler and I didn't hit it off well the first time we met, but the last couple of times I've seen him, he was actually fun to be around.

I wonder what Kent and Abby have planned. Since they don't have family around and she is sick at the moment, maybe they won't do anything. That breaks my heart all over again. Their Christmas party will have to be even more special.

These exciting events coming up are welcome distractions from the things I'm trying to ignore. I almost told James about the possible stalker, but I clammed up at the last minute. He should be one of the first people I tell, but he has his own family to worry about. No one needs to be bothered with something like this.

My phone vibrates on the nightstand. It's time to confront my embarrassment and talk to Kent. While propped up on my elbow, I pick it up. His name shows on the screen, and my hand starts to shake with a mixture of excitement and fear of what he might say.

"Hi, Kent."

"Alexa, are you okay? I've been freaking out over here wondering where you went. I even drove to your apartment."

I sit up straight on my bed. He went to my apartment?

"I'm at my parents. I told you I planned to visit them tonight."

He exhales deeply. "I'm sorry. I forgot."

I fall back onto my pillow. "How is Abby? I'm so sorry about what happened." I cover my face with my forearm.

"Don't ever apologize. What you did for Abby was above and beyond. We can't thank you enough. Not that I wanted you to experience that, but I'm glad she was with you. She said it too and wants to tell you herself when she sees you next. Right now she's sleeping and probably will for the rest of the night. It will take a couple of days until she's back to normal."

Relief encompasses me. "Good. I'm glad she's okay."

"Please, let me see you," he says with desperation. "I don't want to talk about this over the phone. I don't have to work this weekend. I'll drive to your parents if I need to."

He wants to see me even after I left this afternoon? Of course I'd love nothing more than to see his gorgeous face. "I'd love to see you, but you shouldn't leave Abby. I planned on leaving here around lunchtime tomorrow. Why don't you come to my place around three? Or should you stay with Abby tomorrow too?"

"No. We already talked about it. I want to be alone with you, and she's more than excited about that."

So am I.

Abby thinks more about her brother than herself. Their mom might have died too early, but she was alive long enough to bring up two children she can be proud of.

"Me too. I'd love to see you." I can't be any giddier. Today is ending better than I thought it would. He doesn't seem to be mad at me for leaving. If anything, he sounds worried.

"Kent, I need to go to bed. It's been an emotional day for all of us. We can talk about everything tomorrow."

"Anything you want. Thank you for everything today. I look forward to seeing you tomorrow. I'm a punctual person, so I'll be there at exactly three." He chuckles.

"Now you're even more attractive. I can't wait to see what else there is to find out about you."

"You're the first," he says softly.

"I don't believe that for a second, but I'll let it slide for now."

He chuckles. "Get some rest. See you tomorrow, Sunshine."

"Good night, Kent."

I fall back on my bed, wishing it were tomorrow afternoon already.

Chapter 25

Kent

I'm assuming Alexa hasn't received any crank calls the last few days. She hasn't sent me any new phone numbers. I hope that's true, because I'm still annoyed at how easy it is to enter this apartment building.

Abby begged me to buy flowers for Alexa to say thank you, but I reminded her of what Alexa said about flowers and the fiasco with Dominic's lilies. Since she doesn't like flowers, I thought of something else to give her.

I press the doorbell. A few seconds later, the lock clicks and the door opens. Alexa greets me with her breathtaking beauty that knocks me to the core. For a moment, all rational thoughts evaporate. Will she always affect me like this? I hope so.

"Hi, Kent," she says softly as she leans against the door.

"Hi, Sunshine." I hand her an extra-large box of Lucky Charms.

She takes the box from me and looks at it like it's a diamond.

"These are from Abby and me to say thank you and sorry for yesterday."

"This is the best gift anyone has ever given me. It's perfect."

She beams as I walk inside.

"We are truly sorry."

Her smile turns into a slight frown, and she turns away from me. "Please stop saying you're sorry. I'm the one who screwed up and left."

I stop in my tracks. *Is she kidding me?*

She rummages through a cabinet to find a place to put the cereal box. Her white button-down shirt rides up as she stretches on her tiptoes, revealing a patch of ivory skin on her right side. I know this isn't the moment to think about touching her, but I can't avoid it anymore.

I remove the box from her hand and place it on the shelf where she wanted it. I close the cabinet and realize she's avoiding my eyes.

"Alexa, look at me. Please."

She walks away and straightens the kitchen chairs that are already perfectly placed.

I stand at her side. "Please, look at me," I beg with a strained tone.

Her shoulders deflate, and she finally looks my way. Her glistening green eyes reflect sadness.

I gently put my hands on her arms. "We should've never put you in that position. You went out of your way to help us. We told you she'd only be tired. She's never been that sick at home. I would've never ever suggested the idea if I'd have known that could've happened. We're so sorry that you had to deal with that.

"Abby feels this strong bond with you." I stop, but then I don't care anymore. I'm going to say it anyway. "I do too."

She breaks free from my hands and steps away. "I'd do it again for her, for you, in a heartbeat. I don't regret helping her, but when you and Dani came home, I felt completely useless. Useless!" she exclaims. "I just left without saying anything. That's not me. I don't give up. I thought I could handle anything life dealt me, but I guess I was wrong."

"Of course you can't. No one can. But you sure can hold your own in other situations. The way you put up with my shit on Halloween and in front of the café when I blamed you for everything. It's sexy as hell."

A slight smirk forms on her face. "Sexy, huh?"

"You amaze me every time I see you. You have this strength within you that I've never seen before in a woman. Promise me you won't change because of what happened yesterday. You're everything positive, good, and strong. I hate to see your light dim."

She gasps. "That's the sweetest thing a man has ever said to me. But you hardly know me," she whispers and steps backward toward the counter.

I follow her. "It's the truth. Why do you think I call you *Sunshine*? Maybe I'm the only one who sees you the way I do. We both have barriers, but I see them breaking down little by little. From the first moment we bumped into each other, my world tilted in a way that's made me feel unlike anything I've ever known before. Happiness, excitement, hope...it's hard to describe. Every single time you touch me, my body hums for hours. I did everything in my power to stop it. But I don't want to anymore."

She leans against the counter, as if she's afraid of me but not in a bad way. I inch closer to her, take her hand in mine, and press it to my heart.

"Do you feel my heart and how fast it's racing? That's what you do to me. Your bright light shines through the cracks in my wall, and I don't ever want to live in the dark again. No woman has ever possessed me the way you do, and I want more. A lot more. I want to make you feel the connection I do when I touch you." I press my lips to the top of her hand. "Every inch of my body is alert to every move you make. My skin lights up like a flame."

Her eyes sparkle.

"You feel it too, don't you?"

She nods and looks at my lips. "People say I'm too picky, but I've waited all my life to experience this. I've always been a little envious of those who've found it."

I skim my knuckles delicately across her soft cheek. She rests her hand on mine. "I'd do anything to kiss you again."

She grabs a fistful of my shirt, then pulls me down slowly toward her until we're nose to nose. "What are you waiting for?"

Chapter 26

Alexa

He cups my face and slowly lowers his lips to mine, then stops. His chocolatey eyes connect with mine. "Once I kiss you, there's no going back. You're it for me."

"Mmm-hmm." That's all I can say because I'm blown away by his words. His lips are finally on mine, and it feels like I've waited for years to taste them again.

His tantalizing tongue licks my lips, enticing me to open them. I happily comply, and that's when the heat flushes through my veins. My fingers grip his neck and I pull him closer. He kisses me deeper and presses harder against my body.

My stomach twirls in delight. He tastes sweet and minty, like a candy cane. I rub against him, and a moan leaves his mouth. His slightest movements make my pulse increase. I want him to touch me. My body hasn't yearned for someone like this in years, if ever.

He lifts me to the counter without pulling his lips from mine. My arms travel down his muscular back, and he plants himself between my legs. I arch my back as he pulls my hair to expose my neck. He licks and kisses down, and I'm praying he'll never stop.

I unbutton my shirt and let it drop down my arms, revealing the bare skin of my chest, inviting him to taste even more. His arousal pulsates against mine, and all I can think about is how much more of him I want.

"I love how I feel when I'm near you. My body aches for your touch against my skin. Is it too soon to want you like this? To need you like this?" I pant.

His hands stop roaming. "Open your eyes, Sunshine."

I flutter them open.

"Never. I've thought about us like this since the day we met."

I squint my eyes in disbelief. "Even when you hated me?"

His soft lips caress my cheek while he murmurs, "It was never hate. Exact opposite." He continues to the other side.

Everything about him has caught me off guard. I never thought it would happen to me, this need for someone else to consume me. If he is the one, I'd have waited a lifetime to feel him like this. Because in my heart, no one would ever compare.

His fingers trace down my sides as his thumbs brush the white lace over my breasts. Our kiss deepens and lasts for minutes. I don't know what has come over me. I want to devour him.

We're blasted apart when the doorbell rings several annoying times. Both of us are out of breath from our petting and the surprise of the unwanted distraction.

"Are you expecting someone?" he asks, his chest heaving.

"No, and I don't care." I reach out for him. "Come back here. I'm not done with you yet."

His brown eyes turn jet black.

Just as our lips reconnect, the doorbell rings again.

"Are you sure you're not expecting anyone?"

I growl and hop off the counter while buttoning my shirt. "Not that I know of. I want to say it's the mailman, but it's too late in the day."

I step forward to go to the door, but he holds his arm out. "Let me get it. You need to be cautious."

If this doesn't kill the mood, I don't know what will. I walk behind him as he approaches the door and looks through the peephole.

"I don't see anybody. Stay behind the door so I can check the hallway," he whispers.

I'm too busy staring at his amazing ass to care who's outside.

He opens the door slowly and turns around. "Alexa, eyes up here."

My eyes disconnect from his backside, but I laugh to myself.

"Close the door behind me and lock it. I'm going to search the floors and outside. Do not answer the door for any reason."

I shake my head and do as he says.

Who could this person be, and what does he want? Did I do something to deserve this? What if it's someone completely different than we think? Or maybe someone I went on a few dates with months ago? I haven't gone out with many in the last six months. Darren was the latest...I think out of three or four.

I'm picky because I don't fall for assholes. I analyze the guys I go out with on our first date. How they treat other people and me is the first thing I watch for. One thing I didn't like about the guy before Darren was how he treated the waitress where we had dinner for the first and last time. He was downright rude. I left immediately because I was mortified. If a guy is going to treat a waitress so poorly, then how will he treat me?

Then why am I giving Kent a chance? Shouldn't I kick him to the curb? I shake my head. I can't. I won't. My heart speaks to his. Just like he said, this is it. There's no going back. I never thought I would say this, but he has become my forever.

A few minutes go by as I fantasize about Kent doing more to me than kissing. I fluff some pillows on the couch and refold the blanket that's already nicely folded. I nearly jump out of my skin when there's a knock on the door. The heat on my skin while I was dreaming decreases to arctic temperatures.

"Sunshine, it's me. You can open the door."

I let out the breath I was holding and unlock the door. My ears pound as I turn the doorknob and open it.

He's on one knee, staring at something.

"What happened, and what is that?"

He looks up with a stone face. "Do you have any rubber gloves?"

I prop my hand on my hip. "Are you serious? This isn't *CSI*. It's just an envelope."

"Sunshine, you never know. I don't want to get my fingerprints on it."

This is ridiculous. My brain keeps flipping back and forth. This isn't my life. There's nothing to worry about. Then it flips again and makes me a worried mess. Why can't we go back to making out on the kitchen counter? That was so much more fun. I search through my cleaning stuff and find the only pair of rubber gloves I have, red ones, of course.

He tries to put the gloves on, but they're too small. "Can you please put the gloves on to pick up the envelope? But don't open it yet."

"Did you see anybody while you were looking around?" I peek my head out to observe the hallway.

"No. But I'm not sure if this envelope was already here on the ground when I opened the door. It kind of blends in with the mat in front of your door, since it's blood red. I didn't notice it until I got back to the apartment."

I pick it up with two fingers, as if it is full of germs, and walk backward to let Kent in.

He rips a paper towel off the roll on my counter. Using the paper towel as a protective barrier, he removes it from my hands.

After inspecting it, he says, "I think there are pictures inside."

"You're freaking me out. Just open the damn thing instead of guessing."

"I need a knife. I don't want to damage it too much."

I pull one out of the knife holder on the counter.

He slickly cuts it open. "I was right. Please pull them out gently."

I separate them on the table so we can see them. "They're pictures of me at the grocery store, the bank, in my car in a parking lot, at the library, trying on shoes, walking out of a changing room, having coffee at Matt's café, drinking from my beer at Kaleidoscope's, and waiting in the lobby for Abby. Yesterday."

I start to shake. "Wait...wait...wait a minute. I need to get my thoughts straight." I press my temples. I pace the floor. I search through them again. "The picture of me at a changing room. I know where that was." I explain how I saw the man with the scar. "I was looking through the window when I was at Matt's café last Wednesday. There was someone across the street taking pictures of the café. Then it had hit me that he looked similar to the man at the store. He wore a baseball cap...and his clothes were too big."

"Did you see his face at the store?"

I hang my head back. "No. And at the café, the guy had big sunglasses on and a camera in front of his face, so I didn't see him clearly. A bus drove by, blocking my view. He was gone once the bus passed."

"But you said you only saw the man from behind. You never saw what he was wearing because he was behind a full rack. Just the baseball cap. You didn't see that from the front either. Did you see his shoes?"

The vision of his horrifying scalp flashes in my mind, and my stomach churns. "No. I was so shocked when he took off his cap that I didn't focus on anything else."

I close my eyes to erase the disturbing image from my mind.

"So it could be a fluke. But how? When there's a picture of me on that exact day I was at the café with Abby. Which was not even an hour after I was at that store. You can see I have the same clothes on."

I shake the gloves off, and they land on the table, blowing a different picture off it. When I move to toss it back on the table, something catches my eye. It's the photo from the hospital lobby. I zone in on another person in the picture. "I can't fucking believe it." I throw it across the room, and it lands by the couch.

Kent retrieves it and looks at it again. "I don't get it. What's wrong?"

I tap the picture hard. "See this guy in the doorway?" *Tap, Tap, Tap.* "That's Poker. Darren. Whitehead." I snarl. "I have no idea why he's there."

He traces the photo with his finger. Now both of our fingerprints are on the photo. "The way he's resting his back against the doorway and has his head tilted to the right, he was possibly listening to your conversation. He positioned himself so you wouldn't notice he was there. Do you remember what you were talking to the nurse about?"

"If anything, about Abby and what to expect when I take her home. Oh wait. I was talking to a nurse about Abby's scarves. But Darren is the least of my problems when I see these pictures. He wouldn't dare do anything to me if he wants to keep his job."

"Or maybe they're in on this together," he suggests with a bitter tone.

I angle away from him. "How could there be a connection between them? What does this guy want from me? He's watching my every move. Including right now, since I just got home a little while before you came." I want to scream, but I roughly tug my hands through my hair instead. "I keep thinking this is only a dream and it'll go away once I wake up. I don't scare easily, but this is starting to get to me."

He comes up from behind me and wraps his arms around my waist while nuzzling my neck. My blood simmers down just from his embrace.

"We'll find out who he is. I knew all of this wasn't a fluke. He might have watched you come home, but he didn't know someone was here with you. A policeman, no less."

I twist in his arms to face him. "I'm scared, Kent. I'm never scared. You don't understand. These kinds of things don't happen to me. *Ever.* I swear I'm jinxed. That damn fucking black cat." I rest my forehead against his hard chest and inhale his fresh shower scent.

He pulls away slightly and lifts my chin. "What are you talking about?"

I tell him about the black cat on Halloween. "My life has been so fucked up since that day. Granted, it didn't turn out so bad because I met you. But I feel vulnerable. I have no protective barrier anymore. Like a baby in her mother's womb. Protected from the outside, but when it's born, it's completely helpless. That's me in a nutshell at the moment."

"You aren't alone. I promise I'll protect you."

"But how? We have no idea who he is. You can't be with me all the time."

"We have a couple of suspects. That doctor, Darren, and Dom."

"But we can't just show up at their places without proof. This guy had that scar, so it couldn't have been Dom or Darren. And what if it's none of them? This could be anybody."

"What about your neighbors? Do you get along with them? Are they our age? Do any of them act strangely around you?"

"Most of them are married couples. We interact if we see each other, but that's about it."

"You said your phone is also for work. Maybe it's one of your clients."

I shake my head. "I can't think anymore."

"Then let's take the pictures to the station and check for fingerprints. We'll see if we can figure out where the pictures were printed. You can tell them what store you were at, and the detectives can ask to see the cameras from the store. And then I'm going to buy a new lock for your door. The one you have wouldn't protect you from shit. I won't leave tonight until it's installed properly.

"Also, anybody seems to be able to enter your apartment building. Both times I've been here, the main entrance door has been propped open. I closed it before I entered and was still able to open it again without having to ring your apartment. I checked your garage the other night with Abby. The gate to the garage was out of service. Has it been fixed yet?"

"No. I haven't really thought about it. There's a new owner of the building—everything's supposed to be fixed soon. I received a letter about it the other day. As for security cameras, I have no idea if there will be a system installed."

He frowns with disappointment painted all over his face.

I slither in his arms, but he won't let me go.

"I've always felt safe here. That's why I decided to live alone in this apartment after Tina moved out."

Kent tightens his grip around me when my phone rings on the counter. I'm going to lose my shit any second now because my nerves are shot.

He sprints to the phone and brings it to me. "Do you recognize this number?"

I shake my head.

It rings again. "Answer it," I urge him.

He taps the screen and doesn't say a word but puts it on speaker.

"Did you like the pictures I left for you, Goldie? My favorite is of you coming out of the changing room."

I cover my mouth. The way he said *Goldie* makes me want to puke. Kent looks like he's going to blow through the roof. I don't recognize the man's voice. It's as if he's speaking through some kind of cloth. Kent places his forefinger on his lips.

"What, not talking? I guess your so-called boyfriend is next to you. I saw him sniffing around the building just now. Isn't that sweet? But you seem to have more than a few admirers, as you've probably already noticed in one of the pictures."

A tear glides down my cheek, and my body vibrates like a leaf in a storm.

"You listen here, asshole. You stay the fuck away from her because it will be me coming after you. We'll find you, I promise you that."

"You don't scare me. You won't—" He abruptly stops talking and begins to hack up a lung, sounding like an elephant. Just like Dr. Wanker at the café. My throat closes at the sound of it.

"What do you want from me?" I cry into the phone.

Kent covers my mouth, then pulls me to his chest.

The hacking stops when the line goes dead. Kent darts to the door and dashes out of the apartment. I follow him, wondering where he's going. He sprints as quietly as possible to each apartment door on this floor and puts his ear against it. I guess he's listening for someone who's coughing.

He halts at the last door on the right and shakes his head. Nothing. But there's dead silence. I step back in as he approaches my apartment.

"You didn't recognize the phone number? Have you gotten any other anonymous phone calls?"

My eyes bulge. "Yes! I totally forgot because of what happened with Abby yesterday. I had a couple." I unlock my phone and search through my recent calls. "Here. These two numbers are not familiar, and all three are different."

Kent takes the phone and clicks on a number.

"Are you calling one of them? Are you crazy?"

He covers the phone. "I thought you knew that already." He shows off his smile, which makes me feel warm and safe, at least for this short moment.

After a few seconds, he ends the call. "Line is dead. It could be him." He lifts the phone to his ear to call the other one. The mood changes as his eyes turn into little slits.

"That one was Dominic's phone. I got his voicemail."

"Great." I swing my arm toward him. "Now he's going to see that I called. What do I do if he calls back?"

He approaches me and leans down until our lips almost touch. My mind becomes foggy, almost forgetting the severity of what's going on. His dreamy brown eyes soothe me.

"You tell him you're taken by a large, cocky police officer, and you'll never be on the market again." He puts his arm around my waist and tickles my lips with his. "How does that sound, Sunshine?" he whispers against the skin below my ear.

"Funny, that's exactly what I was thinking. Great minds think alike." It looks like he's going to kiss me again, but then he stops.

"Let's go to the station now," he says. "We need to report this as soon as possible now that we have a number and the pictures. So let's move it." He spanks my bottom.

With the rubber gloves back on, I carefully slide the pictures back into the envelope.

"Do you have a big Ziploc bag? We can put the envelope in it."

As I retrieve a bag, I say, "The coughing sound... When I got the call at Kaleidoscope the other week, I thought I heard coughing then too. I wasn't sure if it was noise from the bar or that. After we had that fight at the café, the doctor came up to me again. When he was about to leave, he coughed profusely. It has to be him. But then again, the guy with the baseball hat didn't look like him."

"That's what we're going to find out. Grab your coat."

Reality has sunk in. I have a stalker. A while back, Tina told me to be careful, that one of my men might turn into a stalker. I laughed it off because it sounded ridiculous. Is it my fault this is happening? I'm always straightforward with every guy I date. If I don't want to go out again, I tell him. But some come back for more, as if I'm teasing them. I've occasionally had to block their phone numbers.

People may get the impression that I sleep around because I date a lot of guys casually. But just because I go on a date doesn't mean I sleep with them.

If the stalker is the one with the baseball hat, I'd remember if I'd dated him. So this could be some random guy who saw me on the street, in a store, a doctor's office. When it comes down to it, he could be anybody.

Neither of us says anything on the way back to my apartment. How could they not trace the phone number? In this modern world, and nothing. I'm so frustrated.

"Sunshine, I know you're disappointed and want answers. I'm just as annoyed as you are. It'll take a while for the fingerprints. They'll get on it as soon as possible. The man is smart. He seems to be using burners, just like I thought," Kent says after he closes the apartment door.

I take off my coat and toss it over a kitchen chair. "I understand, but what am I supposed to do now? Do I need to look over my shoulder every two seconds to make sure no one is following me?"

"Yes. You should always be aware of your surroundings. I know this isn't how you usually run your life, but things have changed. Stay in crowded areas. Try to be with someone at all times. I know that's hard, but it's common sense these days."

I hug myself and rub my arms. "Do you really think a new lock will help? If he wants to get in, he'll find a way."

"Come on. Look how pitiful this is." He wiggles the current knob. "The new lock is a hundred times better than what you have now. I wish we'd had time to go to a sports store. I'd buy you a baseball bat."

"Is it too late to change the lock?"

"If it is, I don't care. What—is someone going to call the police? That would be funny." He holds me in his arms and kisses my forehead.

"Shouldn't I notify the landlord that we installed a new doorknob and key?"

"He doesn't seem to care about the safety of this building, so I wouldn't bother telling him. I'm not leaving here until I feel you're safe."

"You make me feel safe when you're around. What will I do when you leave?"

"If you're that nervous, come home with me for the night."

I trace my finger down his neck. "Isn't it a bit soon for sleepovers?"

"I told you when I kissed you. There's no going back. You're stuck with me."

"Promise?" I say as I step on my tippy-toes.

"I never go back on my word."

"Oh really. Maybe you need to kiss me again to convince me."

He lifts an eyebrow. "Is that a challenge, Miss Kramer?"

"Call it whatever you want to. You just need to plant those delicious lips of yours on mine to seal the deal." I tap my lips with my finger. "Then maybe I'll go home with you."

Before he kisses me, he flashes me that heart-stopping smile, and I know beyond a shadow of a doubt that he's the one. Every ounce of me belongs to him, so if anything, he's stuck with me.

Chapter 27

Kent

"The house is dark, so I'm sure Abby's sleeping," I whisper as I lock the door and turn on the alarm, never letting go of Alexa's petite hand.

"Wow, you have a security system. Aren't you cool," she teases.

I hang my keys on the key hook next to the coat rack. "Nothing but the best. What kind of cop would I be without one when I complain about your door lock?"

"A shitty one for sure." She giggles as she follows me to the kitchen.

I sift through a cabinet that I know will have what I'm looking for.

"What are you doing?"

"Searching for this. I knew it would come in handy one day." I lift it in the air.

Her forehead crinkles. "It's an old mason jar."

"Yup." I pat my pockets to feel around for some loose change. My fingers connect with some coins. I pull them out and drop them into the jar, a quarter and a couple of dimes. "Now Felicia has another jar collecting loose change."

She bursts out laughing but covers her mouth to keep quiet. "You're so damn cute." She covers her mouth again.

"I'll let it slip since I put more in there this time."

She shoves me playfully. "You're such a wisea—" She presses her lips together with her fingers.

"But you find me so irresistible because I'm a wiseass."

"There are a lot of things about you that are irresistible."

I'm about to respond, but she raises her hand. "But I'm not going to tell you them now. You're just going to have to wait."

"Fine. Before this becomes a battle, let me show you to my room," I say over my shoulder as I walk away from her. "I just changed the sheets this morning."

She stops in her tracks. "Kent."

I stop at the stairs and see the unease written all over her face. She waves me back to the kitchen.

"What's the matter?"

She wraps her hands around the top of a kitchen chair. "I think I should sleep somewhere else. Don't you have a spare bedroom? Or I can sleep on the couch in Abby's sewing room or down here in the living room."

"Why are you so nervous? My plan was for me to sleep on the couch and you to sleep in my room. My mom taught me how to be a gentleman."

Her cheeks turn red. "It might come as a surprise, but I don't know how to do this. Whatever's happening between us is new to me."

"Am I that addicting that you wouldn't trust yourself to keep your hands off me if I slept next to you?" I crack a smile.

Her cheeks burn even brighter. Red really is her color.

"Come on. It's not funny. And Abby's in the house."

"Sunshine, I brought you here to protect you and to help you feel safe. My goal wasn't to literally jump in the sack with you. Not that I would mind. But I know we need to take it slow. Believe me—it's new for me too. I feel like a teenager who had his first kiss and has no idea how to get to second base."

"Oh, you know exactly where to put your hands, and you do it very well. That's why it's safer if we don't sleep in the same room."

I put my hands up in surrender. "Again, I'll sleep on the hard, old squeaky couch while you sleep in my soft, warm bed."

She crosses her arms and taps her foot on the floor.

I don't think I could resist her if she were lying next to me. I know we're not ready, considering all the shit that's going on. She needs to trust me, and I don't want to miss anything until this guy is found.

"Come on. Let's go upstairs. Do you need something to drink?"

She shakes her head. "No thanks. My phone is off, so I don't have to worry about someone calling in the middle of the night."

I pick up her little red suitcase and walk upstairs. Her hands hang on the back pockets of my jeans. We enter my bedroom, and I place her suitcase on the bed.

"Give me a second," I say and back out of the room.

When I return, she's unpacking. "Here's a towel, if you need one." I toss it on the edge of the bed. "Why don't you get into your pajamas. I'll come back up in a few minutes to say good night. I'll use the bathroom downstairs."

"Okay. Sounds good." She's back to her perky self, with sparkling eyes. "Give me ten minutes." She inspects the towel. "Bright yellow. A touch from Abby, I assume."

"If that color makes her happy, then I'm all for it."

"Me too." She grins as she closes the bathroom door.

I sit on the top stair with my pajamas on as I wait for her to come out. It's been longer than ten minutes. Finally, the doorknob squeaks. I almost lose my balance when I see her. She's wearing a red-and-white polka-dot long-sleeved shirt with shiny matching red sleeping pants. I guess they're satin. Her toenails shine like tiny candy-apple-red Chiclets.

"No socks for such cute little feet?"

She wiggles her toes. "I can't stand wearing socks to bed. Even when it's freezing out."

I don't care about what she's wearing. It's her in general. Is it possible that a woman can become more attractive every time I see her? She's even more beautiful now than before she went into the bathroom. Her hair is in a messy bun, like Abby used to wear, and her face is clear of makeup. She looks sexy in casual pajamas, a devil costume, jeans and sneakers, high heels, business suit, or apron. No matter how she's dressed, she's my very own aphrodisiac. I'm definitely sleeping on the couch. My third leg would be poking her in the back all night if I didn't. I don't need to be the next guy she hates.

While I eye her up, she is doing the same to me. The corner of her mouth tilts up. "You look good in flannel pajama pants. Are you someone who sleeps with or without a shirt?" She covers her ears and squeezes her eyes shut. "No. Don't answer. I don't want to know. Well, yes I do, but no, I don't." She rests her back against the wall.

I walk up to her and pull her hands away. She opens one eye at a time.

I trace a circle on the palm of her hand. "Can I speak now?"

She purses her lips in warning, but her eyes crinkle.

With my cheek almost against hers, I whisper, "Maybe I don't like to wear anything at all."

She swings her hands up to cover her ears again, but I stop her.

"But you'll just have to wait and see. Now go to my room."

I pat her playfully in the butt and trail behind her. "Was the bathroom okay? I scrubbed it down last night. Sorry it's nothing fancy."

She cocks her hand on her hip. "Don't even go there, so zip it. I love your house. Now let me go to sleep in this huge, inviting bed." She points to the left and right of the bed. "Which side is yours, or do you sleep in the middle?"

"In the middle. Sleep any way or on any side you want. Just promise me the bed will smell like you when you wake up."

"For you, I might spray your pillow with my perfume." She picks up one of the pillows and hugs it. "Want to touch, I mean, tuck me in?" She covers her mouth and giggles.

"More than anything." I step to the bed and turn down the navy-blue comforter. "Get in, Sunshine. I don't know how long my willpower will last. I like seeing you in my bedroom a little too much. Let's get you covered up."

She lies on her side, facing me. I tuck her in tightly, then kneel on the floor next to her, with our faces close together. A hint of mint passes my nose. "Sweet dreams, Sunshine."

She smiles contently with her eyes closed.

"Don't think about the hell from today. When you do, distract yourself by thinking one day you'll be lying next to *me* in this bed. Because I promise you will be." I gaze at her as her breathing becomes long and steady.

Chapter 28

Alexa

He's promising me something I already know. I'll sleep in this bed, his bed. But one day it will be *our* bed. He's no longer my beast. He's my prince.

Oh, man, do I have to pee, but I'm wrapped up like a cocoon. I haven't slept this good in weeks. I stretch my tight arms and legs out, then rub my desert-dry eyes. I have no idea what time it is, and my phone is nowhere to be seen. The sun is shining through the curtains though. There is no clock in this room. Who doesn't have a clock in their bedroom? It doesn't matter, because I don't need the embarrassment of peeing in Kent's bed.

My feet connect with the soft cream carpet as I focus. Anyone close to me knows I'm not a morning person until I have a cup of coffee. But who is? Even if it's just a sip, my peppiness magically appears.

I peek out of the room and listen for any movement. God only knows what I look like. My hair is usually a total rat's nest. I tiptoe on the hardwood floor in the hallway in hopes it won't creak. Just as I reach the bathroom, the door swings open and steam billows out. As if in slow motion, I note movement within the steam. I don't go in, because cold fear drowns my body. I step backward as the figure becomes clearer. In seconds the fog lifts, and floating in front of me is Dr. Walker.

"Hello, *Goldie*," he says as his beady eyes zone in on my knees.

I look down and gasp when I realize I have only a miniskirt and high heels on. Where are my pajamas?

"Surprised to see me? Kent suggested I take a shower before I could see you." He turns his head to the left. "What do you think of my new haircut?" He traces the red, oozy, swollen jagged scar, like the one the guy had in the store. "Do you like this braid? I did it for you. I want to look better than Kent. I even had your name shaved into my hair on the other side."

When I get a glimpse of the other side, my stomach begs to empty. I take a few shaky steps behind me and find myself drifting back, as if diving backward off a diving board. My arms flap to catch me from falling down the stairs. My scream burns my eardrums as my body trembles with force.

"Alexa. Alexa." I hear Kent's panicked voice yell in the distance.

"Wake up, Sunshine. You're scaring me. Please wake up."

"What's going on? Why is Alexa here?" Abby's shaky voice asks.

I flutter my eyes open as Kent cradles me in his arms. "Shh, shh. You're okay. It was just a bad dream." He rocks me back and forth in a soothing rhythm.

His grip on me is like a vice, but I like it. I lay my hand on his chest and only feel skin. Warm, baby-soft skin with a sprinkle of hair. I inhale his familiar scent.

"Do you want to tell me about it?"

I shimmy out of his grip. "It was him. The doctor. You need to check him out. Or we need to. I know where he works."

I replay the dream for them. Abby squeezes her cheeks together in shock.

"I can't do this anymore. We need to find him. Can't you question him or search his apartment?" I say in desperation as I squeeze his arms.

173

"Unfortunately, it's not that easy. We need a search warrant. I'll talk to the detectives this afternoon when I go to work."

He holds my chin and pecks my lips. "We'll find him. I'll do everything in my power. I promise." I believe him.

I nod and glance at Abby. "Hi, Abby. Isn't this the best thing to wake up to?"

She giggles. "It actually is when I get to see my big brother cuddle with a woman. I never thought I'd see the day. That is, until you came along." She jiggles my feet. "I'll go make some coffee for you both, and tea for me."

I reach out to her. "How are you feeling this morning?" Seeing her without her head covered doesn't shock me so much this time.

A slight smile appears. "I'm much better, but that's not what's important right now. I'd rather focus on you. I have a feeling there is more to this story. I'll be right back." She turns back to us again and waves her finger between us. "Behave, you two. No making out when I'm in the house."

Kent throws a pillow at her, almost knocking a picture frame off the dresser. Light chuckles float through the hallway and then down the stairs.

"Give me a second. I need to go to the bathroom."

He nods and lies back on the bed. Within a few minutes, I'm back. I had to brush my teeth. You never know. I climb over him and lie down. He tucks me under his arm, pulling me against his half-naked body.

"You are so toasty. How is it possible to be so warm while shirtless in the middle of November?" I snuggle closer to him. I would love to lie on top of him, but it might cause a problem...an enticing problem, but not when Abby will come back soon.

"I always sleep without a shirt. I have for years."

I toss my leg over him and land on something long and hard. He jerks and choke-laughs, if that's possible.

"I may seem relaxed, but one part of me isn't, so I suggest you don't move, or you'll come up with another name for me."

"Do you mean like this?" I wiggle my leg and feel him get harder. *Sorry, Abby, but I wish you weren't home.* Maybe it's better this way though.

Within a blink of an eye, he flips me on my back and hovers between my legs, teasing my sensitive spot. "Sunshine, you're killing me. You have no idea how hard it was to leave this room last night."

I giggle.

"No pun intended." He eyes me. "Unless you want to finish what you've started, I'm going to leave this bed and take a long, cold shower."

"I can't wait for the day I can finish it and then start it again." I wink as he stands up, giving me an even better view of his chiseled deliciousness. My imagination sparks when I see the tent in his pants. My mouth waters. He's the complete package of any woman's dreams. I squeeze my eyes shut as I kneel on the bed. "Leave the room now," I demand as I point to the door. "Because in a few seconds, I will beg you to finish me."

"I'm coming back up the stairs. I don't want to know what you want to finish, but it's gross when it's my brother."

Kent and I giggle as he quickly covers his nether regions, then opens his closet.

"You forgot your glasses in the kitchen. Do you need them?" Abby asks as she hands him black ones, then leaves the room.

He wears black glasses?

"Thanks. I left them there last night." He takes them from her, then puts them on.

I can't see his face, so I inch over to get a better view of it. He sifts through the orderly uniforms and regular clothes. He pulls out dark-blue jeans and a gray shirt, then lays them on the end of the bed.

He looks up. "You're quiet all of a sudden. What's up?"

I rest my hands on my hips. "Seriously? Glasses? Can you get any hotter?" Man, my hormones are going to erupt any second, like an explosive volcano. "Are you testing me this morning?"

He pulls me to him. "Is it working?"

"You could be a model. I can imagine you posing for a romance book cover or a calendar. You have the chiseled bod, crazy beautiful hair, and glasses. I would buy the book myself even though I don't read romance novels."

"You don't need a book. I'm all yours, and the only one I'm posing for is you."

I wrap my arms around his shoulders and kiss his neck. My fingers brush against some raised skin on his left shoulder. It's about two inches long. A scar. I come back to reality and remember what he does for a living. It's probably something he got when on duty.

I trace over it with my finger again. Goosebumps form on his skin within seconds. "How did you get this?" I ask, already regretting it. I'm not sure I want to know.

He squirms out of my arms and shuts the closet. "I broke up a bar fight about two years ago. I was off duty but helped anyway. A couple of guys pulled out knives. One of the knives grazed my shoulder. It was summertime, so I was only wearing a T-shirt."

Abby returns as she covers her head with the purple head scarf Tina would love. "Coffee will be done any minute."

Why does this feel so normal? Like we've hung out in our pajamas before. I can't believe I'm kneeling on his bed, looking the way I do and not caring at all. He doesn't seem to either. I like it that we're taking it slow and are comfortable with each other. Who knows what would've happened at my apartment if we were never interrupted. Would we have ended up sleeping together? I'm enjoying the buildup, and I think he is too.

"Who's in the mood for bagels?" He glances at Abby. "If you're feeling better, then I know you are."

She gives her typical thumbs-up.

"Alexa?"

"Of course. There would be something majorly wrong with me, since I'm a Jersey Girl. Don't worry. I'm not a carb counter."

I should be since I canceled my gym membership. Going to the gym is time consuming. I've never been one for exercise. My body has natural curves that I need to take care of, but I'm too lazy. Since I'm jinxed, I'll probably wake up tomorrow the size of a rhino.

"Good. Let me shower quickly, then I'll go buy some. Write down how many you want and which kind." He kisses my cheek and strolls out of his room.

I wait for the bathroom door to click. Just as I'm about to say something to Abby about Friday, she beats me to it.

"I'm so sorry about Friday." She squeezes her hands together, like she's begging. "I know that Kent already apologized to you for me. But I needed to say it myself. My reaction was unexpected. I'm so embarrassed that you saw my naked chest."

I probably shouldn't ask this but, "Do you plan on getting breast implants? Usually it's done when you get a mastectomy. Did something happen?"

"I wanted to get through chemo as fast as possible. I'll worry about implants next year. That's another thing I'm trying not to think about right now."

My shoulders droop. "Sorry I brought it up."

"No problem. If it means anything to you, if I had to choose who I wanted to be there with me, it would've been you. You made me feel safe. I can never say thank you enough."

I embrace her hands in mine. "I'm glad Dani got there in time to help you. She took control right away. It was amazing."

"Yeah, but she has no bedside manner. You radiate compassion. Don't get me wrong—Dani is an excellent nurse and a good friend. She knows her stuff, but there is a lack of warmth there. We clicked with her because she's around our age and doesn't have a lot of family here, like us."

Even though I've only hung out with Dani a couple of times, I have the same impression of her. But she apparently has a heart, considering her profession and the way she took care of Abby.

Abby looks down, as if she's shy all of a sudden. "I'm afraid to say it, but you're like the sister I never had, and I really like it."

I reach out to give her a quick hug. "I don't want to talk a lot about this because I don't want us to cry—but I feel the same way. You can come to me about anything. You won't be getting rid of me anytime soon."

She shocks me by wrapping her arms around me. When she releases me, she wipes under one eye. "Sorry. Tears came anyway."

We giggle.

"Want to see what I looked like with hair and some meat on my bones?" She picks up the picture frame that was almost knocked off before and hands it to me.

I'm stunned. "Wow. I think you're beautiful now, but with that long, chestnut-brown wavy hair... I'm sure the guys were running after you."

"I had a couple of serious relationships. My last one was at the time I was diagnosed. He took off when I had my first treatment. Kent was ready to kill him. I only had to say the word, and he would've been out the door." She sits on the edge of the bed. "I thought it was love, but I guess not. I was devastated at the time, but surviving was more important. I had to focus on me. I never heard from him again. Kent kept me together, and he still does."

In the picture, a woman is standing next to Abby, but she's about six inches shorter. She has the same smile as Kent. "This is your mom, right?" I point at the picture and sit next to Abby on the bed.

"Yep. It's our favorite picture of us. It was taken at my college graduation. She was so proud of me. I thought she was going to burst that day. She was the same when Kent graduated from the police academy. Everything was perfect for a while, and then it wasn't. After she died, it hit Kent hard. Just when things were getting back to normal for us a couple of years later, I was diagnosed. I don't know who was more upset, Kent or me."

This is hard for me. I have no idea what to say. I've already said I'm sorry for what they've been through. Then it hits me. Maybe it's pushing it, but after seeing her sick and what she's said about me, I think anything goes at this point.

I bounce on the bed when I turn to her. "Hey. What are you doing for Thanksgiving? Does Kent need to work?"

"We have no plans because he has to work Thursday and Friday. I haven't thought too much about it because I had no idea how I'd feel. Dani asked me the same question last week."

I bounce again. "Why don't you come home with me and spend Thanksgiving with my family? You can meet my brother and his wife. And a whole lot of other people. We can do girly things on Friday, like shopping or get facials."

She bites her lower lip and looks down.

"My treat. You don't have to do anything. Think of it as an early Christmas present."

"What about Kent? I can't leave him here alone."

"I'll talk to him and see if he wants to come on Saturday because my brother's having a big party at his house. Matt and Kayla will be there too. We can talk about the Christmas party, and there will be lots of yummy food. I can promise your stomach will hurt from laughing so hard. It'll be awesome."

A smile sprouts on her face. "You don't have to ask me twice. My life is a new blank page. It's time to fill it up."

Chapter 29

Kent

As soon as I'm in my truck, I dial Vince's number and put him on speaker.

I hear shuffling. "There better be a good reason to call at this time," Vince moans.

"Sorry. More shit happened with Alexa. She slept at my house last night."

"Hold on," he groans. "Let me get out of bed."

"Is Dani there?"

He snorts. "No. We had a fight last night, and then she left."

"Do you want to talk about it?"

"Negative. It's nothing I can't handle," he claims. "So shoot. What happened last night?"

As I drive to the bagel shop, I tell him the short version.

"You've done all you can do. You have to let the detectives do their job. You're personally involved with Alexa, so you need to take a step back."

"You know I can't fucking do that. This guy is out there. Maybe he's all talk, but I'm not going to take the chance. And who knows what this Darren guy is up to. Like she needs to worry about him too."

"Is she taking it seriously now? When we were at her apartment that night, she was relaxed about the whole thing. She didn't seem fazed at all."

I park my truck in front of the crowded bagel shop but don't get out.

"He got her attention last night. She's scared now. Again, that's why she stayed with me."

"But she can't stay at your house every night. You hardly know her."

"I love her, Vince," I blurt out. "I never believed in this love-at-first-sight shit, but I do now. I'll do anything to protect her."

"Dude, you need to slow down. I'm happy for you, but it's a bit fast. Are you sure you aren't just trying to save her because you couldn't save your mom or Abby? You had no control over their illness, but this you do."

"Fuck you, Vince."

"Come on. Think about it. I've known you for years. You hated it that you couldn't do anything for them except watch."

"Yeah, and you should know that this has never happened to me. You know I felt like this about Alexa before I knew anything about this stalker. You seemed all for it the other day, telling the station that I found my future wife. What's the sudden change? Is it because you fought with Dani last night?"

"Forget about the fight. I just want to make sure you know exactly what you're getting into. You're emotionally involved, and that can cloud your judgment."

"Are you telling me if Dani were in the same situation, you wouldn't get involved?"

He growls, and silence follows.

"The difference is that I'm not in love with her," he snaps. "That's all I'm going to say about this."

"Then what do you suggest I do?"

"You let the detectives do their job, and on the side, you protect her, and if any clues pop up, you tell them. Don't do it on your own, because you know you'll get shit for it. I'd also keep your mouth shut about her stalker. She should be quiet too. The fewer people involved, the better. Now that he knows you might have a trace on him, he might stop. Then the problem is gone.

"Think with your head man, not your dick."

I keep replaying the conversation with Vince in my head. Is he right? Am I in love with her, or is it my chance to finally save someone I care about? Can't it be both? No woman has ever gotten my attention like she does. It's not just sexual attraction. If that were it, I would've done more than tuck her in last night.

I glance in my rearview mirror and see Dani park her car in the street. She's up early. Since she fought with Vince last night, she'd better not try to get me involved. I don't want things to get awkward between the three of us if things don't work out between them.

I open up my truck door when she comes up the driveway. She jumps. "Damn, Kent. You scared me," she gasps. "What are you doing in your truck so early in the morning?"

"Good morning to you too. I should ask you the same. Why are *you* here?"

"Didn't Abby tell you I was coming over this morning before work? I want to see how she's doing. I brought you some of the donuts you like from the bakery down the street." She raises the box in front of me with a big grin.

"No. She didn't say anything, but we've had a distraction this morning. Come inside. It's too cold, and the ladies are waiting patiently for bagels."

Her smile fades. "Ladies?"

"Alexa stayed the night. We'll explain during breakfast," I say as I follow her through the front door.

"I'm home and I smell bacon," I yell down the hallway.

Alexa comes prancing out of the kitchen but stops short. "Dani. Hey. What a surprise." She fidgets with her pajamas and pushes her hair away from her face.

Even though she seems uncomfortable in her pajamas in front of Dani, I love it that she still has them on. She didn't feel the need to shower immediately. It shows that she's comfortable here. I want her to feel at home. What I wouldn't do to lie around all day with her in just our pajamas—or nothing at all.

"Hi. Great pj's. Did you have a sleepover with Abby?" she asks as she opens her coat and unravels her scruffy black scarf.

"Ah no. More stalker issues. We thought it would be better if I stayed here last night."

"Come on. I'm sure it's not that bad." she asks. "Where's Abby?" She glances in the living room.

"She's in the shower," Alexa responds.

"Do you have time to stay for breakfast? We have the donuts you brought, and I just bought bagels." I shake the bag of bagels.

"Abby told me to make bacon for Kent. There's plenty for all of us. We just need to add a plate for you." Alexa sniffs the air, then scurries to the kitchen. "It's not burnt. *Phew.*"

"I can stay for a half hour. So tell me what's going on. What did this stalker do now?" She air quotes the word *stalker*, then rolls her eyes. "I'm sure he'll give up eventually."

"That would be a blessing, but it doesn't seem like it," Alexa says while she keeps an eye on the hissing bacon.

"Alexa, where's your phone? Show Dani the pictures of Darren at the hospital. I'm glad we took pictures of them before giving the originals to the detectives."

Dani pulls a mug from a cabinet and pours herself some coffee. "Who's Darren? And detectives are involved now?"

"He's the drunk from Kaleidoscope. It turns out he works for the same company as me. The stalker took pictures of me, and Darren's in two of them that were taken at the hospital. He seems to be watching me too."

"I don't remember what he looked like." She stuffs her scarf in one of the coat sleeves and hangs the coat off the back of a chair. "Let me see the pictures," she adds as she sits at the table.

Alexa runs upstairs to get her phone. I take the strips of bacon out of the pan and place them on a plate with a paper towel on it.

"Are you really taking this seriously? I'm sure it's just a joke. Women like Alexa will always have issues like this."

I cross my arms over my chest. "What the hell is that supposed to mean?"

"You know, how flirty and nice she is. She makes your teeth hurt, she's so sweet. Guys take it the wrong way. It's nothing against her. That's just the way she is," she says dryly.

Alexa returns before I can respond. I hope she didn't hear what Dani said. I need to ask Vince again what they fought about. Dani doesn't seem to be over it.

"Hey, my brother told me you called him last night but didn't leave a message. Did you finally call him to thank him for the lilies he sent you?"

"I called your brother?" Alexa laughs. "You've got your story wrong. He called me. I had several calls from different numbers. We rang them back, and one of them was Dominic's. It slipped my mind about the flowers. I'm assuming you gave him my number. Next time ask before you give someone my number. I don't want to know how he got my address when he sent me flowers. Did you give him that too?"

She droops in her seat. "I don't understand. Why won't you give him a chance?" she presses, ignoring my comment.

"For a guy to like me so much, why is his sister talking to me instead of him? I thought he was Mister Confidence and Persuasion?" Alexa glances at me and then to Dani again. "Just back off about it. It's not happening."

Dani stares at a chocolate donut as if trying to come up with an excuse.

Alexa nods with satisfaction and says, "It doesn't matter anyway, because I'm taken."

Dani's head shoots up. "Taken? By whom?"

I walk over to Alexa and pull her to my side. "Me."

She slaps the table in amusement. "You two are together? That's hysterical. Seriously now, who is he?" She cackles.

"We're not joking," Alexa says happily as she squeezes my side.

"Is it official? You're together?" Abby appears out of nowhere. "I'm so excited." She wraps her arms around us. "My brother's finally off the market. Woo-hoo!"

"Hi, Dani." She sidles over to her and gives her a big hug too. "Thanks for helping me on Friday. I don't know what I would've done without you and Alexa. Hopefully, that was the last time you'll ever see me like that. You deserve a big breakfast with us. It's the least we can do."

Dani strokes Abby's upper arm. "How are you doing? You were pretty bad. I'm glad I got to the house in time. A couple of days rest were good for you. You look great this morning."

Abby twirls around. "I'm still tired, but I feel like a human again. Let's eat. I'm starving."

"Dani, here are the pictures of Darren. Let me know if you recognize him. It'd be normal for him to be around the hospital since he's an oncology sales rep. But I don't know why he's following me. Well, I possibly do, since both our jobs are on the line. He seems a bit desperate though."

I stack the bagels in a basket and put them in the middle of the table. "I bought a bunch of different cream cheeses. Help yourselves."

"Here, Dani." Alexa hands her the phone as she sits down next to her. "This guy." She points at the screen.

Dani analyzes it for several seconds, then shakes her head. "Sorry. He doesn't look familiar. I zoomed in, but I don't think I've seen him around the hospital. I'll keep an eye out for him from now on though." She gives Alexa her phone back.

"So tell me what happened yesterday," Dani says as she cuts a powdered donut in two.

"Yes. I want to know too. We didn't have time to talk about it." Abby taps a hard-boiled egg on her plate.

Alexa and I explain what happened and how we reported everything.

"Okay. Now I can see why you're worried. That must have totally freaked you out, knowing that someone is watching your every move."

"I feel safe when Kent's with me, but he can't be with me all the time. He bought me some Mace for my apartment and my purse."

"When I'm not working, I plan on being with you a lot." I wink at her as she traces her foot up my thigh and places it between my legs. I shift in my seat.

Dani coughs and drops her donut on the plate, knocking the knife off. "Sorry," she sputters as she covers her mouth with a napkin. "Damn powder."

"I'd appreciate it if you don't say anything to anyone. I want to keep this just between us in this room. Of course, Vince knows. I don't want this psycho to know that detectives are involved now. Alexa, you need to act like everything is normal."

"That's true. I don't want to tell my family. They already don't like it that I live in Hoboken. Don't even tell Kayla and Matt. They shouldn't have to worry. I'll be at my parents' for Thanksgiving. I'll be safe there."

I don't know if it's right not to tell her family. But I understand why she doesn't want to. But what if this guy goes after her family? Would he go that far?

"Ooh, look at the time." Dani shoves a last piece of donut into her mouth, then wipes the crumbs off her scrubs. "I'm going to be late. I have to go," she exclaims. Her chair scrapes back as she pushes away from the table. "Thanks for breakfast. Be careful, Alexa." She hugs Abby. "Get some rest." She grabs her coat. "I'll call you guys soon."

In seconds, the front door slams hard.

I'm glad she's gone. It's more peaceful without her negative attitude. I don't like how she talks about Alexa or constantly brings up Dominic. Though if she pushes Alexa's buttons, Alexa makes her opinion clear.

"Alexa, did you talk to Kent about Thanksgiving weekend?"

"Nope. I didn't have the chance, with Dani here."

I finish my orange juice. "Talk to me about what?"

Alexa pushes her plate away. "About Thanksgiving. Abby said you have to work on Thursday and Friday. I'm going to my parents on Thursday morning. Would it be okay if Abby came with me? Then on Saturday, my brother's having a big party. Kind of like a Thanksgiving Christmas party. Matt and Kayla will be there. Would you like to come?" She props her chin on her folded hands. "It should be fun."

"I want to go with her. *Please* come on Saturday," Abby begs. "Then I can go home with you. We need to do new things. When's the last time we went to a party?"

"Are you going to let me talk?"

We all laugh.

"Will your parents be there?"

Alexa sits straight up in her chair and pinches her lips together. "Um. Yes. Would that bother you?"

"Yes."

Her face drops, and Abby gives me her famous death stare.

I chuckle. "I'm just kidding. Your parents need to meet the man who'll be around for a very long time."

Alexa's eyes sparkle as she walks over to me. She bends over and wraps her arms around my neck. "You'll be the first man I've brought home in a very long time."

And the last one.

Chapter 30

Alexa

It's like I have my own bodyguard. "Thanks for coming with me to the store." I turn the key to unlock my apartment door. Kent was right. This doorknob is much sturdier than the old one.

I step forward, but he grabs my elbow softly. "Let me go in first. You never know." I step aside for him to check. Then I follow and close the door. He places the grocery bags on the kitchen table and tosses his uniform and jacket over one of the chairs. He walks around to check out the kitchen and living room.

After what happened yesterday and then the dream I had, I like that he's cautious. What am I going to do when he's not with me? Freak out maybe?

"Does anything look out of place?"

"Not that I can see. Want to see my bedroom?" I wrap my finger around one of his belt loops and flash him a sexy grin.

"Don't tempt me," he growls.

We stand in front of the door. "You open the door. I'm a bit freaked out thinking that maybe someone was in there."

After we inspect my bedroom and the office, we agree everything seems kosher. The office still smells faintly of lilies. I put my suitcase in my bedroom and walk back into the kitchen. Kent is busy placing the groceries on the counter. He bunches up the last plastic bag and leaves it near the sink. I lean against the counter and wonder how he's the same man as the one I bumped into at the hospital.

"How sweet. Thank you for doing that for me." I quickly put the cold stuff into the refrigerator. "What time do you have to leave for work?"

"In about forty-five minutes. I need to change into my uniform before I leave."

Goodie. I get to see him in it before he goes.

I sit on a kitchen chair. "Are you sure you're okay with being alone on Thanksgiving if I take Abby home with me?"

"It's good for Abby to be with someone on Thanksgiving. I was already dreading the thought of her being alone while I work overtime on Thursday and Friday."

"Tell me the truth. Do you really want to come to my brother's party on Saturday? I don't want you to feel pressured, you know, with my parents being there. I can drive Abby home on Sunday."

He slides a chair in front of me and sits down so we face each other. He places his hands on my knees. "I want to spend as much time with you as I can so we can get to know each other better. Abby is ecstatic, as you've seen. So why wouldn't I want to be there?"

"You'll meet my parents. Doesn't that make you nervous?"

I bite my fingernail. Something I've started since my nerves have skyrocketed.

He moves my hand away from my mouth. "I guess any guy would be worried, but with you nothing scares me about us anymore. I'd meet them eventually, so why not now?" He gently kisses my fingertips one at a time. "It'd take a lot more than meeting your parents for me to hit the road."

Him kissing my fingertips gets me all riled up. I can't imagine what will happen when his lips touch other parts of my body.

"It's new for the both of us. It's like ripping a Band-Aid off...just get it over with."

He picks up his phone off the table and flicks through his apps. "I want to ask you something before I go to work, but I hope it doesn't come across the wrong way."

I lean closer so I can see his screen. "What's up? You can ask me anything. I've got nothing to hide."

"Can I put a tracker on your phone?"

Huh?

"Don't look at me like I have three heads. Let me explain. I have an app that I use with Abby. It links her phone with mine. I can see where she is, or at least where her phone is, at all times. It works both ways. She can also see where I am. With your situation, can I link your phone with mine? It would quiet my mind to know you're safe. Or if I can't get ahold of you, I'll be able to see where you are. It's invading your privacy, so if you aren't comfortable with it, just say the word and I won't ask again."

I take his phone out of his hand and place it on the table. "You're awfully protective, Officer. It's quite a turn on."

His eyes turn black as I straddle his legs and rub my chest against his.

"Is that a yes?" he says with a husky voice.

"I'm not sure you're going to need it, because you'll be plastered to my side during our free time."

I never thought I needed someone to take care of me. I've never met someone who wanted to. Now that I know what it's like to have a man in my life who honestly cares, I'll never let him go.

His hands land on my backside, and he pulls me closer. "I'd spend all my free time with you if I could. You're addictive."

The last twelve hours have been such a tease for us. Now that we're finally alone, I think we're afraid to act on it.

"What do you say? Or do you want time to think about it?"

His hands roam up and down my thighs and then up my back. A trail of fire follows behind, and my breathing increases. I close my eyes because I can't think straight.

"Maybe we can come up with a password that only you and I know. One that you can use if you're in a situation when you need my help. You only need to say the word, and I know what it means."

"Can we talk about this later? I'm kinda enjoying your hands roaming all over me."

He smirks. "Do you mean like this?" He pulls me closer to him.

My eyes grow heavy as I release a low moan. "I love how I feel when I'm near you. My body begs for you to touch me."

He cups my face with his hands and gently kisses me. I tease his lower lip with my tongue. He's the most delicious thing I've ever tasted. Our kisses deepen and last for minutes. Just as I'm ready to remove his shirt, he separates our swollen lips and leans his forehead against mine.

"Sunshine," he says in between shortened breaths. "I need to get dressed for work."

I reach for the bottom of his shirt and lift it up. "Do you need help?"

"If I let you help me, I'll end up naked in your bed and jobless."

"Ooh, did you say *naked* and *bed* in one sentence? I've already seen the top half of you. I can't wait to see the bottom. But I know how much you love your job, so I'll let it pass. Next time, you're mine, and you're not leaving." I nip his neck, then suck on it, but not long enough to leave a mark.

"You tempt me like no one else. But I'd gladly die just to lie naked with you. I have a weird schedule. I'll have more time off after Thanksgiving."

He lifts me off him and holds me in his arms. "Before I do anything, can I load that app on your phone? Once we find this jerk, I'll remove it. I promise." He puts me down and pecks my lips one more time.

Cop mode is back on. I readjust my clothes and pull my hands through my hair. "You're lucky I trust you with my life. Just remember—I can see where you are at all times too."

"I have nothing to hide. Just keep it to yourself that I'm tracking you. Remember to have your phone on you at all times. As for a secret word, think about it, and let me know if you come up with something only you and I would know. I'll try to think of something too."

I twist him around and pat him on the ass. "If you don't want me to attack you right this second, go get dressed and leave. You've turned on a button that I don't think you'll ever be able to turn off."

After he leaves, I get a text message from him. *Garlic?*

At first, I have no clue what he means, but then it clicks. Our secret password.

Perfect, I type back. I get a smiley face with hearts, and I swoon. Over an emoji.

Chapter 31

Kent

"I was going to call you but heard you would be in soon," Detective Griggs says as he approaches me. "Come to my office. We have an update for you on Alexa Kramer's case."

I hate his office. Someone with OCD would have a coronary if they came in here. There are stacks of paper everywhere. It's a modern world, but he prints everything even though it's on his computer. He claims he has a color system, but I don't see any colors on any of the stacks or documents. I hope no one ever turns on a fan in here.

"Cool. But probably not the answers we're looking for," I comment as I sit down.

"Did she get any more phone calls?" he asks as he pops an orange Tic Tac into his mouth. He extends the rattling plastic box to offer me one. I shake my head.

"No. It's been quiet since last night."

He relaxes in his chair and twists and pulls on a rubber band until it snaps. "Unfortunately, we're at a dead end. There were no fingerprints on the pictures, and we couldn't track down where they were printed. Most likely the man printed them himself but was very careful. He knows what he's doing."

"What about the mobile numbers? Nothing there either?"

He sifts through one stack and pulls out a piece of paper. "We have no trace on the numbers you gave. But the one used last night was detected about a block from the apartment building." He hands it to me, then points at the location on a map. "But that was the last location of the phone. No trace after that. If he's using burners, he probably uses the phone once and throws it out."

"What about videos from the clothing store Alexa was at?"

He taps a pen repeatedly on the desk. It drives me nuts that he can never sit still. He has to play with something at all times.

"Those will take a little longer to get. Oh, and we ran a report on the doctor. He has no criminal record. Squeaky clean."

I rub my jaw out of frustration. "So what's she supposed to do now? Just hope nothing else happens?"

"She has my card and knows to call me if something else happens or if she remembers anything else that might be useful. You know the drill. This is about all we can do at this point."

"It's hard to sit and wait around. I want him caught."

"You do your job, and I'll do mine."

Chapter 32

Alexa

Before Abby and I left for James and Lisa's house this morning, I packed a bunch of my mom's Christmas decorations in my car for Abby's party. Mom won't even know they're missing.

Abby and I helped decorate Lisa's entire house all day. Lisa wanted it to look extra special with all the guests coming to the party tonight. Abby took a nap in between. I almost did too.

Abby and I have had a blast these past few days. We went shopping with Lisa and Tina yesterday and ended the day with facials. Of course, they asked Abby a million questions about Kent. Both are still shocked that I have a real boyfriend. They can't wait to meet him, and I can't wait to introduce him to everyone. What a novelty.

I asked Abby not to mention the stalker in front of my family and friends. The only thing I talked about was work and Darren. Tina and Lisa know I can handle myself in those situations, but they wouldn't feel the same if they knew everything else. My parents would move me back home and lock me in my old bedroom. They're glad Kent's a police officer—they think I'll be safer. They act like Hoboken is downtown Newark.

Abby ate like a horse on Thanksgiving. The only person missing was Kent. I wish he could have been there, but maybe it would've been more nerve racking. Tonight he'll meet everyone all at once. But he said several times he wants to meet my family. I'm still nervous, even if he's not.

"Gerry, you've outdone yourself," I say as I pat him on the back. I snag a stuffed mushroom as Tina places several on a silver platter.

"Tina, I can't imagine having a chef as a husband. I'd be as big as a whale." I sample the mushroom, which melts in my mouth.

She wipes her hands on a dish towel. "Believe it or not, I've had to up my exercise routine. German food is so damn good. Since he likes to work out at home, I have a hot exercise partner."

"I'm sure you find some creative ways to sweat other than yoga and lifting weights." I wiggle my eyebrows.

"We do, don't we," she whispers into his ear as she wraps her arm around him. "Remember that time on the weight bench?"

My mouth drops. She throws the dish towel at me, and they both laugh. "Just kidding."

I chuckle as I walk over to help Abby put some other mouth-watering appetizers on the buffet table, and the doorbell rings. Who's the next addition to this crazy large group? More people were invited than I'd thought. It's not Kent and Dani, because it's too early.

Dani spent Thanksgiving alone because she had to work and Dominic flew to Arizona to see their parents. I felt bad for her so I told her to come with Kent to the party.

"Hey, everyone, it's Tyler," James yells.

Abby tugs my sweater sleeve. "Remind me. Who's Tyler again? I can't keep track of all the people I've met this weekend."

"He's Kayla's brother. He lives in California, but he's moving back to New Jersey or maybe New York. I'm sure we'll find out."

I hear the guests greeting him for a few minutes, then he approaches the kitchen. "Gerry, how did I know you'd be in the kitchen? You can't stay away from the stove for five seconds," he jokes but then gives him a bear hug.

I nudge Abby with my elbow. "There he is." She doesn't respond. I glance her way, and she looks like a mannequin. I wave my hand in front of her face. "Are you okay? Do you need to sit down?"

She ignores my question and mutters, "He's gorgeous. Why didn't you tell me he was so hot?" she says as she readjusts her head scarf, then fiddles with her earrings. "How do I look?"

"You look fab."

No freaking way. She's attracted to him. Should I worry about this? They're adults. I haven't seen him in a while, so who knows what he's like now. I don't know if I could trust him with her.

Tyler slowly makes his way over to us.

"Alexa! It's great to see you." He embraces me like he's on top of the world.

When he finally lets me go, I readjust my sweater. We make small talk, but Abby stands there mute. She gawks at him like he's a famous actor. It's hysterical.

Tyler glances at Abby and does a double take. Their eyes lock, and it's as if they're the only two in the room. The electricity crackles. I'm surprised the lights aren't flickering. I introduce them to each other, but they don't acknowledge me. Abby babbles like crazy, as she usually does when she's nervous. This is awkward. I know when to walk away.

"Abby, can I get you a drink?" he asks with a suave tone.

She bites her lower lip. "Um. Yeah. Sure." Her voice squeaks.

I whisper in Tyler's ear, "I'll warn you once. Don't go there if it's for games. You know I will kill you in your sleep." I turn away but whisper again, "And her brother, my boyfriend, is a cop. A big one. He'll be here soon."

He only nods with a massive grin. If he could only see himself.

Funny enough, they leave the kitchen, not even getting a drink. But what just happened there? Did I just witness a love-at-first-sight encounter? But why does it have to be with Tyler? I still hold a grudge against him after he humiliated Tina at Matt's bachelor party. I remind myself that he was drunk and had a bad night. The couple of other times I've seen him, he was different in a good way. But Abby is vulnerable and doesn't need a guy to play games with her and get her hopes up.

Maybe I'm getting way ahead of myself.

"Where's your brain right now?" Kayla asks while lightly knocking on my head.

I duck out of reach.

"You're so deep in thought." She bumps shoulders with me. "Come on. Tell me. Fantasizing about Kent's handcuffs?" she whispers behind her glass.

"Kayla! You have a dirty mind."

She nudges me with her arm. "Come on. I know you do. We all have fantasies."

I nod with a simper. "Anyway, what I was thinking about is how your brother just walked off with Abby, and they both looked smitten." I point to them in the living room. "Should we be nervous about that? Abby just finished her treatments and is sensitive about the way she looks. Would he be able to deal with that? I don't want to see her get hurt."

"Slow down. They just met. I know you have issues with Tyler, but he's not as bad as you think. He's matured and is stoked that he's moved back to New York City."

"He's already moved back? Where does he live?"

"Out of complete luck, the couple who were renting Gerry's apartment in Hell's Kitchen moved out a couple of days ago. As soon as Gerry heard they were moving, he told Tyler. My brother will stay there until the small penthouse he bought in the city is ready. His new office will open right after Christmas. He's already sniffing around for new investments."

"Sounds like things are going well. Good for him, but I'm still leery, though I'd be like this with any guy right now. I already warned him that he'd have to deal with me and then Kent."

She giggles. "You've got it bad."

"Huh? What do you mean?"

"You're already attached to Kent and Abby."

I don't even attempt to refrain from smiling.

"Yeah. Yeah. I thought so. But just remember when you met Kent. He had a bad attitude and was far from nice to you. Now things have changed. Just like Tyler has changed. So please don't worry so much. He'll also have to deal with my wrath if something bad happens."

"Okay. You're right."

Especially since I have enough to worry about as is.

"Speaking of Kent. Shouldn't he be here by now?"

I check my watch. "Yes. He's over thirty minutes late. It's unlike him, since he's Mr. Punctuality. I hope everything's okay." I pat the pockets of my jeans and pull my phone out. No messages.

"You should marry him just for that." She giggles. "Are you nervous for him to meet the family? There are a lot of people here."

"Sort of. I couldn't tell you the last time I had a real boyfriend. One that I wanted around for more than a couple dates anyway. I think he'll fit in well with James and Gerry. He already knows Matt. I think my dad will have the hardest time because he's probably dreaded this moment since I was born. Lisa, Tina, and especially my mom are dying to meet him, as if our relationship is the biggest news announcement of the year."

"Well, it kinda is. We've never seen you excited about your men, and this time you're introducing Kent to your family after you've been together for only a short amount of time. We're thrilled for you because you're too awesome not to find your perfect match." She sips her red concoction through a straw.

"Hey, that better be without alcohol," I say.

She coughs, and the red drink dribbles down her chin. I hand her a napkin from the table.

"What do you mean?" She avoids making eye contact.

"You know exactly what I mean." My eyes zone in on hers, and then I let them drift to her belly. "You better be announcing it tonight."

She plays nervously with her shirt collar, but she's saved by the bell. The doorbell, that is.

Chapter 33

Kent

Why is it that I get so damn nervous every time I wait at a door to see Alexa? This time it's warranted. As soon as this door opens, I'll be thrown into the middle of her friends and family. I've never been in this situation, when I actually cared so much. I'm glad Abby has been with Alexa for the past days. She would've warned me if this was a bad idea. She's said only good things about everyone.

"Stop worrying. If they don't like you, then screw them. You still have Abby and me," Dani says.

"Did Alexa respond to your text message about us being late?"

She flips her hair over her shoulder, almost hitting me in the face. "Nope. I guess she's having too much fun to check her messages. Or she's mad."

"Can you cheer up? I know you had a bad day at work and Vince is on duty, but try to have some fun."

I hear laughter behind the door and then a click. The bright light I always see when it comes to Alexa greets me as the door opens. Her warmhearted smile calms my nerves in an instant.

"Hey, you two. I was worried. Come in. It's cold." She waves us in.

Once she closes the door, she reaches out to hug me, but Dani jumps in the middle and hands her the bottle of champagne I bought. Dani told me Alexa's family is rich and probably only drinks expensive champagne. That doesn't sit right with me, but I bought a bottle anyway. It makes me wonder if Alexa is out of my league.

"Wow. I love champagne. I only drink this on special occasions, but today is one for a lot of reasons. Thank you!"

Alexa steps around Dani and wraps her arms around me.

"Hi, Sunshine," I whisper in her ear. "You look beautiful, as always."

Her gorgeous eyes dazzle. "I've missed you," she whispers, tightening her arms around my waist.

I kiss the tip of her nose.

"Sorry we're late. Did you get Dani's text? She locked her keys in her car, so I had to help her with that." Dani drove us here tonight because my truck fits only two people comfortably.

Alexa glances at Dani. "That's funny. I checked a few minutes ago, and there was no message from you."

Someone clears their throat. I follow Alexa's gaze and register several pairs of blinking eyes fixed on us. Dani's head toggles between them and us.

Alexa lets go of my waist but wraps her arm through mine. "Everyone, this is my boyfriend, Kent. He's Abby's brother." She swings her arm out. "Kent, this is everybody."

Dani steps forward.

"And this is Dani. She went to the same high school as James and me and just happens to know Kent and Abby too."

After Alexa introduces us to a lot of people, both of them wander off to get some drinks. I don't see Abby anywhere.

"Who are you?" asks someone with an angelic voice while tugging on my pants.

I turn around to find the sweetest little girl with the clearest green eyes I've ever seen.

I kneel down to her level. "I'm Kent, pretty girl."

She giggles.

"You must be Felicia." She nods as she sways back and forth in her ruffled red dress.

"Do you like Superman? Aunt Lexa says she wants to smoosh Superman."

"I said I have a crush on Superman. I don't want to smoosh him," Alexa explains as she hands me a beer, then picks up Felicia and tickles her. "You're telling him all my secrets. He's not supposed to know I have a crush on a superhero."

They look so much alike, Felicia could be her daughter. Blond hair, gorgeous eyes, and a charming personality.

"I had a feeling you did." I wink at Alexa. "But I told Alexa I have to earn the name Superman, so she's not allowed to call me that. But you can if you want."

Her face lights up. "Really? So I can tell my friends I know Superman?"

Alexa and I chuckle with her. It's hard not to be excited when you hear her contagious laugh.

"Are you flirting with Kent like your aunt does?" jokes a woman as she takes Felicia from her. "Since the day you were born, I knew you were just like your Aunt Alexa." She props the girl on her hip.

"Kent, this is Lisa, my brother's wife. She's been hiding in the kitchen with Gerry—whom you have yet to meet."

I shake her hand. "Nice to meet you. I've heard a lot about you and your family."

"We love Abby already. We were counting down the minutes until we could meet the mystery man who's finally captured Alexa's heart."

I pat down my pants pocket. "Felicia, before I forget, I have something for you."

Her eyes widen.

I pull out a small but heavy plastic bag full of coins. "These are from your aunt Alexa and a little bit from me too."

Lisa and Alexa laugh as Felicia jiggles the bag.

"Don't forget about me. What are you laughing about?" interrupts another woman. "I'm Tina, Lisa's sister and Alexa's old roommate. Abby told us all the gory details about you. But we love you anyway."

"Tina, I don't want him to run out of the house and never come back," Alexa exclaims.

"I'm just kidding. But Alexa did tell us she's madly in love with you and says you look hot in a uniform."

Alexa's mouth drops, and she turns the shade of strawberries.

I pull her to me and kiss her temple. "Good to know." I tickle her side. Alexa hits Tina in the arm.

A man sneaks up behind Tina and says, "Are you talking about me again?"

She rolls her eyes with a smile, "Of course, my love."

"I'm Gerry."

We shake hands.

"Gerry's the chef who agreed to cater the Christmas party at your house, along with Matt. I need to talk to Dani about the party. Where is she anyway?" Alexa looks over everyone's shoulder. "There she is with James."

She points to Dani, standing by the drink table, opening the champagne with James.

"Abby's inviting everyone to the party, so beware of the size it will be," Alexa divulges.

"As long as she's happy, I'm happy," I say.

We chat for a few minutes about the party, or at least they do. I'm overwhelmed. Let's see if my knack for detail helps me connect the names to the faces.

"She's better than happy. Let's see if she's still in the living room." She intertwines her fingers with mine and leads the way.

In the corner of the living room, under the cathedral ceiling, is a massive Christmas tree with white lights. Train tracks run underneath, and Christmas songs play lightly in the background. I don't even remember the last time I listened to Christmas music. These folks are starting the holiday off right.

My eyes scan the rest of the cream-walled room and land on Abby, next to the burning fireplace. She's sitting with some strange guy, deep in conversation. Who the hell is he? Their knees are touching, and I catch him whispering something in her ear. She grins and touches his arm. They look a bit too cozy. Warning signals go off.

"Abby, Kent and Dani are here," Alexa says. "I'm surprised you didn't hear them arrive."

She jumps up and gives me a big hug. "I'm so glad you're here."

I squeeze her back, but my eyes zone in on the guy.

Alexa rests her hand on my arm softly, as if she's picked up on my negative vibes. "This is Tyler. Kayla's brother. He just moved back from California."

He gives me a firm handshake and doesn't look the least bit flustered, even though I'm shooting spears at him and am several inches taller than he is. This has trouble written all over it. She's my little sister, and she's just won the battle of her life.

"Let's go see if the food is ready. Champagne is also calling my name. I hope Dani didn't drink it all," Alexa suggests, trying to break up the tension only she and I feel. "Abby, we need to talk to Dani about the party. Let's go find her."

Alexa leads me to the kitchen as her brother, James, says, "Attention everyone. We have some special announcements."

Alexa yanks on my arm in excitement. "Oh my gosh. I think I know what it is."

"I'll let the lovely Tina and Kayla tell you all." James motions to them both.

Alexa's face lights up like Felicia's was.

"Do you know what's going on?"

She pulls me down so she can whisper in my ear. "I think they're pregnant."

Alexa said *pregnant* at the same time Kayla and Tina yell it. The room roars with excitement. I'm almost pushed over by all the women running to them to say congratulations. Alexa and Abby are two of them. Their smiles couldn't get any bigger.

I watch them for a while. Within just a few weeks of Alexa being in our lives, she has changed Abby and me for the better. Abby and I laugh and talk more with each other. Alexa has given us a whole new family. I can already see that Tina and Lisa have pulled Abby into their circle. Warmth spreads through my chest, knowing how happy that makes Abby. She needs sisters and new friends.

It's amazing how being angry made me feel like I was suffocating. I wasn't living. Now that happiness has found me, I never want to be without it again. Without Alexa again.

A hand squeezes my shoulder. "I think you need to hang with the guys for a little while," James offers. "Don't worry. My dad doesn't bite."

"I think you're right. Lead the way."

I pass Alexa on the way and whisper, "I'm going to hang with the guys."

Her eyes bulge, and then she squints at James. He does the same, then laughs.

"Don't worry, Sunshine. I can hold my own." I kiss her on the cheek and whisper, "Have fun talking about babies. It just might be you one day."

Her jaw drops, but she doesn't say a word, but her smoldering eyes do.

In shock myself, I walk away with James. I can't believe I just said that.

The next hours fly by. My eyes were mostly on Tyler and Abby, when I had a clear view of them. He hasn't left her side since I got here.

I cross my arms. "So, Tyler, what do you do for a living?"

"I'm an investor. If I see a good idea, I jump on it."

"Like one of those investors on the TV show *Shark Tank*? I love that show," Abby says.

"Just like that, but I'm not as successful. Maybe one day."

"Why did you move back here?" I'm like a father interrogating his daughter's first boyfriend. That's not fair though. I just met Alexa's parents, and they were so welcoming. They didn't give me the third degree.

"Most of my work is here, and I'm near my family again. I just moved to the city."

Alexa slips her hand in mine, instantly calming me down.

"Tyler, maybe you can give us some advice. Abby makes her own head scarves. Isn't the purple one she's wearing beautiful?"

He looks at Abby like she's a precious diamond...the way I look at Alexa. *Shit.*

"She's thinking about selling them. I thought I'd help her out, since I have a sales background. Maybe you can give us some advice."

The three of them talk among themselves, and I stand back. I glance to the left and notice Dani reading something in the living room.

She talked about Vince the entire drive here. She asked if anything was wrong with him and said the same thing that Vince said about her—that he's the one in the mood all the time. I can't stand being in the middle. I tried to change the subject, but she kept at it. I don't know what to do with her.

I don't want to leave Alexa, but I'm beat. I don't think I've socialized this much since Abby became sick. Alexa's parents are down-to-earth, good people. Not at all what I expected after Dani told me that this was a wealthy, snobby area. They welcomed me as if I've been around for years. It was nice to be a part of a family gathering. I've missed it after all these years.

"I wish you didn't have to go." Alexa mopes as we stand outside near the front door. "I miss you already."

She has a jacket on, but her teeth are chattering. I open the front of my coat and wrap her in it. "I hate it too, but I need to work tomorrow. I've always hidden behind my job to distract myself from everything, so I worked all the time. Now I don't want to, because I have you to explore. If you know what I mean." I nuzzle her neck.

Abby finally makes it to the door, with Tyler next to her. Now she's the one beaming. He kisses her cheek, says his goodbyes to us, and walks away.

I'm not liking it.

"Do you have all your stuff?" I ask Abby.

"Yup. Dani took my bag to her car."

Right. Let's see if she even made it there. I think she drank the entire bottle of champagne I brought. "Yeah. I'm driving since she's drunk. I should drop her off at Vince's house and make him deal with her."

"Don't be mean. Just let her crash on the couch in the living room with a bucket next to her," Abby suggests. "She's helped me so many times. I'm sure she needs to sleep it off."

I whisper to Alexa, "She won't be sleeping in my bed."

"Don't worry. I'm not the jealous type. But there's no reason for her to be in your bed anyway."

Abby gives Alexa a hug and thanks her for the weekend.

"So get a move on, you two. You have a long drive. Send me a message when you get home," Alexa says.

Abby walks to the car.

I cup Alexa's face in my hands. "Don't forget, you can watch me on your phone. But I'll text you anyway." I lean in and watch her eyes close in anticipation. My lips tickle hers as she opens for me. At first, I tease her, but finally I give in to her sexy taste of strawberries and champagne. I can't wait until we can be alone. I need to know what the rest of her body tastes like.

"Okay, lovebirds, I'm tired," Abby yells from the car.

Chapter 34

Alexa

The entire Thanksgiving weekend was perfect. From Abby being with me to Kayla's and Tina's pregnancies. And best of all, Kent met my family and he's still alive. They loved him.

Now that I'm back in Hoboken, a sense of dread washes over me. I remember my real life. Stalker and my job on the line. I haven't had any strange phone calls since last week though. Maybe Kent's threat scared him off.

I'm disappointed the detectives didn't find any clues. With this modern world, why *can't* they find anything? This guy can't be that smart.

When my phone rings in my car, I yelp. The screen flashes Kent's number. I also programmed it to play the *Superman* theme song when he calls. I can't wait to see his face when he hears it.

"Hey, babe," I answer the phone with a smile. "I just parked in the garage. The connection's not the best down here. Just give me a second, and I'll call you back when I'm in my apartment."

It's ridiculous how much I smile when I hear his voice. I'm a happy person in general, but now I understand what happiness truly feels like. What I've been missing. I never thought I needed anything else. I was content with my life.

But my high spirits get sucked away when I run up the stairs to reach my apartment as fast as possible, constantly looking over my shoulder. I slow as I approach my door. There's a box in front of it. It's pink and might be a Victoria Secret's box. There's an open note on the top that says, *Early Christmas present. I couldn't resist.*

I giggle while I call Kent. He picks up after one ring.

"Aren't you the romantic."

Silence. "What do you mean?"

"Don't play stupid. You're so sweet to have left me an early Christmas present in front of my door." I lower my voice. "Is it Victoria's Secret?"

"Alexa, I *did not* put anything in front of your door. Did you touch it?" he asks with a cold, authoritative voice.

"You're scaring me. No, I didn't touch it. I just saw it and called you. I haven't even gone into my apartment."

"Do not touch it and do not go into your apartment. I'm not far from there. I'll be there in a few minutes."

The line goes dead.

I press my shaking body against the wall. "No. It can't be." I try to convince myself. But what if it is from my stalker? What could be in it? A bomb? I fucking hate the guy who's doing this to me. My life was fine before this shit started. Now I twitch with every little noise I hear. I don't like me as this person.

Sirens blare in front of the building. Was that really necessary for just a box in front of my door? He couldn't come quietly?

Seconds later, Kent and Vince come around the corner and run down the hallway to me. Kent pulls me into his arms. Vince kneels down and puts on some gloves to inspect the box.

"Are you okay?" Kent says as he rubs up and down my arms.

"I'm fine, but I hate that I'm paranoid about every fucking thing right now." I point to the box in front of my door.

"Alexa, you need to be cautious. You don't know what this man is capable of."

"I understand that, but it's my life that's affected by this. I can't even get into my damn apartment. And how do we know it's even from him?"

"Come on. Look what he's already done. Maybe we're wrong, but let's just assume it's from him and be glad if it's not."

"Fine. So what do we do? Can we deal with this in my apartment? I don't want my neighbors to see. Can't we take it inside and open it?"

"Yes. Walk around it and wait inside."

I unlock the door and step over the mat. Kent hands me my suitcase and handbag. I set them near the couch and wait for the guys to come in.

They're still kneeling there, staring at it. "Guys, pick up the damn thing and bring it inside. How dangerous could it be? I'm sure it's not a bomb." This is ridiculous, but my inner voice says it's not.

"Alexa, let us do our job," Kent remarks. "We could call in a whole team to do this. Would you like that?"

Time to zip my lip. "No. Let's get this over with."

After minutes of them poking it and examining the box...not what's in it yet...Kent carries it in and sets it on the kitchen table.

"Okay. Alexa, stand farther away."

I move a few steps back, even though I want to see what's in the box. My patience has flown out the window.

"Vince, I'm going to flick the top off. Are you ready?"

"Yes. Get it over with."

Thank you.

"On the count of three. One, two, three."

In one swift move, the lid flies off. Both jump back and yelp.

I jump. "What is it?" I ask as I creep behind Kent.

Kent shoots his arm out. "Stop, Alexa. Vince, get the cover. Fast."

I look between them and see the black things crawling around. *Spiders. Fucking huge spiders.*

A shriek leaves my mouth as I bolt to my bedroom. I slam the door and jump on the bed as if they're crawling on the floor around me. I collapse on my knees and rock myself, trying to focus on something else, but the panic sets in. My chest grows heavier and heavier, making me gasp for air. I cover my ears and start counting. *One, two, three, four...*

Visions of my brother and his friends dumping spiders on me while I was tied to a tree replay in my mind like it was yesterday. I was only seven years old. They were stupid and young, never thinking about how it would affect me. I was terrified. I avoid spiders at all costs now. James has never forgiven himself for that. He was grounded for a month.

The spider legs scurry along my skin. I wipe down my arms frantically and shake my hair. My mother had to pick spiders out of my hair. My brother's friend had bought the spiders for his damn pet lizard, but he used them to torture me instead.

"Alexa," Kent yells with concern.

The bed dips, then a gentle hand caresses my shoulder. I hurl myself at Kent and squeeze him tightly. "How did he know I'm deathly afraid of spiders? Hardly anyone knows that. How did he know? How?" My body quakes in his arms. "I'm sorry. You were right all along. This is more serious than I wanted to believe. Please find him."

"We will. I promise. I know I've said it before, but we will, even if I have to do it myself. I called the detectives on your case, and they're on their way over."

"Did you kill them? I don't know if I can stay here."

"We took care of them. You have nothing to worry about. I wonder if you'll get a phone call from him. Can you please get a new phone number? Ask your boss if you can have a new one even though you use it for personal calls. Have two phones if you need to."

"I'm supposed to go into the city tomorrow with Abby and Dani to see Tyler. I can stop by the office to ask. I'll send a message to my boss later tonight."

The buzz of the doorbell trickles through the doorway.

"Do you want to come with me to talk to the detectives?"

I shake my head.

"All right. If they want to talk to you, I'll send them in here. Is that okay?" He kisses my hand. "Hmm?"

My nervousness subsides, and a little confidence returns. I push my hair away and clean off the mascara that I'm sure is running down my face. I should use waterproof until this guy is caught. "Yes. Send them in here. I want this over with."

Chapter 35

Kent

It takes everything in me not to lose it right now. I want to punch the wall. Vince keeps giving me *calm down* looks because I'm pacing back and forth. Alexa spoke to the detectives. But again, it's a waiting game: fingerprints, trace where the spiders were bought, question all the occupants of the apartment building, check cameras—but there aren't any. The detectives want to call the landlord regarding the lack of security in the building. Maybe there are cameras, but we don't see them.

Tomorrow, the detectives should receive the videos from the clothing store she was at. Hopefully, we can see the guy and make a match. If it's the doctor, they better do more than just check his record. If they don't, he'll have to deal with me.

Chapter 36

Alexa

Sleeping at Kent's can't become a habit. But the thought of sleeping in my apartment last night was unthinkable. He promised they killed all the spiders—even had an exterminator in—but it didn't matter. I ended up hanging out with Abby until he got home from work. I'll see if I'll have the nerves to go back tonight.

Kent has been nothing but a gentleman. This is the strangest relationship I've ever been in. With the stress of everything, we haven't approached the subject of sex. Last night we snuggled together on his bed with sweatpants on, but he still slept on the couch when I fell asleep.

I apologized several times about him having to deal with my problems. He didn't sign up for this. But if I could pick anybody to be by my side through this, it would be him. I know he'll do anything to protect me.

Kent urges me to tell my family, but I can't. There's no need to worry them, especially with Christmas around the corner. I've always taken care of myself, and I'm not going to stop now. They'll find out once the stalker is behind bars.

"Today is going to be fun," I say to myself in the mirror. I need to hide my fears behind my mask. I have to forget about disgusting spiders crawling all over my body and try to enjoy myself. It's

Christmastime in the city, and all the decorations are out. How can I not be in a good mood?

Once Dani gets here, we'll head out. Natalie called me back last night and said we could meet up right before lunch. She has something to discuss with me, but she wouldn't say what it is over the phone. Dani and Abby can go shopping while they wait for me. After that, we'll meet Tyler at his apartment and go for lunch somewhere in Hell's Kitchen. I suggested a good burger joint or sushi place.

"Alexa, Dani just pulled up in the driveway," Abby says through the door. "I'll be downstairs."

I put the final layer of holly-red lipstick on and fluff my hair. "I'm ready," I say as I open the door. "Don't forget to bring a bunch of different head scarves to show Tyler. But I think he'll only be looking at you the entire time we're there," I yell from over the railing as she walks down the stairs.

"Ha-ha. You're funny. Don't make me even more nervous. Don't get my hopes up either. Why would he want a bald, boobless wonder?"

I trot down the steps and find Abby in the kitchen. "I can't say I know what you're going through, because I don't. Just be excited about the prospect with your scarves. Tyler can give us some great advice. If romance sneaks in there, let it be. He's fully aware of what you've been through. Kayla gave him an earful yesterday, with several warnings included."

Kayla called me Sunday before I left Lisa's house. She had a long talk with Tyler and explained Abby's situation. She was open with him because Abby is someone special and deserves to be treated like a queen. If he's not willing to do that, then he should leave it as just business.

So I'll see how it goes today. I have a suspicious feeling they'll end up together. Or maybe I'm becoming a hopeless romantic. *Eek! Not me!*

The doorbell rings.

"Let's go," I say. "We'll probably hit some traffic, but I know where to park. Remember—no discussing anything that's going on with me in front of Dani and Tyler. If Tyler finds out, he'll probably tell Kayla. Get my point?"

"You know I won't tell anyone. Your secrets are safe with me."

"Why didn't we take public transport? This traffic sucks," Dani whines.

"As I've said many times, I hate taking the train. The traffic should break up once we're out of the tunnel."

She rests back in her seat. "Whatever. Wake me up when we're there."

My phone rings, and Natalie's name shows up. "Hey, Natalie. What's up? I shouldn't be too much longer."

"Yeah. Um, sorry. I need to cancel our meeting. Something came up last minute, so we need to reschedule," she says with hesitation in her voice and then hushes someone.

"Is everything okay? Is someone in the office with you?"

"Um...um, only my secretary," she stutters. "She's gone now. Anyway, let's reschedule soon. I have to go."

"Sure. I'll call you later this week."

"Sounds good. Bye."

Something's up. She's never that distant on the phone. I hate that I question everything about my life right now.

"What do we do now? Should we call Tyler to meet earlier? I'm already starving for lunch," Abby asks.

"Sure. By the time we get to his place, it'll be around noon."

My oh my, love is in the air. Abby and Tyler walk in front of Dani and me. Abby's her nervous self, talking a mile a minute and arms flying everywhere. But that's what I love about her. I wonder when she'll slow down. It's time to get some food in her mouth. I giggle.

Dani leans toward me. "What's so funny?"

"Nothing really. Abby has such a crush, and it's sweet. She deserves some excitement."

"He seems like a good guy. I spoke to him for a little while at your brother's. Not that I remember much about what we talked about. That champagne went down pretty smoothly. Thank God Kent took care of me that night."

I guess taking care of you meant he helped you to the couch and Abby put a blanket over you.

"Hey, Abby and Tyler. You just passed the sushi place. It looks busy. I'll go in and see if there's a table for four."

"Or two and two. I can sit with Abby at another table if necessary," Tyler suggests.

He's so sly.

I enter the restaurant, and there aren't any tables available. The host says it'll be about a thirty-minute wait. I say no thanks and turn to leave, but I freeze and dip down. In the corner of the restaurant, looking cozy, are Natalie and Darren.

I hide behind a customer and apologize when the host thinks I'm hitting on him. I explain what I'm doing, and they both agree to help me. Natalie has a new but unflattering hairstyle. Either she hasn't washed it in days, or she's using the wrong hair products—it looks greasy. Horrible. Darren leans in close to her and proceeds to brush his hand through her hair, but it gets stuck in the knots. I duck to choke down my laughter. What fucking idiots. I peek over this poor guy's shoulder again, and Darren is still trying to get his fat hand out of her bird's nest. While he's doing that, Natalie covers her face in embarrassment.

I shouldn't find this funny. She's screwing around with him, and she could end up being his boss. She's my boss. He's an asshole and an alcoholic. And he has something up his sleeve with me.

I wonder if I should walk up to them or keep it to myself until I figure out what's going on.

"Are there any tables?" Dani asks from behind me. "It's damn cold outside."

"Shhh." I grab her arm and pull her down. "There's Darren with my boss."

She stands up and practically yells, "Who's Darren again?"

"Would you be quiet," I snap as I yank her down again. "You don't recognize him? He was the drunk at the bar and in the pictures I showed you."

"Oh. Right. Maybe we should leave so they don't see you. She obviously doesn't want you to know."

"You're right. Let's go."

We bolt out the door.

"What's up? No seats?" Tyler asks while blowing in his hands. "We're freezing."

"Long wait. Let's go to the burger joint. There's another reason I don't want to go in there. I'll tell you when we get there."

Thirty minutes later, we're enjoying our burgers. I decide not to tell them why I didn't want to eat at the sushi place. We focus on Abby instead.

"Peeps, it's time to discuss the Christmas party. We need to focus on the decorations. We need a tree. The clock is ticking."

A phone rings, and we each check our own to see whose it is. It's mine, and it's Detective Griggs. I had added him as a contact so I wouldn't assume his number is from the stalker.

"I need to answer this. I'll be right back." I scoot out of the booth and grab my coat.

"Hi, Detective Griggs. How are you?"

"Hi, Alexa. I wanted to let you know that we have the video from the store."

My churning stomach makes me regret the burger I just ate. "Really?"

"Can you come in today to watch it and see if you know him? We have a perfect view of his face."

I shiver from the frigid wind trying to knock me over. "I'm in the city right now, but I can be there late afternoon. Say around four. Does that work for you?"

"Yep. We'll be here. We're one step closer. See you at four."

"Thanks."

I cut the line and call Kent. Hopefully, he can be there with me. The next hours are going to crawl.

As the day grows darker, it gets colder, like it's preparing me for what I'm about to see. I'm afraid to see the guy's face. What if it's someone I don't know?

Kent said he'll wait for me in the station. I need him there because we're a team now. I can rely on him if I freak out again. His presence will keep me calm, or at least calmer than if I were alone. This is when I need my family. I know they'll kill me, but I'll worry about that later.

When I pull into the parking lot, Kent's already outside, waiting for me in his snug uniform. I'll never get sick of seeing him in it. Well, I'll never get sick of him period. I look in the rearview mirror and see him approaching my car.

I open my car door, and his hand is there to help me out. "Hi, babe," I say. "Will we ever find time for just us, and not for something like this?"

"Even though I don't like this, I'll take you any way I can."

He convinces me of that with his lips on mine. Each time he kisses me, I think it's the best one, but it always gets better. He kisses me like I'm his last breath.

"Are you ready to do this?"

"Yes. I hope I know who it is. I want this over with so I can move on with my life without looking over my shoulder or imagining spiders crawling on my body. I would rather you crawl on my body."

"Stop, or we'll get arrested for indecent exposure." He pecks me on the lips. "Lock your doors and let's go."

Within fifteen minutes we're sitting in the room with a monitor. A detective says I can watch it as many times as I need to, in case I can't identify the man right away. My palms sweat and my leg bounces. Detective Griggs walks in, and Kent trails behind him. When Kent sits next to me, I grab his hand and squeeze it like it's a stress ball. He doesn't flinch.

The video begins, and at first I don't see anybody, but then I appear, looking through the racks. In comes a strange figure in a baseball hat. He makes his way to the corner, as if he knows there's a camera somewhere.

When I go into the dressing room, he moves a few feet forward but still has his head down enough that I can't see his face. He removes something from his pocket. A camera, not a phone. I look on the screen for a salesclerk, but no one is around. He hides behind a rack and rests the camera on it. It looks like he's waiting for me.

It's disturbing to watch the scene unfold from the security camera's vantage point. He hunches down as I come out of the dressing room. I remember it clearly, how he took his hat off after I paid for my pants. I watch myself, but in the police station, I have a completely different reaction when I see his face.

I stand up and look closer. "Pause it please." He isn't entirely clear, but I know it's him. "It's Dr. Walker." *But it isn't him.* "What the hell's wrong with him? He looks emaciated. He didn't look like that a month ago."

"Are you sure it's him?" Detective Griggs presses.

"Positive, but it's obvious he's sick, with a scar like that on his head. I can tell you where he works, if he even works anymore, with the way he's behaving. I saw him at the cancer clinic, but I didn't know why he was there. Play it some more please."

We continue to watch me leave the store. There's a point where he starts coughing. "Freeze it." I point to the screen. "That's what everything has in common. See him bending over in a coughing fit?"

"Does he look like the man who took pictures of you at the café?"

"One hundred percent. He was skinny and with the same hat. I'm positive he's the same man. The pictures all connect with the video."

"You said you haven't had any verbal contact with him since the pictures were delivered."

"Correct. I assumed I would've gotten a phone call after the spider incident, but one never came."

"Thank you, Ms. Kramer. Good job. We'll take it from here. As soon as we find him, we will let you know. In the meantime, call if something else happens."

Kent and I leave the station and walk to my car hand in hand. "How can someone change so drastically in such a short amount of time?" I ask.

"It happens. He most likely has cancer. It felt like my mom changed from one day to the next. I told you she looked nothing like her vibrant self. Cancer is an ugly, despicable illness. Watching the females in my life suffer is one of the hardest things I've had to bear. But yeah, he could have changed that quickly."

I wrap my arms around his neck. "That's crazy. Is that why you're so protective of me? An urge to be able to save someone you're close to?"

"I'll admit it's partly that, but I care for you more than any other woman I've been with. Please don't think this is only a mission for me. I want to be with you, and no one is going to take you away from me."

He hugs me tightly and then pulls away. "You know what? We've never been on a date before. How about tonight? Have you ever been to Mario's?"

"Yes. I love the pizza there. We can walk from my apartment, even though it's freaking cold. I'll go home and get ready." *I need to ignore the fear I have of being in my apartment alone.*

"You always look perfect no matter what time of day it is. I'm hooked on you, so you don't need to impress me."

"I don't just do it for you. This is me, how I've always been. I like to look nice. I want this to be a real first date. I want to be nervous for you to knock on my door. I want to look in the mirror a thousand times to make sure I look good. Maybe change my outfit two or three times. The difference with this date is that I'm more excited than I've ever been."

He opens the car door for me.

"Our relationship didn't start off the normal way. It started with hate then like, and who knows where it'll go from here."

"I already know." He backs up from my car with a cocky grin. "Just let me know when you figure it out."

"Do me a favor—wear the glasses tonight, but no flowers or candy." I wink at him and get in my car. I know where our relationship is going, but I'm not ready to say it out loud.

Chapter 37

Kent

Alexa wraps her red knit scarf around her neck and pulls the matching hat on. It has a giant fur pompom on it that shakes when she moves, and it matches her lips perfectly. She closes and locks her apartment door, then reaches for my hand.

"I made a reservation so we won't have a problem getting a table," I say.

"Cool. There's always a wait list."

She swings our hands back and forth. "This is perfect. Let's promise not to talk about my problems. I want us to have fun and get to know each other without depressing things getting in the way."

"You're not too cold?" I say as I wrap my arm around her shoulders.

"Not when you're around. It's refreshing to walk in the crisp, cold air. It helps clear my head."

We walk down the block, admiring the Christmas decorations. White lights and snowflakes drape from one side of the street to the other. Store windows feature Santa Clauses and snowmen. In front of Mario's, a young man plays Christmas carols with a saxophone, hoping to make some money. The sound reminds me of my mom. She loved listening to music with saxophones. Her favorite Christmas CD was from Kenny G. She listened to it nonstop, and I always complained about it. Every time I hear similar music, I think of her, and it breaks my heart that I had always told her to turn it off. I throw some money in the basket.

"Ooh, I forgot to tell you what happened today," Alexa bursts out as the server walks away with our drink and food order.

She explains that her boss, Natalie, canceled their meeting and that she saw her with Darren.

"I never met your manager, but do you think she'd get involved with him, since she's his boss? Is she even his boss?"

"She's his potential boss. Supposedly his manager quit when the merge happened, and they won't hire a new one until they know what's happening with the combined sales forces. I have to wonder if it's just to keep his job. There's something that makes him nervous. I can't pinpoint it, but after seeing him in those pictures, he's definitely up to something. But what pisses me off more is that Natalie's falling for his crap."

"You're worried that he'll screw with your job."

"Of course. Since Natalie and I have worked together for so long, I'd think she'd be more loyal to me. But she has such low self-esteem that when a guy gives her attention, she falls for it immediately. I've seen it firsthand."

"So you've had a fun-filled day," I say, full of sarcasm.

"It was entertaining, but my favorite part is being here with you. Believe it or not, you're the first man I've ever wanted to spend this much time with."

I reach over the table and hold her hand. I caress it with my thumb. "Sometimes I think you're out of my league. We're opposite in so many ways, but then opposites attract."

"Does it still bother you that I work for the pharma industry? We haven't talked about it, and I don't know if we've been avoiding it."

We lean back in our chairs for the server to set our table. Her white wine and my beer are placed in front of us. She reaches her hand out for me to hold it again.

"I'll never like the pharma industry, but it's not enough to keep me away from you. I had the wrong impression of you and assumed a lot. I didn't want to like you, so I used that as an excuse. You've shown me how caring and compassionate you are. You watch over Abby like she's family. You're passionate about everything you do. I watched how you interact with your friends and family at your brother's. You light up every room you walk into, and that positive energy spreads to other people. It was impossible not to fall for you."

The corner of her mouth lifts ever so slightly, but I see it.

"But in a way, it's the same from my point of view. Your job frightens me. The world is a scary place right now. There's more violence and crime. More cops get injured on the job. But just like me, you love your job. You like to protect people and solve their problems. It makes me so proud of you. And to top it off, there's nothing better than a man in a uniform. Don't even get me started with your glasses."

I laugh out loud. "I don't understand what the big deal is with these glasses. Abby said that women would fall at my feet if they saw them on me. I only wear them after I take my contacts out."

"They're an added perk for me." She flutters her eyelashes.

"And your opinion is all that matters." I kiss the top of her hand just as the pizza arrives.

Time flies by as we devour our salami pizza. Alexa relaxes in her chair and drinks the last sip of her wine. "I couldn't eat another delicious bite."

"I guess that means no dessert."

She shakes her head. "Not for me, but you can."

"I'll just ask for the check." I pull my wallet out of my jacket and place it on the table.

She moves to retrieve her wallet. I grab her hand. "You are not paying for dinner."

"Let me pay half."

"I know you're Ms. Independent, but can we do this the old-fashioned way? A real first date, where I knock you off your feet." I close the gap between us.

"You've already done that." She traces her finger along my jaw. "So I don't need you to pay for dinner."

I hold her chin. "You are stubborn, but I like that about you. But you lose this time. I'm paying whether you like it or not." Before she can say another word, I plant my lips on hers. I feel her lips form into a smile.

"Stop trying to distract me, you big hunk."

I pay the bill and put my wallet back into my jacket pocket. "Let's go." I stand up, but Alexa yanks me back down to my seat and looks away from the entrance.

Chapter 38

Alexa

"What's the—" He falls back into his chair.

"Don't look now, but Tongue Boy just walked in with a blonde. I don't want him to see us. Just wait until he's seated." I peek to see if the coast is clear. "Okay. He's in the other corner. Let's go."

We stand, and Kent helps me put my jacket on. As we move away from the table, he wraps my arm in his and whispers, "I know this is childish of me, but follow me."

He leads me to Dominic's table. I'm not sure this is such a good idea. As we get closer, Kent and I glance at each other in surprise because the blonde looks exactly like me. Her hair is the same color but looks bleached. She notices us approaching, and I see her eyes are green too, but not as bright as mine.

Her eyes flicker as she scans me up and down. She seems to have the same thought as we do. She clears her throat and nudges Dominic's hand.

He looks up from his menu and snarls, "What?" in utter annoyance.

She gasps in surprise, as do I, at his abrasive response. He just proved he's an asshole.

"Now that's no way to talk to your date," Kent jabs with a cool tone.

I squeeze his hand, warning him not to make a scene.

A slow smirk forms on Dominic's face as he sits up tall. He instantly zeros in on Kent holding my hand. He crosses his arms, his hands noticeably gripping his biceps. Kent has been teaching me how to read people's body language during my sleepovers. Dominic's is typical of someone who's angry or uncomfortable. I suspect angry.

He scopes out who's around us, then says, "It's none of your business what I do."

"Oh really?" I chuckle. "It's funny how we ran into you tonight." I focus on the blonde. "You look very familiar. I can't quite pinpoint why though." I tap my chin. I like toying with him, but I feel sorry for his date.

She glances at me for a split second while she fidgets in her seat. "Who are these people?" she says under her breath to him.

He kisses the top of her hand. "No one for you to worry about."

His tone switched to fake kindness. I wonder if he licked her hand too.

A server approaches the table.

"Can you give us a moment please?" Dominic says.

"They went to the same high school and recently met up again. We're friends with his sister," Kent says.

"Hey, Dominic, I saw that you called me the other day. Was it something important? You didn't leave a message."

His posture relaxes as he drapes his arm over the back of her chair.

"I called you? You wish. You're the one that called me."

I teeter my head back and forth. "Really? That's not how I recall it, but whatever." I readjust my handbag strap on my shoulder. I glance at Kent. "We should get going."

He places his hand on my lower back.

"Good to see you again. Enjoy your meal. Ask for extra garlic. Dominic *loves* it." I recommend it to her with a big smile.

Kent and I turn around at the same time and calmly walk out of the restaurant. Once we are far enough away from the windows, we break down laughing.

"That was so wrong of us, but I couldn't help it," I say in between giggles. "I feel sorry for her."

"It's creepy how much she looked like you, but in a processed way. I could tell she noticed it too."

"Hopefully, she won't fall for his slimy personality."

Kent glances back at the restaurant. "It's strange that he showed up there on the same night we did."

I grip Kent's jacket and pull him close to me. "Do not overanalyze it. I can hear your brain spinning like the wheels on the Polar Express. He's not following me. It was just by chance. Yes, it's weird that she looked like me, but who cares. He probably prefers blondes. It's Dr. Walker who's following me, not Dominic."

I release his jacket, then grab both of his hands and pull him with me in the direction of my apartment. "Now you're going to take me home and kiss me at my door, like a good first date would end. Then you're going to walk away with a giant grin on your face."

"I get only one kiss? That's not fair."

I put up my finger. "Only one, so you better make it good. I need it to last me until I see you again."

He holds out his hand. "Do you have any mints or gum?"

I chuckle. "Of course. Why?" The sound of me rummaging through my bag fills the air.

"If I'm going to give you the best first-date kiss, I have to make sure I don't taste like garlic. It'll ruin my reputation."

I drop my head back and laugh, my breath turning to smoke from the cold. "Good thinking. You're one step ahead of me." I pull out a pack of gum and hand him a piece.

He waves me on. "Maybe give me one more just in case."

I roll my eyes but find it sweet that he cares so much. I toss a piece into my mouth too. Maybe I'm the one who'll taste like garlic.

"Come on. Let's finish the best date you've—I mean we've—ever had." His grin is brighter than a streetlamp.

I have no doubt it will be mine.

Chapter 39

Alexa

"Girls, we got a lot done today. Let's go to my apartment and crack open a bottle of wine. We deserve it."

"I don't know if I can carry these bags anymore. We went a little overboard with the Christmas decorations for the party, but I love it," Dani says. "I can't wait to wear my new dress too."

This is the best mood I've seen Dani in since the day I met her. I don't want to ask her why, since it might come off as rude. I don't want to pop her happy bubble. Maybe things are going well with Vince again.

I look over my shoulder toward Abby. "You okay over there? Those bags aren't too heavy, are they?"

"Thanks to my power nap before we went shopping, I'm strong like a bull."

Dani chuckles. "That you are, my friend. That you are."

"Good. You know where we are. My apartment's just around the corner."

My phone rings. It's Kent. My hands are full, so I don't answer it.

"You have the *Superman* theme song as your ringer?" Dani scoffs.

"So? It's Kent. Remember how I picked on him about being Superman when I ran into him on Halloween? It kind of stuck with me."

"I think it's sweet," Abby chimes in.

Now Abby's phone rings just as we turn the corner, but I think I know why. "What the hell is this?"

"Holy shit. What happened?" Dani bursts out.

In front of my apartment building are three police cars and a couple of plain black ones. An ambulance slowly pulls away. Two police officers guard the front entrance. My stomach plummets. I drop my bags and call Kent.

"Alexa, where are you?"

"Across the street from my apartment with Dani and Abby. Where are you? Why are so many cops in front of my building? What happened?"

"I'm inside, but I'll come out to the front. Wait for me there." The line goes dead before I can say anything else.

I yank my bags off the ground and speed-walk to the building.

"Alexa, what's going on? What did Kent say?"

I ignore them and keep going.

"Answer Abby," Dani snaps. "What did he say?"

"Chill out. He said he'd meet us out front. If your bags are too heavy, then give them to me." My adrenaline is so high that I could carry fifty bags. My ankles are going to snap with these damn high-heeled boots.

I whip my head back and forth while watching the traffic. "Come on. Let's cross."

Just as we reach the other side, Kent storms out the door and rushes over to us.

"What's going on? Does this have to do with me?" *Stupid question.*

"Yes. The detectives are here, and they need to talk to you alone." He looks at Abby and Dani. "I'm sorry. Can you go to Matt's café for a little while? One of us will call you when you can come back."

"No," Dani says. "I have my car not too far from here. Just give me the bags with decorations, and I'll drive Abby home. Maybe Abby and I will start to decorate. I hope everything is okay."

We switch bags, and then Kent and I head up to my apartment. "I'm scared. Why do so many cops need to be here?"

He squeezes my shoulders gently. "They found him."

I swallow deeply.

"But you're not going to like to know where. Detective Griggs will tell you everything. They're waiting in front of your door."

"You'd better not leave me here by myself," I shriek as we run up the stairs.

"I will *never* leave you. I'll be in the room with you. Let's go. They're waiting."

We approach my door and find Detective Griggs and another person. I slow down because one part of me isn't sure I want to hear what they have to say. But the other side is excited that this might be over.

"Hi, Alexa." Detective Griggs's extends his meaty hand. I shake it. He introduces me to the detective next to him.

"Can we talk in your apartment?"

I nod and unlock the door.

I drop my things on the kitchen table. "Please sit on the couch."

"I think you're the one who should sit." Detective Griggs points to the couch. "Because this will be hard to take in."

"Would you please get to the point?"

Kent comes to my side and sits down with me.

"Kent said you found him. Where?"

"In an apartment on the top floor."

I spring off the couch, and Kent follows. "In this building? Where is he now?"

Kent clears his throat as he holds my hand. "He's dead."

I pull my hand away and wrap my arms around my torso. "What do you mean? Did he kill himself?"

Griggs shakes his head. "From what we have seen, it looks like he died naturally, but it'll take a few days before we know that for sure. We also think he's been dead for several days."

I take a few deep breaths. "I'm sorry. This is absolutely crazy." *In and out. In and out.* "But I still don't understand why he was here."

Detective Griggs waves his hands. "Let me start from the beginning. We went to the last address we could find. The place was vacated, with no forwarding address. We then went to his practice. Supposedly he sold it for a large sum of money, and no one has heard from him since. We received some tips and found out that he had an aggressive brain tumor. After some procedures and surgery that didn't work, he had chosen to stop his treatments."

"That's why he looked the way he did." I touch my scalp and cringe. "That explains the scar on his head." I massage my forehead. "But what does that have to do with this building, other than me?"

"After more research, we were told that he bought this building and has been living here for months."

I pace back and forth. "That can't be true. I never saw him here. I only saw him around town, but never here."

"You told me that there was a new owner, didn't you?" Kent asks.

I rub my temples. "Yes, but I never paid attention to the name. I pay my rent and do my own thing. As long as things work in this apartment, I don't have contact."

"You wouldn't have recognized the name. He used his mother's last name. It seems this was planned well in advance. He bought this building from the previous owner for more than it was worth and paid cash.

"We thought there were no cameras, but there were. He watched you daily. There is a whole security system up there, but from what we briefly saw, it was only videos of you coming and going from this building."

"Were there videos of me inside my apartment?" I cry. I cover my chest, as if I'm naked in front of a crowd. I feel violated.

"I want to say no, but we don't know for sure. If you give me permission, I'll have your apartment checked for cameras. We still have to see what he recorded. My team needs to do their jobs, and we'll let you know everything once we've connected all the dots. My detectives will also interview everyone in the apartment building again."

Kent pulls me into his arms. "The main thing is that he's gone and it's over. You don't have to worry about him anymore."

I bury my face in his neck. "I'm so glad you're here with me," I whisper.

He gently caresses my hair. "Always," he responds softly against my temple.

I don't know why I'm crying. Maybe it's because everything finally has come to a head. Or I finally understand how dangerous he really was. He could've hurt me the next time. I should be excited and relieved this is over.

"One more thing." Detective Griggs interrupts our cuddle moment. "I can't guarantee this won't get to the media."

I pull away and wipe the tears from my cheeks. "You mean my friends and family might hear about this through the TV or newspapers?"

He nods.

"I never told my family, and I want to keep it that way." My voice rises with determination.

"I suggest you tell them now, because I'm sure they'd rather hear it from you than to see you in the newspaper or on TV."

My head hurts just thinking about how my parents will react.

"I'll tell them after your team leaves. Am I allowed to leave the building? Can I drive to my parents' in Cleartown?"

"Yes. We'll call you if we need anything."

Kent hugs me again. "Pack your bag. I'll go with you to your parents', and then you're staying at my house."

For some reason his firm demands make me chuckle. I tap him on the chest. "Since when did you get so bossy?"

His eyes lock with mine. "When my favorite woman in the world just had the scare of her life, I'm going to be there to pick up the pieces."

I'm running on empty at this point. Kent parks my car in front of his house. When we near the front door, Abby opens it for us. On the way to my parents, I'd called her to explain what happened. I made Kent drive because of my nerves.

She wears sympathy like a mask on her face. "How did it go?" she says as she steps aside to let us in.

"They acted like any parents would. They were distraught that I didn't tell them what was going on. There was a lot of yelling and more crying than were necessary. By the time the yelling stopped, I felt worse than I already did. Mom wanted me to stay, but Kent and I convinced them that the danger is over and said that I'd be staying here tonight. They love Kent even more now." I squeeze him around the waist.

"So everyone in your family knows now?"

"Yes. They were all there, including Tina and Gerry. James said he would tell Matt and Kayla for me. But enough of this now. I don't want to talk about it anymore."

We've been standing in the foyer the entire time, but I hadn't noticed the decorations.

"Oh, Abby. It looks beautiful in here. I'm sorry I didn't notice right away. How could I have missed it? You and Dani did an awesome job with the garland and white lights. The party is going to be such a hit. There's so much we need to do still though."

"It's only Wednesday. There's plenty of time. All you should do is go upstairs and relax."

I can't even think about the party because I need to let the shit from today go out the door first. Maybe with a good night's rest, I'll feel more festive in the morning. It's Christmastime, Abby is healthy, I'm safe again, and I have Kent. I couldn't ask for more. *So snap out of it, Alexa!*

She nudges Kent. "Maybe this big guy over here will give you a massage."

I tilt my head. "Now that sounds like a good idea."

Chapter 40

Kent

She moans when I press on a knot in her shoulder.

"Where did you learn how to give such good massages? I don't want to know who else had your magical hands on her."

I stop and sit up on my knees. "Not to gross you out, but I learned how to do this for my mom. I would massage her hands and feet to help her relax when she was in so much pain."

"That's so damn sweet. Can you make my heart melt any more than you already have? Soon, I won't have one left," she says with a muffled voice. "Why don't you try my hands?" She wiggles her fingers on her right hand. "Let's see if you can beat my manicurist. She's the best. I always get a quick hand massage every time I go to her."

I squirt more body lotion onto my hand.

"The door's closed, right?" she asks softly.

"Yes. Why?"

She flips her half-naked body over and extends her arm out to give me her hand. I can't see her hand because I can only focus on her perfect pink-tipped breasts. "Do you have to tease me like this?"

"Yes," she says without hesitation. "You want me to relax. So that's what I'm doing. But I have a question. Do you give frontal massages?"

She's smooth. I'd do anything to give her a massage that would feel good for the both of us. I'm hesitant because I want to be with her when her focus is entirely on me, not only to forget about what's happened.

"Is that an invitation?"

"What do you think?"

"Let me see." I adjust myself so that I'm kneeling over her, her body trapped between my legs.

I tickle her with one finger in a circular motion around her belly button. Goosebumps form on her rosy skin. She props her head on her left arm. Her other hand slowly rubs my thigh.

After a few circles, I rest both of my hands on her hips, then trace my fingers up the sides of her waist and rest them right below her breasts. She gasps and wiggles as I graze her skin. Our eyes never waver.

"How's your frontal massage going? Enquiring minds would like to know." I repeat the same movements. Up and down. Her hand movement on my thigh mimics mine. When I go up, I go slightly higher and tickle the undersides of her breasts more each time. Not high enough to touch her nipples, but close enough that I know she's about to burst.

"Why are you teasing me like this?" she says between heavy breaths.

"Because I want to turn you on the way I am every time I'm near you. It takes every ounce of energy to not make love to you each time you're in my bed." I slowly crawl up her body, kissing, licking, and nibbling on her feather-soft skin. I nudge myself between her legs. "Do you feel what you do to me?"

"Mmm-hmm." She places her hands on my backside and pulls me to her, grinding against me.

"Kiss me," she demands.

"Now look who's bos—"

She cuts me off. Her lips are on mine, and I become dizzy. Nothing ever tasted as good as she does, like the ripest red berries bursting in my mouth.

Her hands graze through my hair as she angles her head to the side, exposing her supple neck. I suck gently below her ear and down her neck, stopping at her chest. My lips graze one of her nipples. She covers her mouth as she lets out a low groan and arches her back.

"I wish we were alone so we could make as much noise as we want. Will that ever happen?" she asks with a sultry voice.

I lick between her breasts, then trail kisses back up her neck. "Open your eyes." Her pools of green focus on me. "I'm off after Friday for a week. We'll find the time."

She exhales in frustration. "I love Abby, but I feel like we're teenagers sneaking around our parents and could get caught any minute. I just want it to be you, me, and a bed." She traces my jawline with her finger. "Or the floor."

"Or the shower." I cock an eyebrow.

"Kitchen table?" She pulls me to her again and sucks on my lower lip.

"It better have sturdy legs." I ease to my side and wrap her in my arms.

She caresses my face with the back of her fingers. "Sleep with me tonight. I don't want you away from me anymore. I need your warm body next to mine." She kisses my cheek, then nuzzles her head into the crevice of my neck.

I drape the comforter over us. "You'll never sleep alone again."

Chapter 41

Alexa

Phones are my enemy right now. Mine is ringing on the dresser, but I'm not in the mood to talk to anyone. I should have turned it off before we went to bed. I let it ring. If it's important, they'll leave a message.

Kent stirs and flips so he's spooning me. He pulls me as close as possible to him, like a child clinging to a teddy bear. My heart gushes with love for him, but I keep that little secret to myself. We stayed up late last night talking and laughing. Even though I wanted to jump on him, it was nice just to relax. Well, kissing and petting did interrupt us sometimes. I can't help but smile right now.

He told me sweet stories about his mom from when he was a child. She sounds like she was a wonderful woman. I wish I could've met her. They've all endured so much. Any time Abby or Kent mentions their mom, I want to grab my phone to call my mom to tell her how much I love her. I should tell my dad that too.

"Stop thinking so much," he says with a hoarse morning voice.

I squeeze his arm that's curled around my waist. "I'm just dreaming of you and thinking how happy you make me. Today's a new day."

"You smell good in the morning. Let's stay in bed all day. You deserve it after what happened yesterday."

"I would *love* that, but you have to work, and I have a couple of appointments this afternoon. Hopefully the person who called was canceling one of them. I also made sure I have off tomorrow to prepare for the party."

He growls. "Fine. But does that mean you'll sleep over again tonight?"

"Sure, but I need to go home and get some clothes. Especially my sexy outfit for Saturday night. Let's see if you can resist me then."

I pull his arm off me and sit up in bed. I reach over to the dresser to get my phone. I look at the time. "It's eight already. Don't you need to be at work soon? Maybe I'm a bad influence on you."

He sits up like someone zapped him. "Shit. I need to be there in thirty minutes." He whips the blanket off and briskly walks to the bathroom. I could get used to this, waking up together and having breakfast before we go to work.

I scan my phone and notice it was Natalie who'd called. I ring her back. She answers on the first ring. She screams into the phone about how she read about me in the newspaper. I'm not surprised she read it so early this morning. She reads the newspaper every morning like the Bible at the exact same time. Not on the internet, but the paper.

After I explain everything, she asks if I could meet her at her office. Some things have come up at work that are urgent, she says, and she needs to talk to me face to face. Knowing my luck, I'll lose my job today.

I pinch myself. No. I was handed my life back yesterday. I'm not jinxed anymore. It's time that things get back to normal. Once this day is finished, I have a long weekend ahead of me and I need to have some fun.

"I don't know how you can be so calm about this. Who knows what could've happened to you?"

"He's dead, and life can resume. I'm not going to stop working and not live my life. It's done with."

"The spider thing gives me major willies." Natalie shivers in her chair. "I can't believe you didn't tell me about it. I vaguely remember you mentioning your phobia once when we saw a small spider in my car."

"I would've told you if you hadn't canceled our meeting the other day." Let's see how she reacts to that comment.

She straightens everything on her desk. Pens are lined up next to each other. Papers already in neat piles are restacked. She wipes off the desk with her hand. She re-sticks Post-its on a file. Who does that? Someone who's hiding something.

"Let's get to the point of this meeting. Is there an update on the layoffs?"

She sits up straight like a rooster and folds her hands on her desk. Sometimes I can't take her seriously as a manager.

"Something has been brought to my attention, and before it gets out, I need to get your side of the story."

I point my thumb at my chest. "My side of the story?"

She holds her hands up. "Listen to me first. There's a rumor going around that you are trying to ease your way in with some of the oncology medical staff at LCCI."

My chin just about hits the top of her desk. "What the hell are you talking about? Who did you hear this from?"

She folds her hands again, but this time she grips them tightly. Her fingertips are white. "I know you've been spending a lot of time at the library there. Have you been in contact with any of the doctors or nurses at the hospital?"

I've not told her anything about Kent and Abby. "I have been in contact with the staff, but it was never for work purposes."

She shakes her head in disbelief. Wow, she thinks I did something wrong.

"I was told that you had a meeting there recently? Is it true?"

"Am I on trial? You don't even know my side of the story."

She leans back into her chair like she's the queen. "So tell me."

For the next half hour, I explain to her about Abby's chemo appointment and my involvement with Abby's scarves.

"But are you trying to sell those scarves to get ahead in the oncology sales business? To pull away the staff from other sales reps?"

I rub my forehead. "This is mind blowing. Do you hear yourself? I'm not even an oncology sales rep. Why would I get involved with them? Yes, I'm trying to learn, but I've had no contact with anyone regarding my job in sales. That's the least of my worries right now, with all the other shit that's been going on." I stand up from my chair and lean over her desk.

"Tell me who told you that I had a meeting the other day." Before she has the chance to answer, it hits me.

"You heard this from Darren Whiteman, or, I'm sorry, Pushead." I smack my forehead. "My bad. I mean, Whitehead. He told me his last name was Whiteman when I went on a date with him."

Her eyes turn into giant saucers.

"Remember Joker the Poker? Guess who he was?"

Now her neck is red and blotchy. I struck a chord. Good. This is the time she should be wearing a turtleneck.

"I don't know what you're talking about. Why would Darren have anything to do with this?"

"Um, maybe it's because I have pictures of him spying on me at the hospital. He's threatened me more than once." At least one good thing came out of Dr. Wanker's psychotic behavior.

She shakes her head, but in a twitchy way. "Again, he has nothing to do with this."

"Why did you cancel our meeting the other day?"

She looks everywhere but at me. "I had a bad toothache and went to the dentist."

I burst out laughing. "I didn't know that dentists serve sushi in their waiting rooms. Is that covered under medical insurance?"

Her face pales. "How did you know?"

"Let's just say we seem to have the same taste in sushi restaurants."

She wisps hair away from her face.

"Don't try to defend him to me. He's an asshole and will do anything to save his job. There's something weird about him. Why he'd go to this extent to try to get me fired is beyond me. If he wants my job so badly, he can have it."

"He's not a monster like you describe him," she blurts out.

"Seriously? He has you so wrapped around his finger. But why? And why would you even fall for his shit? I guess you enjoy his poker."

She jumps up from her chair. "That is completely uncalled for."

"You know what's completely uncalled for, *Natalie*? Is that you're taking this asshole's side when you've known me for years. I considered you my friend. I take my job very seriously, and I've never been unethical. And you know that. But you are so damn desperate for a man's affection that you'll believe his lies."

Her eyes water. I don't care. She's just another person fucking with my life.

"I want proof that I've done something wrong. I want the names of these so-called doctors or nurses I had meetings with."

"The only name I was given is Michael." She sniffs.

"As in, Jackson? Are you sure?"

She pinches the bridge of her nose. "Maybe it was Miguel."

I point my finger at her. "If I don't get his correct first and last name by Monday, I will go to human resources and report your little alcoholic boyfriend. And because you're involved with him, that just might come back and bite you in the ass."

I grab my jacket and purse and storm out of her office, slamming the door behind me. I guess that black cloud is still hanging over me. But I'm not going to let this ruin my weekend. I'll tell Kent about it next week. No need to piss him off more than I already am.

Chapter 42

Kent

I knock on Detective Griggs's office door. He waves for me to come in. "Hey, Hayes." He shakes my hand.

"I just wanted to say thanks for the help on Alexa's case. It took a while to calm her down yesterday, but she was feeling better this morning."

He sits on the edge of his desk and plays with another stupid rubber band. "Alexa would've been worse if we'd told her how much we found in his apartment."

"What did you find?" I clench my teeth.

"A shitload of pictures. They were taped all over the walls. That was another reason we didn't want you to go into his apartment."

I ball my fists. "Were there cameras in her apartment?"

He shakes his head. "No. No. We found nothing."

"Then what are they of?"

"Just everyday stuff. You saw the pictures he left on her doorstep. So you get the point." He stands up. "You were in one." He walks over to a stack of pictures and hands them to me.

I recognize where we were that day. It's one of us when I gave her the parking ticket. I chuckle to myself. I know this is serious, but when I think of what a smartass she was that day, it makes me fall in love with her even more. *Huh? Where did that come from?*

"He seemed to follow her everywhere. He probably knows more about her life than she does."

I shuffle through the pictures quickly because it makes me sick to my stomach knowing that this disgusting piece of shit was following her.

"He had a notebook of her daily routine. Which was very irregular. I don't know how he kept track of her. We still don't know what his motive was."

"Sometimes there is no main motive. He was obsessed with her. He probably just sat there watching the videos, waiting for her next move." I'm getting even more pissed, and this guy isn't even alive anymore.

"We're slowly going through the videos to see if we missed anything. I don't think we have, but we need to keep an eye open until we get the autopsy results back. I think it'd be best if you don't discuss the case with anyone."

"Understandable. I'll tell Alexa."

"Why don't you sit down? Relax for a minute." He motions to a chair as he sits in his. "I've seen a big change in your mood lately. Practically a one-eighty. It's like you found your old self again. Does Alexa have something to do with it?" He raises his eyebrows.

I can talk to him about things like this because we worked closely when I was training. We got to know each other pretty well. "Yes. She's shown me the way back. I'm happier than I've ever been." I try to cover the smile that's the size of Alaska on my face.

"Good for you. That type of happiness is worth everything. There's nothing better. Sounds like she's a keeper. You deserve it after all you've been through."

"She's stuck with me whether she likes it or not." I laugh out loud.

"Is she aware of that?" he jokes back.

"Definitely. But listen. I need to get back to work. I have some reports to fill out." I stand up to leave.

"Give me one more minute. Let's talk briefly about something else. Sit back down."

I get comfortable again. "Shoot."

"How's Abby doing?"

This is what he wants to talk about?

"She's doing great. The treatments are done, and now she can find her way again. That'll take time, of course." We talk a few minutes about her and how she wants to sell her scarves.

"Are you still interested in becoming a detective? You did really well during training. It was a pity to see you stop. I think you'd make a great detective. We have an opening, and you would train with me if you would consider it again."

I lean forward. "This is unexpected, but I would love the chance to do it again. When would the training start?"

He rolls closer to his desk and rests his elbows on it. "Not until January. Before you agree, go home and think about it for a couple of days."

I rise from my chair with an obvious grin. "Thanks for thinking of me." We shake hands. "I'm off next week, but I'll call you during the week with my answer. I'm pretty sure it's yes though."

"I'll be in touch if anything comes up. Say hi to Abby and Alexa."

Chapter 43

Alexa

This house couldn't be more festive if we tried. Garland with shimmery white lights and red beads trace the archways of the different rooms and up the banisters outside and inside. Big dark-red velvety bows add the last accent to them. Candy canes hang from ribbons that run along the top of the front windows on the first floor. A beautiful wreath hangs over the fireplace.

My favorite is the Christmas tree. Kent and Vince surprised us with a seven-foot-tall obese real tree. I was in the living room with Abby and Dani when they came barreling in with it. It almost didn't fit through the door. Needles flew everywhere. We had to rearrange the furniture to make more space for it. The scent of pine instantly swirled throughout the house.

I wish I'd had a camera to capture the glowing smile on Kent's face. It had given me a glimpse of the future. That is what I want, with him, every day, for the rest of my life. I can't wait until the moment I tell him that I love him. It has to be at the right time.

We cleaned the crap out of the dining room to use it for the food buffet. Dust bunnies were everywhere. Abby checked for spiders in every corner. Kent told me they hadn't used this room since his mom had died. That's going to change tonight. The room screams *Redecorate me*. But it's not my house.

"I did..." Abby's huff mixes with Nat King Cole's "The Christmas Song" playing in the living room. "I did go a little overboard with the mistletoe," she says with her hands propped on her hips. "Look at the size of it. It looks ridiculous hanging from the doorframe. The guests will have to duck to walk into the dining room, or they're going to think it's a piñata."

"You're crazy." I chuckle. "Let's just find another place then." I stand by the front door and weigh the options. I motion up and down the hallway. "The ceiling is high in the hallway leading to the kitchen. Let's hang it in the middle. What'd'ya think?"

Abby's eyes roam the hallway. "Good idea. I'll add it to the list of things we need Kent to do when he gets back from the liquor store. He'll be thrilled, I'm sure."

I hang a small ring of jingle bells on the front door handle. "He's been a good sport this entire time. He's not a Grinch this year, like you said he was the last couple of years."

She wipes her brow. "Thank God. I think back to last Christmas and see how much has changed for the better. I never want to relive that again."

I squeeze her hand. "You won't."

We both jump when my phone alarm goes off. I fetch it from the table. "Look at the time. Who gets the shower first?"

"You," we say in unison and laugh.

"You go first. It takes me two seconds because I don't have any hair. I hope it starts to grow soon. But will you help me with my makeup? Since Tyler's coming, I want to look extra special."

"I hope you aren't nervous."

"We've been talking every day, and I find him so freaking *amazing*. But what if—" She looks at the floor.

"What if, what?"

She lifts her head and looks at me. "When he sees me again tonight." Now the speed mumbling starts. "It'll be a reminder to him that I'm not a normal woman physically. Why would he ever want to get involved with someone who has the problems I do? I have no boobs. Men love boobs." She looks down at her chest and sighs.

"You're scheduled for reconstructive surgery in January. You won't be a boobless wonder like you say for much longer."

She giggles.

"You were open with him from the beginning about your medical issues. But I think Tyler looks beyond your physical beauty and already knows what a beautiful woman you are inside. Love is blind. It's time to celebrate *you* and the start of your new life. Don't focus on Tyler and question every second what he's thinking. I was drawn to you the moment I saw you wearing a head scarf. If you can do that to a straight woman, why can't it happen with a man? If you are unsure of Tyler's intentions, talk to him. Don't do it tonight though, or at least wait until the party is over."

Her shoulders droop. "I wish I was strong like you. This week you found out your stalker is dead and was living in the same building as you. You walk around like it didn't even happen. I would be traumatized."

I sit on one of the dining room chairs that we lined along the wall to make room for tonight. Abby leans against the doorframe. "I am freaked out. I've been avoiding going back to my apartment. Other than that, I handle things differently. He's dead, so now I can wipe my hands clean of it and resume my normal life. It's not like I was physically harmed or anything."

Abby juts out her hip, not looking convinced.

"It's hard to explain. I don't wallow in things. Yes, I'll be more alert to my surroundings from now on, but I can't cut myself off from the world. My life has changed so much since October, I can hardly see straight. But most of the changes are positive. Those are the things I want to focus on most."

Even though Natalie is fighting her way into my head. I dread Monday. I should ask Dani or even Abby if they know a doctor or nurse named Michael or Miguel. The hospital is big though. If it's true that someone complained about me, it could be anyone. It's better that I keep it to myself tonight. I still haven't told anybody.

I leap from the chair when the doorbell rings. "Okay, maybe I'm a little jumpy," I admit with my heart in my throat.

Abby strolls over to the door and opens it. The jingle bells jiggle against it. "Hey, Dani. Come in. We just finished up and were chatting."

"Chatting about what? Anything fun?" She drops a big duffel bag on the floor. "Man, it's cold today."

"I was telling Alexa how strong she is and how I wish I were like her."

Dani looks at Abby and me with disappointment.

I raise my hands. "Sorry. Not that juicy."

She pulls her hat off, and the static pops in her hair. "If that happened to me, I'd be in a corner twitching and would probably never talk to or go out with another guy again." She pulls her hand through her hair. "What is with the static today? There's enough electricity in my hair to light up New York City," she complains.

"I contemplated that, but now that I have Kent, I don't want to date anyone else."

"That's sweet. Now let's focus on the party."

Dani assesses the rooms. "The decorations are so classy. Alexa, you went a little crazy with the mistletoe though. I guess you want to be kissed a lot tonight," she jokes as she traces her fingers over it.

"I bought it," Abby says. "I'm not sure I'll be kissed though."

Abby points to Dani's bag. "What's the big bag for? Moving in?"

Dani unwinds the extra-long multicolored scarf around her neck. It looks like a snake. "If I drink too much, I thought I could crash here. Vince is acting all weird, so I'm not going to rely on him to drive me home. Dominic's out with another girl tonight, so he's not going to pick me up either."

"I'm sure you won't be the only one who wants to crash. You can stash it in my room so it's not in the way," Abby offers.

Dani unzips the bag and pulls out a large dirty pillowcase full of clothes. "Our washing machine broke yesterday. Would it be okay if I wash a couple of loads here?"

"Sure. You know where it is."

"Since we're done here, I'm going to shower. Kent should be home any minute. Tina, Lisa, Kayla, and the guys will be here within the hour to set up the food."

As I climb the stairs, Dani whispers something about me. Then more chatter, and Abby says, "Mark my words—they'll be engaged by the summer." I don't listen anymore, because I'm floored that Abby would say that. But I'm even more shocked because I hope she's right. I laugh at my bright smile in the bathroom mirror.

I hear Dani tell Gerry where to put the food as I slip my black fitted silk suit jacket on over my red lacy push-up bra and button the three buttons in the front. I bought this pantsuit a while ago but this is the first time I've had an event I wanted to wear it to. It's too sexy and fancy for work.

Abby's in the shower still, so I have time to go downstairs and say hi to everyone.

The doorbell rings again as I step off the bottom stair. As I approach the kitchen, I overhear Kent firmly say, "Back off about Dominic. What is it that you don't understand? Alexa and I are together. *Together.* I don't care what our differences are or how much Dominic likes her. Believe me—we got a glimpse of how much he likes her when we ran into him the other night with a plastic replica of Alexa. That's just sick. And it's funny how he just happened to show up at the same restaurant we were at."

I stop short and move to the side so I'm out of sight. What the hell just happened? She must have said something horrible if Kent responded to her so harshly. If she's pushing the Dominic issue again, then she deserves it. I thought I made myself quite clear about it.

"I'm sorry. I'm sorry." Dani lowers her voice in defeat. "I thought it was my brother's last chance with her. I just wanted to help him. Things aren't going so well with Vince, so I'm all out of sorts. I know I shouldn't take it out on you or Alexa."

"Did something happen?" Kent asks with concern.

I press myself flat against the wall, hoping that no one sees me and yells my name.

"No. That's the point. Maybe he's found someone else. He's in the living room and has hardly spoken to me. I'm all dressed up, and he hasn't said a word. Do you like my red dress? Do you think I look sexy?"

"Alexa, you look ravishing as usual," Kayla shouts from down the hall.

Damn it.

I peel myself off the wall and pretend I just came downstairs. "Merry Christmas," I respond as I meet her halfway and greet her with a hug. "How's the baby bump coming along?"

She opens up her navy wool coat and glances at her flat belly. "Nothing there yet. It's still too early. Maybe in a couple of weeks I'll be showing a little bit. Tina is a couple of weeks ahead of me, and she has a little pooch."

"Before you know it, you'll be complaining your pooch and butt are too big."

She slaps my hand. "You're bad, but probably right."

"Give me your coat and go have some fun. In a few minutes, I have to go upstairs to help Abby with her makeup." I motion for her to come closer to me. "She wants to look extra special for Tyler."

Kayla clasps her hands in front of her chest. "She's all he talks about. It's so sweet." Her face then turns to stone. "But I'll kill him if he plays with her."

"Okay, before you get all hormonal, missy, can you please take charge of the Christmas music? Kent has satellite radio in the living room."

She salutes me and walks away.

I hang her coat in the closet and walk toward the stairs. An arm embraces me from behind to stop me. His other hand tugs my ponytail to one side, and then he nips the nape of my neck.

"Where do you think you're going, Sunshine?" Kent's breath tickles my ear. "You smell and taste good enough to eat. I love your hair pulled back like this. It reminds me of Halloween. My little devil."

I spin in his arms and stand on the first step so I'm almost the same height as he is. "I told Abby I'd help her with her makeup."

"You're looking mighty fine in this heart-stopping sexy pantsuit. I'm curious what you're wearing underneath." His hands graze my backside, then pull me closer to him. "I thought you'd be wearing red tonight. But black suits you with these fiery-red lips of yours."

When his hungry lips capture mine, everything around us disappears. My lips willingly part and welcome his familiar taste of peppermint. It's a kiss that's slow and passionate, as if he's trying to tell me something. I melt into him as I wrap my arms around his muscular back, deepening the kiss even more. I'd blame this on the mistletoe, but it's nowhere near us.

"Psst. Alexa."

I want to scream, and I think Kent does too, because his grip tightens on my hips. When will we ever be alone?

"Sorry to interrupt the seduction scene down there, but can you please help me?" Abby waves me up.

"Sorry. Duty calls." I turn away from Kent but quickly turn back. "That will hold me off for now, but I don't know for how long." I suck on his lower lip one last time, then go up one stair.

He wipes around his mouth.

"Don't worry. I finally bought the lipstick that doesn't come off. I could kiss your entire body for hours and it'd still be on my lips only." I pucker my lips, then blow him a kiss.

"That's not helping when you do that," he growls, then adjusts his black pants. *Yummy.*

"Then maybe I shouldn't tell you I'm wearing red but you just can't see it," I whisper as I trace my finger down my chest.

His eyes flicker with pure lust as they follow my finger.

I go up one more step, bracing myself on the railings. "I need to escape before I give in and show you. We'll be down in a few minutes. Go and socialize." I lower my voice. "And find out what's going on with Vince and Dani."

His forehead creases, and then the lightbulb turns on. I wink at him and go up to Abby.

Chapter 44

Kent

What is taking Abby and Alexa so long? Everyone has arrived and is hanging out by the food and in the living room. The common conversation topics are what happened to Alexa and what it's like to be pregnant. I try to change the subject, but it doesn't work. I politely excuse myself and walk down the hallway, laughing about the mistletoe. Even hanging it from the high ceiling, it misses my head by a mere half an inch, if that.

Most of the guys are in the living room by the TV. Vince stands by himself while staring out the window. I pretend to look for something, to see where Dani is. She's in a circle with Lisa and Tina in the dining room.

"Hey. What's up with you? You're pretty quiet. That's what Dani said anyway. Did it get worse between you two?"

He scratches at his chin like a dog does with fleas. This isn't going to be good.

He moves closer to me and whispers, "I think I need to break up with her man, but it's Christmas."

"She cornered me in the kitchen. She thinks you might have found someone else. Have you?"

He looks over my shoulder several times. "Of course I don't have someone else. I would tell you if I did. I like her, but she has become paranoid and jealous like hell. I'm convinced she has an alcohol problem too."

"Why haven't you mentioned this before?"

"I don't know. Our schedules haven't matched, and I didn't want to bother you with this shit. I thought it would stop. I can deal with her typical moodiness, but this is more than I can handle."

"But you both said you were nothing serious, so it's not like you're engaged."

"Exactly. When do you think I should do it?"

I point my thumb to my chest. "You're asking me? I'm in a relationship, but I don't know what the hell I'm doing most of the time. I can't give you any advice." I raise my hand. "Wait. I can. If you don't want to be with her, be honest and walk away. Don't string her along if she's more into you than you are her. It'll make things awkward for all of us."

I turn around when I hear giggles and Abby's name from the women. I stand to the side to observe Tyler. I don't know what his intentions are with Abby. Is it only a business relationship, or is it more? I see how flustered she gets when his name comes up. I'm not stupid.

Abby finally comes around the corner in a beautiful deep-red dress and a matching head scarf. On the scarf is a silver snowflake pin that's covered with diamonds. I forgot she had it. It was our great-grandmother's, and it was passed down from generation to generation. Abby looks like her old beautiful self. She's wearing makeup that adds a bit of color to her pale face. Her smile is contagious. I never thought I would see her like this again. Her doctors all told me she would survive, but I never believed them. Until now.

After a few minutes of the other women fussing over her, she turns in the direction where Tyler stands. Tyler's eyes blink nonstop, as if he can't believe what he's seeing. Gerry nudges him to go to her. He gives her a hug and kisses her cheek, then whispers something in her ear. Which she seems to like, because she chuckles and traces her scarf gently with her fingertips. I'm starting to believe what Alexa said about them. But if he's messing with her, I'll fucking kill him.

I part from the guys and walk toward Alexa as she jokes around with Tina and Lisa in a corner.

"What are you ladies laughing about?"

Alexa pretends to slit her throat to be quiet. But she giggles again.

"Lisa and I were asking her if she's seen your gun yet and how big it is," Tina says.

They all laugh again. Why do I have a feeling they aren't asking about my real gun, as in handgun.

"Every time I want to show it to her, we're interrupted. I guess it's just not meant to be."

Alexa smacks my arm in a childish warning.

"She told me she doesn't like guns anyway. So I keep it wrapped up safely. But maybe one day I'll show her how to use it."

Now I get the elbow from her.

"What? I'm telling the truth. By the look on your faces, your minds are in the gutter. I'm going to tell your husbands on you." I pretend to look around the room.

"We like you, Kent. You're a keeper. We only need to convince Alexa of that."

Alexa presses herself against me. "He's done that already."

"I need to go have some more of that German cabbage salad. I didn't think I would start craving things this early in the pregnancy. I could eat a gallon of it," Tina says.

Lisa pretends to gag, then pushes her along the table.

"Talk to you guys later," Lisa says.

Alexa pokes me in the side. "Don't be talking like that and not expect me to get all worked up."

I put my hands up. "I don't know what you're talking about. I'm innocent until proven guilty."

She shakes her head. "You're bad. But let's change the subject since I'm not getting anywhere with this one. I forgot to tell you a million times that I finally got an appointment to get my car door fixed. I have to drop it off at eight o'clock Monday morning. You're still coming with us to see the Christmas tree in the city that day, right?"

"Of course. I told you I have the week off."

"Now that I have to drop the car off, I need you to stay at my apartment because everyone is coming over for breakfast. Maybe you can entertain them for me. I might also have a conference call with human resources that morning. Hopefully it won't be necessary."

"Is something going on with your job?"

Alexa puts her arm out. "Lisa, I'll take the dirty dishes. You don't get out much. Go and socialize."

I remove the dishes from Lisa's hands. "I'll clean up. You both go and have fun."

"Just like we said, he's a keeper," Lisa responds with a big smile.

"That's what I thought about Vince. Kent, have any love to spare?" Dani interrupts with a loud slurred voice, then walks away with an empty champagne bottle.

Alexa shoots spears out of her eyes.

"Ignore her," I whisper to her.

She purses her lips. "Oh. I'm trying."

I search for Vince. He's on the phone in the corner of the living room. I'm going to kill him. I feel like we're in high school.

Alexa kisses me on the cheek, then whispers, "Don't forget about meeting me under the mistletoe later."

I swallow hard as I watch her walk over to Lisa. I need to come up with a plan to get us out of here tonight.

Slowly, guests are leaving. James, Lisa, Tina, and Gerry left a while ago since they have a longer drive than the others. Gerry knows his stuff. He calculated just the right amount of food for the number of guests. There's hardly anything left. Matt made extra desserts. Abby can eat them so she can gain some weight again.

There's not much more we need to do until after everyone is gone. Time to find Alexa. I stop under the mistletoe just as she walks out of the kitchen. I lean against the wall and look up at it. She saunters over to me with a goofy grin, like I probably have.

She gazes over my head. "Would you like a kiss?"

I grab her hand and whisk her away with me. "Where are we going?"

It's not the most romantic place, but I pull her into the laundry room, close the door, and lock it. Before she can speak, I press her against the wall, my lips on hers.

She gives as much as she receives. Our hands are all over each other. "I can't take it anymore. Every time I see you, you're even more intoxicating. I want to rip this jacket off you."

"Come home with me tonight." She captures my lips with hers. "You can do whatever you want with it as long as it ends up off me," she says while I gently kiss down her chest. "We'll help clean up tomorrow." She guides my hand to her breast.

I devour her sweet lips again, then wrap one of her long legs around my hip. She moans into my mouth as I rub against her. Her hands move frantically to my hair and pull me closer. I release my tingling lips from hers to catch a breath.

"I'm way ahead of you. I already packed my bag."

"Really?" she asks with excitement. She slowly lowers her leg to the floor.

I rest my sweaty forehead against hers, hoping my heartbeat will slow down. "I already spoke to Abby. I want us to be alone and to stay at your place. When we leave this room, go straight upstairs and pack your bag. Then we can sneak out the back door."

"When you act this authoritative, I'm not sure I can wait until we get to my place."

When we hear the squeak of the doorknob twisting, we both gasp and rapidly adjust our clothes.

"Who locked the fucking door? We need the mop in there," says Dani's angry, muffled voice.

The knob wiggles again. "Stand behind me," Alexa commands.

She unlocks the door and swings it open. "What's the problem?" Abby chuckles, but Dani's cold stare could freeze us to death.

"Abby knocked over a glass of champagne, and it shattered on the floor. We need the mop and dustpan." Dani barges in with little patience.

While she adds cleaning fluid and water to a bucket, Abby gestures at Alexa's chest and then does a weird shimmy movement. Alexa looks down and readjusts her jacket. I turn away and help Dani.

"Dani, go back to the living room. I'll clean up the mess."

"This is a party, and people are still here, and you're in here fucking around. Real nice." She flashes me a look of disgust.

Abby gasps. "Dani! That was uncalled for."

My blood pressure skyrockets. "What Alexa and I do in this house is none of your damn business. If you don't like it, then get the hell out."

She backs up, and her demeanor changes within seconds. Her face droops in sorrow, but I don't care anymore. "Whatever problems you have with Vince, don't take them out on any of us. If I have to, I will throw you out myself."

Abby stands between us. "Dani, take the dustpan and see if you can clean up some of the glass. I'll be there in a minute."

Dani walks out with her head down.

Abby waits several seconds, then whispers, "She keeps whining about Vince. Sneak out of here, and I'll deal with her. She's pretty out of it. I'm sure she'll pass out soon."

"Are you sure?"

"I'm more than sure. You and Alexa need time alone. Tyler said he'd stay longer to help me." Her smile grows ear to ear.

"No wonder it's okay." I can't help but smile and worry at the same time. "Please be careful. I don't want to see you get hurt."

"I don't either, but life's too short not to give something a chance. I can't ignore what I feel."

"Then don't. That's what you told me when I first met Alexa."

"Abby?" Tyler says, then looks at me. "Sorry to interrupt, but Dani asked me to get the mop right before she dropped onto the couch. I think she'll be out for a while. Maybe we should put a bucket next to her."

Abby puts a hand over her mouth to hide her laughter.

"Where's Alexa?" I ask Abby.

"I'm right here," Alexa responds. Her eyes dazzle with mischief. "Let's go."

Chapter 45

Alexa

I didn't think I would look forward to being back in my apartment, but the anticipation of finally being alone with Kent erases all worries from my mind.

Kent locks the door behind him. I slowly turn and let my coat slide off my arms onto the floor. My heart pumps faster than a cheetah's at top running speed. He doesn't move from his spot but observes me like I'm his prey.

I kick my shoes to the side. "Do you want to tear it off me, or should I undress painfully slow?" I purr as I trace the buttons of my suit jacket with my fingers, then walk backward toward my bedroom. His eyes follow my fingers down, then burn my skin as they rise to meet mine again. He tosses his jacket on the couch and removes his shoes.

My pulse spikes as he moves quickly, then halts and leans over me. "I can't promise you I won't be rough. My control is at its limit."

I grip his shirt. "And I'm impatient."

He pulls my hands away from his shirt and holds them behind me, pushing my chest forward. His hot lips press on my skin where the V of my jacket meets the three buttons. The slight stubble on his chin tickles my sensitive skin, causing tingling sensations to travel to every pulsing spot on my body. He lets go of my arms. Agonizingly slow, his lips graze my skin as if following a honey trail up to my heart.

He hovers where my heart beats, making it speed up even more. His lips form into a smile.

As he moves toward my neck, his powerful hands squeeze my hips, then brush up the sides, pushing my breasts higher, landing on the buttons. He pulls my jacket forward and jerks it open, and a cool breeze blows over my stomach and chest. The buttons scatter on the floor. I hear a gentle thump as the jacket hits the carpet.

He leans away and smiles. "Red is definitely your color. Too bad it won't be on for long." He picks me up and wraps my legs around his hips. I giggle as I unclip my bra and throw it behind him when he walks us through my bedroom door. His sexy mouth feasts on one breast, then the other. Both of us know nothing is holding us back anymore.

He lays me gently on the bed and hovers over me. I pull his shirt over his head and toss it away from us.

"I want to taste every inch of your body. I've craved you for too long," he whispers.

I roll onto my stomach and gaze at him over my shoulder. "If you want to do that, you need to help me. My zipper is in the back."

His fingers trace down my spine and then run along the edge of my pants. He unzips them, then carefully tugs them off, exposing me in a way he's never seen me before. "Move a little higher up the bed. I need to get something from my bag."

"Don't go," I growl out of frustration. I can't wait any longer. "I'm on the pill and had my yearly checkup in September. I'm clean."

"Me too, Sunshine."

As I move up, I hear another zipper, and his pants topple to the ground. I want to see him, but the anticipation is even more riveting.

There's movement on the bed, and then his hands and lips massage my calves and then the backs of my thighs. His fingers wrap around my thong and pull it down and off, adding to the pile on the floor.

"You're even more enticing now. How is it possible that I can call you mine?" He says softly as his hands skim from my dimples up my back.

I glance over my shoulder again. "Because my heart was waiting for yours."

Chapter 46

Kent

She flips over onto her back, exposing every tempting curve of her body. Her eyes drip with desire.

Her satiny hands tease my already warm skin as she squirms underneath me. "I've dreamed of this moment for so long." She spreads herself open for me. "I don't want to dream about it anymore. Touch me the way I know you want to. The way I want you to."

As I climb over her, something snaps my restraint. She places her arms over her head as her back arches. I tease her succulent nipples with my tongue as she releases soft, painful whimpers of pleasure.

"I love the way you sound when I touch you."

One of my hands holds hers in place over her head. She watches my every move as I position myself between her thighs. Her moans become louder as her eyes glaze over.

I slowly glide into her, overwhelmed with the sweet tightness that turns my blood into fire. She gasps as I fill her completely. I let go of her hands and allow them to roam my backside with fervor as our bodies sway together. She pulls me in deeper.

"Kent," she says breathlessly. "I never knew it could be like this. Feel like this. It's indescribable."

Hearing her voice reflect the passion and love I feel for her transcends me into a world surrounded only by her light. I increase my speed as our wet bodies cling to each other.

"Sunshine" slips off my tongue before our mouths connect as the wave of euphoric pleasure peaks and convulsions of pure bliss rattle us. Our deep moans continue until the pulsating high decreases, rendering us motionless.

Her legs remain wrapped tightly around my waist, her arms spread out to the sides. I separate my pounding chest from hers. As I lift my head to gaze at her face, our eyes connect, and we just know. We will never be apart again. Her soul belongs to mine. All those years of being on our own will never compare to the perfect future we'll make together.

Chapter 47

Alexa

I shuffle through the refrigerator and realize I forgot to buy a pomegranate yesterday. I want to make a special champagne punch that has pomegranate juice and seeds in it.

"What's the matter?" Kent says as he slinks his arms around my waist from behind.

It's become his signature move to show me affection. I twist around, and my hormones spin out of control because he's shirtless, with low-hanging jeans.

"Must you do this to me this morning, when I need to leave?" I inhale his fresh soapy scent. His sexy wet hair drips on my shoulder.

He tickles my side, then walks over to the coffee machine. "How does this fancy thing work?"

I place the cup under the spout. "I set it up for you already. Just press this button and that's it."

He pushes it and it beeps. The smell and sound of ground coffee beans circulates through the air.

"Anyway. I need to go to the store again. I'll pass one when I walk back home after I drop the car off at the dealer."

"Let me go with you," he says as he pours milk into his coffee.

"It's only a couple of minutes away. It's not necessary. Everyone's supposed to show up between eight and eight thirty. James and Lisa are notorious for being early, which means Tina and Gerry as well, since they're coming together. I need someone here. I would've told Dani to stay, but that changed since she can't come now."

Dani left a message on my phone saying how sorry she was for acting the way she did on Saturday night. She was asked to work an extra shift today and decided that working would be better, with the mood she's in. It was a pretty long-winded message. Kent got a call from Vince, who told him he'd broken up with her yesterday. She's been a bitch these past days, but I feel bad for her. I called her back to try to convince her to come anyway, but she didn't answer her phone. Kent told me to drop it. It's probably for the better. I want today to be special since we're going into the city to see the Christmas tree. It was never a big deal for me, but this year feels different.

He leans against the counter. "I don't know why you told them to come so early."

"Once we eat breakfast, we'll still have a huge chunk of the day to hang out in the city. Lisa and James need to get home at a decent hour because of Felicia."

"Felicia should be coming with us. We could've taken her to see Santa."

I wrap my arms around his neck. "Well, aren't you the sweetest. I'm starting to think you like kids."

"I do. Especially ones that have your eyes." He kisses my lips like a feather.

I push him away. "You need to stop talking or we'll end up naked again and I need to leave in two minutes."

"I'm half-naked already, so it'll save time. I wouldn't mind spending the entire day in your bed again like yesterday." He pulls me to him.

I give him one big, yummy kiss, then break from his hold while laughing.

My phone chirps in my purse. I dig it out, and it's a text from Darren saying that we need to talk. I roll my eyes and throw it back into my bag. He can kiss my ass. I know he has something to do with this Michael person. I plan on calling human resources before we leave for the city. Not the optimal time, but I've waited long enough and haven't heard from Natalie.

"Who was that?"

"Only work. I don't want to deal with it right now." I still haven't told Kent what's going on. "Okay. I'm off. I shouldn't be more than half an hour."

He opens the door for me. I block him with my coat. "You don't have a shirt on. I don't need my neighbors drooling on my welcome mat because of my hot boyfriend. Also, I don't think my brother wants to see your muscular body. He might get jealous. Please go put something on."

He turns me around and nudges me forward. "Then leave."

I blow him a kiss and walk toward the garage. I know he'll watch me until I'm out of sight. This weekend couldn't have been any better. I'm floating. Now I understand love songs and romance books and even Lisa and Tina. They'd tried to explain to me what it's like to be completely in love with someone, and now I understand. That zap of lightning that everyone talks about is real.

I shiver once I step into the garage. My car lights flicker in the darkest parking spot in the garage. I speed-walk over to it since I'm still antsy after everything that's happened. I slide into my seat and close the door, locking it immediately. The leather on the backseat squeaks, which makes my hair stand on end.

Before I can turn around, there's something over my mouth and nose. I try to scream, but the cloth masks it. I yank on the door handle to get out, but my vision blurs and my body becomes weak. Then there's only chilling darkness.

Chapter 48

Kent

Alexa must have forgotten something, since my phone's ringing. I pull my shirt down over my head and grab my phone off the table. It's not Alexa. It's Detective Griggs.

"Hey, Griggs. It's early. What's up?"

"I tried to call Alexa, but she didn't answer."

"Really? She's in her car, so maybe she doesn't have it hooked up."

"I have some updates. Let me finish before you react."

"What do you mean, react?" I snap.

"Kent, hear me out. We got the autopsy results back. Dr. Walker died of natural causes due to his illness. But the time of death and when Alexa received the spiders, they don't line up. He died days before. We watched the videos to see if we could see who delivered the spiders. We assumed he'd been the one, but it was someone else. Unfortunately, the way the person was dressed, we couldn't tell who it was. We guarantee it wasn't Dr. Walker."

Chills run down my back.

Alexa.

I cut the call and look at where Alexa is on the app, already running toward the door. It takes forever to reload. When it does, my heart sinks. She's still here. I open the door and bang into James and the others.

"Alexa's in trouble," I yell as I bolt down the hallway. They run behind me like a herd of elephants. I jump down the stairs as if I have springs on my shoes. But it's not fast enough. I burst through the exit doors and run to her parking spot. My adrenaline spikes when I see her car's still there. I look through the window, and she's slumped over the steering wheel. *No!*

"James! Help!" I whip the door open and am shocked to the core. "Gerry, call nine one one. Now! She's unconscious and bleeding."

I pull her gently out of the car and carry her to where it's brighter. I sit on the floor, cradling her. *No, no, no!* I rock her in my arms. "Come on, Sunshine. Wake up. Please wake up."

James removes his jacket and covers Alexa with it. "Let me look at her," he pleads. His hands shake as he examines the gash on her head.

Lisa pulls tissues out of her bag and hands them to him. "The cut isn't too deep. She won't need stitches."

Then Lisa cries, "Look at her hair. What kind of monster would do this to her? I thought the asshole was dead."

Gerry runs up to us. "The ambulance and police are on the way. Tina and I will wait on the street." They run to the garage exit.

"Why won't she wake up?" I drill James.

James utters medical terms in frustration and angst, but I can't concentrate or understand. A sick person did the unthinkable. Who could be so fucked up to do this? I've never felt such rage to the point of wanting to kill someone.

I press my cheek against hers. "Don't leave me."

Chapter 49

Alexa

Why do I feel like I'm on a roller coaster? Sirens scream at me from every direction. *Make it go away.* I shake my head but stop when a sharp pain pierces the back of my ear.

"Sunshine. Open your eyes," Kent cries.

I can't open my eyes because a black cloud hovers over me, luring me back.

Instead of fighting, I fall back into the murkiness that surrounds me.

"Alexa, baby, please wake up."

I hear my mom's shaken voice in the distance. She's scared and crying. I feel her soft hands kneading mine like dough.

"Mom." My voice cracks. "What's the matter?"

Then it all comes back to me in flashes. I squeeze my eyes and shriek. My arms fly out, fighting to get the person's hand off my face. My mom cries out.

Someone grabs my wrists.

"Let me go," I scream.

"Alexa. Calm down. Breathe. You're safe now," James whispers in a soothing voice. "Try to open your eyes. I know it's hard, but try anyway."

I inhale a few times and flutter my eyes open. The light is blinding. "Mom. James." I reach out for them.

"I'm here." Mom hugs me.

"I'm so scared. What happened to me?" My vision starts to clear, and I see Mom in tears next to me and James on the other side. He stands up and whispers something to my mom.

"What happened?" I yell as I move my head to the side.

Something isn't right. My head feels bare and cold, as if naked. My free hand goes straight to my head.

"No. Don't!" Mom yelps as she grabs my wrists.

She loses her grip. I skim my free hands all over my head in search of my hair, but I only feel stubble with random painful indentations. I rub even faster as I panic, realizing my hair is gone.

I spring up. "Where's my hair? What happened to my hair?" I cry as my lungs try to find air.

James sits next to me on the bed. "Alexa, you need to calm down. We can't tell you anything until you relax."

"Where's Kent? Why isn't he here?"

"He's talking to the detectives in the waiting room. Dad's with him."

I can't handle this. It's only a dream. A sick, fucking dream, and soon I will wake up safe in Kent's arms. We're supposed to go to Rockefeller Center this afternoon.

"Please tell me what happened. What happened to my head?" My chin quivers as tears sting my eyes.

"The asshole..." James's jaw clenches. "The asshole shaved chunks of your hair off. In parts, so deep that it cut through the skin. When you arrived at the hospital and were examined, the doctor shaved the rest of your hair off to clean the cuts and ensure there were no other injuries."

"Give me a fucking mirror."

He starts to say something else.

"Now," I demand, my focus on Mom. "You *always* have one in your purse."

She wipes under her eyes and takes her bag from the chair. When she finds her mirror, she hesitates.

"Please, Mom," I whisper in desperation, my energy almost gone. The fear of what I will see makes my body vibrate.

I snatch it from her and lift it in front of me with my eyes closed. My lungs expand, but when I open my eyes, all the air spews out. I shake my head. This can't be real. My hair is completely gone. There's a swollen gash above my ear. I look like Abby, but the difference is I look like a monster in a horror film. Abby is beautiful.

I throw the mirror across the room, and it shatters. Little metal shards and plastic pieces fall to the ground.

"I want to be alone. No visitors. No detectives. Especially Kent. I don't want to see him."

"Kent won't care. He's a nervous wreck. Don't shut him out," Mom cries.

"Do you see what I look like? I look like a fucking freak. Just like that psycho who started this. If he's dead, who did this?" Anger quakes through my body. "Please leave. I want to be left alone."

Chapter 50

Kent

My fists ball at my sides. "There was a tracker under her car? This asshole has been watching her all along. He has to be connected to the doctor. But I don't understand how they knew she was leaving at that specific time. I don't think they would've stayed in there overnight."

"That's a good point. Who else knew she was taking her car to the dealer this morning? You or I need to talk to Alexa," Griggs suggests.

James comes up to us and stands next to his dad. "As expected, she refuses to see anyone." His eyes droop. "Including you, Kent. I'm sorry."

Someone taps my shoulder. I turn, and it's Abby, with tears streaming down her face. She pulls me aside and wraps her arms around me. "I can't believe it. Is she going to be okay? Are you okay?"

"Let's talk somewhere else." I grab her hand and walk away from the waiting room. "The doctors say she'll be fine. There were no major injuries. But you had to see her." I put my face in my hands. "What he did to her hair and head. All the memories came back to me from when you and Mom began to lose your hair. She was hanging over the steering wheel." Tears of anger and sadness flow again. "Why does something happen to every woman I love?"

Abby squeezes me. "Have you seen her since she woke up?"

I shake my head. "She refuses to see anyone, including me. She doesn't want me to see her like that."

"I know how it feels. It's humiliating and something a man would never understand. Most men look good bald, but it hits women hard. It took me a long time to deal with it. It still bothers me, but I don't have the energy to care anymore. Thankfully, hers will grow back with no problem."

"Maybe she'll see you. You can talk to her for me and convince her to let me see her. I have to see her. She needs to know that I love her no matter what."

She taps her chin and purses her lips to the side. "I have an idea. Do you know how long she'll be in the hospital?"

"Until tomorrow morning."

"Stay here. I need to go pick up something at the house. I think I can be back within the hour. I'll ask Tyler to go with me."

"Please be careful," I say with the little energy I have left. My body deflates against the wall.

I watch her leave with Tyler. I run my hands through my hair, and then I freeze when an idea comes to mind. "Abby," I yell. "Wait a second."

I catch up to them and ask Abby to bring one more thing to the hospital. Well, two things. It just might be what's needed to convince her that I'm in love with her.

When I return to the waiting room, Alexa's mom approaches me with bloodshot eyes. Mr. Kramer is right behind her.

I shake my head. "I'm so sorry Mr. and Mrs. Kramer. We thought we got him."

"We know, Kent. We don't blame you." She squeezes my hand. "And please call us Kathleen and John."

I nod with a slight grin.

Kathleen turns to John. "Honey, can you get me some water, please? I'd like to talk to Kent alone."

I swallow hard.

"Sure." He kisses her cheek and walks away.

"Sit with me, Kent." She gestures toward some chairs and takes a deep breath. "I'm worried about her. I've never seen her like this. She's so angry, which is completely warranted. Since she was little, she's had this aura around her that shines on everyone. When someone is with her, they can't help but feel her glow, her fire. It's as if every person who comes in contact with her gets a little dose that could light them up for days. It's like a drug."

"I know. It's what I love most about her."

She cracks a smile, but it disappears as fast as it came.

"My biggest fear has always been that someone will steal that from her. Did this disgusting man accomplish that today? Did he put out her flame?"

"I don't know, but I'll do everything I can to make sure he didn't."

She nods. "I know. She loves you and Abby. You keep her on her toes, that's for sure. I love it that she's finally found someone who appreciates who she is. All that she is, not just how she looks. She's beautiful inside and out."

"Here you go, honey," John says and hands her a bottle of water. "Kent, Detective Griggs would like to talk to you again before he leaves."

I push off from the chair. "Again, I'll do everything I can. I'll wait here as long as I have to until she'll see me."

John extends his hand. I shake it as if it's my acceptance into their family. It gives me the strength I'll need until we find this bastard.

I jog back to Detective Griggs. "We need to trace this tracker. Find out who bought it. Once I can see Alexa, I'll find out who she told about her car appointment today."

"I'll get on it. Call me when you get any information from Alexa."

Chapter 51

Alexa

I can't stop touching my hair. Or should I call it *scalp*? I have no idea. My hair is so short that there's practically nothing there. So many unwanted emotions drown me right now. I'm angry, depressed, embarrassed. *Ugly*.

I replay the moment in my car when someone's hand goes over my mouth and nose. I try to remember a voice or sound that would give me a clue as to who it was, but nothing comes to mind. Why would someone do this to me? I rack my brain to remember something I might have done to piss someone off. Nothing, other than telling a guy I don't want to see him anymore. And this person is still out there. He must have been working with Dr. Walker. There's no other explanation. How did he know I was going to the car at that time?

I'm startled by a knock on the door. "Who is it?"

"It's me. Abby. I'm alone."

She's the only one who would understand how I'm feeling. What if Kent is with her? I physically ache for him. I want to see him, hug him, kiss him. I want him to tell me everything will be okay and that he still wants me. But why would he want me when I look like this and have caused him nothing but problems? He's already endured so much.

"Alexa, can I please come in? Please."

"Only if you're alone," I say as I sit Indian-style on the bed.

The door creaks open. Abby slithers in so no one can see inside. She leans against the back of the door and observes me.

"I don't know what to do. But all I want to say is, I'm sorry."

I motion for her to come to me. She runs to my bedside and encompasses me with her entire body.

"Of all people, you don't deserve any of this. Kent is losing his shit out there. Please let him see you. He loves you."

"How do you know that? He's never said it to me. Once he sees me like this, he'll never want me."

She pulls her neck back. "Are you kidding me? Of all people, Kent would understand and still love you." She points to her head. "What am I? I'm bald. Does Kent still love me? Yes. Did he still love my mom when her hair fell out? Yes! Why would you think he'd ever feel any differently of you?"

I focus on my folded hands. She's completely right. "I don't know. Physical looks were always part of my appeal. I don't want to say that's what got me to where I am in my life, but it didn't do any harm."

"It's just hair. It will grow back. You're so beautiful in and out. It won't make a difference."

"I want so badly to believe you, but it's hard." My shoulders slouch.

"Please let Kent see you. He's a mess," she pleads. "He has something special for you." She lifts her hand to shut me up. "No, it's not flowers or cereal. I promise you—you won't be disappointed."

"I'm scared, Abby. I'm scared that when he sees me, he'll see me the way I was when he found me in the car."

"You won't find out until you talk to him. Let him in. Let him take care of you."

I don't say anything, but I'm sure she hears the wheels spinning in my head.

"I have something for you." She lays a bag on my lap. "Open it."

"Abby, you didn't have to get me anything." I slowly open the old bag. I look in it, and my eyes well up. I pull out a teal-colored head scarf with Swarovski-like crystals on it. Just like the one I saw weeks ago and loved.

"Oh, Abby. It's gorgeous."

"Thanks. Can I put it on you?"

I nod.

"I thought this color would make your pretty eyes pop, something different than red," she says as she wraps it around my head with precision. She stands up and moves away from the bed to examine how it looks. "Gorgeous. I think you'll have to be a model for me."

I throw the bag at her. "You're out of your mind."

I swing my legs off the bed. "I guess it's time to look in the mirror." I drag myself to the bathroom with my head down, bracing myself for what I'll see.

"Just look. It's perfect."

I pop my head up and rotate back and forth. It's weird to see something like this on my head. My fingers adjust it even though it doesn't need to be.

"I wouldn't say I'm beautiful, but it's better than the mess I was two minutes ago."

"Please let Kent see you. I know you want to see him, but you're too damn stubborn."

"And vain." I roam to the window and lean my forehead against the glass. "You can tell him to come."

She squeezes my shoulders. "You won't regret this."

I gaze out while hugging myself to stop the shaking. What will I say when he walks in here? All I want to do is jump into his arms. Relationships are so damn stressful. That's why I avoided them. But he's worth it. I wouldn't give him up for anything, but does he feel the same? I thought so this morning, but now...I'm terrified.

I stiffen when the door opens and then clicks shut. Neither one of us says anything. How can silence be the worst sound in the world?

His shoes scraping along the floor give life to the room. He stands behind me, so close he's almost touching me. My skin absorbs his alluring body heat.

"Turn around, Sunshine."

"I don't feel like sunshine anymore." I trace a circle with my finger on the frigid foggy window.

"Let me see you. Please turn around. I can't stand this anymore," he says as if he's in physical pain.

I pace to the left, then turn to face him. *Huh?* He wears beanies? I may be depressed, but his sexy meter just shot up. His smile grows, as if he knows what I'm thinking. And just like that my insecurities drift away because he sees me, the real me.

He opens his arms, and I jump into them and cry into his neck. He sits on the bed and cradles me.

"I'm sorry I wouldn't let you see me. It wasn't to hurt you."

"I know. It could've been worse. I thought I'd lost you."

He urges me up, and I straddle him. He swirls his hand over my head. "You with no hair doesn't mean jack shit to me. You being here with me forever does. You are the most beautiful woman I know, and it's not because of how you look. When we met the first time, I saw a blinding light right before we collided. When I went to take a breath, I felt like I'd inhaled some of that warm light. It was your light. Part of your soul." He taps on his chest. "It's inside me now." He places my hand on his. "Our souls found each other."

I lean in to kiss him, but he pulls back gently. "Not yet. Let me finish."

I push out my lower lip.

"For the rest of my life, I will make damn sure that light is always burning there. In you and in me. Maybe this will make you understand."

He fists his hat and pulls it off. I lean back too fast and almost fall off his lap.

"You shaved your beautiful hair off. Are you crazy! What were you thinking?" I rub his peach fuzz with both hands. It's so damn soft and warm.

My hands fall to my sides.

"That I am in love with you and I'll do whatever I have to do to convince you of that. You gave me a new life, one I look forward to, and it will only stay this way if you are in it."

He cups the nape of my neck. "Do you understand? I love you, and I'll never leave you. I didn't lie that day when I kissed you the first time. You are it for me."

I wrap my arms around his neck and inch closer so our lips are almost touching. "I love you too. Since day one I've felt our connection. I've always been on my own, but now I can't imagine being without you. You are my forever."

"Just like I've always wanted." He pulls me to him and caresses my lips with his. When we join, it confirms everything we've just said. I am his, and he is mine, and *nothing* will split us apart.

Our kiss becomes heated, but we pull apart because we're in a hospital. Gross. But there's also the other subject we haven't addressed, and it's hanging over us like a dark cloud.

I slide off his lap. "I wish we could forget about what happened this morning, but we can't. When do I need to talk to Detective Griggs? Was there anything found in my car? Any clues? Were there hidden cameras down there?"

He explains to me about the tracker and how the timing of the doctor's death and the spiders don't add up.

"But the guy who delivered the spiders could've been a delivery guy."

"Maybe, but Griggs doesn't think so because of the body movement and the timing of the delivery. It was less than thirty minutes before you got back from your parents. With the tracker under your car, this person knew exactly when you were coming back. No videos were found connected to the garage. The security gate is still out of order, so the person had no problem getting to your car."

"And no problem breaking into my car. What about the tracker then?"

"Detective Griggs will find out where it was bought and under whose name. Our main question is how this person knew you were going to be at your car at that specific time this morning. Did you tell anyone other than me?"

I pat my cheeks as I pace around the room. "Thursday or Friday I got the call. We were so busy with the party that I didn't think much about it. I believe I only told you, because it wouldn't have affected our plans for our trip to the city. But anyone could've heard me. I got the call right after a meeting. If this person is watching me, then they could have overheard the conversation."

I throw my hands up in the air. "Holy shit. I completely forgot to tell you something. I didn't want to mention it this weekend because of the party." I sit on the edge of the bed and tell him about my meeting with Natalie. "I got one text message from Darren saying we need to talk. He sent it right before I left the apartment this morning. I didn't respond. I haven't heard from Natalie, so I planned to call human resources this morning to report what happened between her and me. What if it was Darren trying to prevent me from going to HR? I don't get what he's doing. I can't imagine he would go as far as attacking me like that."

Kent's face gives nothing away. No emotion, so I know he's having an internal battle. He's connected with me, but he's also in law enforcement and has to go by the rules.

I cup his face. "You need to stay calm and not do anything rash. Let Griggs connect the dots."

"You need to tell Griggs every little detail. Anything can be helpful. I'll call him and tell him to come by as soon as he can. I have to warn you—this could affect your job if Darren is involved," he says with caution.

"At this point, I really don't care. My life is more important than a stupid job."

"I'll call Dani later and ask her if she knows any doctors with the name Michael or Miguel. She left me a voicemail asking how you're doing. She's working the night shift this week."

"I wish I didn't have to stay here until tomorrow. I don't know how James likes to work in a hospital all day. It's depressing and smells."

"Speaking of James. Your entire family is in the waiting room. Can I tell them to come in?"

"I guess so. But about tomorrow."

"I'll pick you up, and you'll stay at my house as long as it takes to find this guy. I have a security system, and your boyfriend is a pissed-off cop. We will find this guy and make him pay for what he's done." He pecks me on the forehead. "I love you. I'll be back."

My heart will never get tired of hearing those words come from his perfect lips.

I drop the *People* magazine on my lap when someone knocks on the door. I don't have the head scarf on, but I don't care.

"Come in."

The door opens, and Dani's head peeks in. "Is this a bad time? I know it's early, but I'm off with the time, given my work schedule. Did Kent tell you I planned to visit you this morning?"

This is when I can see she is an oncology nurse. It doesn't seem to faze her that I'm bald. She doesn't have the twitching eyes like others who are uncomfortable looking at me.

"No, but it doesn't matter. Thanks for visiting. I'm going stir crazy here. Kent had to go to the station for something, and he'll be back when I get released, which I was told would be any minute. He's supposed to take me back to my apartment so I can pick up fresh clothes. I'll be staying with him until this guy is caught."

She sits on the chair next to my bed. "I'm so sorry about everything and for not taking this scary situation seriously. When I heard what happened, I was shocked to the bone. I'm so relieved you're okay."

And there she goes with the flicking of her hair.

As if God answered my prayers, the nurse walks in and tells me I'm allowed to go home.

"At last! But I don't know when Kent will be back."

"I don't have to go to work until the evening. Why don't I drive you home for your stuff and then take you to Kent's? Then you don't have to sit around waiting."

"That would be great. Let me call Kent to make sure he's not on his way here."

I dial his number, and he answers on the second ring. "Hey, babe. I can go home now."

"Great. I'm on my way to my truck now."

I hear ruffling. "Kent, what's the matter?"

"Son of a bitch. One of my tires is flat, and I don't have a spare. Shit! It doesn't matter. I'll take a patrol car."

"No. Don't be crazy. Dani's here, and she offered to take me back to my place for some clothes. Get your tire fixed, and I'll meet you at your house."

"No way. I don't trust you being anywhere near your apartment without me."

"Fine. Can't you ask one of your police buddies to meet us at my apartment building to watch us? Is Vince working? Ask him."

"Vince is on duty, so that's a good idea. Can't you wait an hour until I can pick you up? Will it bother you that much?"

"You know I hate being here. I just want to get to your house as soon as possible. Dani will be with me, so I won't be alone."

All I hear is him huffing and puffing. "Please call Vince. Tell him we're leaving in two minutes. Give him my phone number if you want."

"You still have the pepper spray in your bag, right?"

"Of course."

"Please call me as soon as you get to your place. I'll call Vince and then send you a text message."

"Sounds good. Love you."

Dani springs from her chair. "So are we good to go? Is he allowing you to leave?"

I raise my eyebrows. "Is everything okay?" I ask with caution as I wrap the teal scarf around my head.

She waves her hand. "Yeah. Just twitchy from the lack of sleep. Let's get going."

"Damn it's cold. I wish I owned a fur coat." I shiver as I close the car door.

"You don't have one? You seem like the type who would."

Great. Dani's back to her insulting self. Just what I need.

"I don't like fur coats. Animal cruelty isn't my thing."

Kent hasn't sent me a text message yet. I hope he's able to get a cop over to my place. I'm a bit antsy.

Dani's phone rings, and she picks it up on the first ring. "Hey. Yeah. I'm on my way. Bye."

"Was that Vince?"

"Um. Yeah." She scratches her cheek and then her leg.

"Are you sure you're okay? You're making me more nervous than I already am. Is it because Vince will be waiting for us? Does that bother you?"

She jerks the car to the right but straightens right away. "I don't care if he's there or not. Do you mind if we stop somewhere else first? I was supposed to pick up something for my brother and take it to his office, but I forgot. He'll be pissed if I don't drop it off."

"I actually do mind. Vince will be waiting for us, and I want to go to Kent's."

My phone rings. "Hi. We're on our way."

"Vince won't be at your apartment, but another officer will be there. He'll be waiting at the entrance."

My stomach flips. *Shit!* I steal quick glances at Dani.

"Good. This is so stupid to ask you this now, but can you please pick up two large cloves of garlic before you get home? I want to cook something for you and Abby tonight."

"Alexa, what's happening? Tell me what's going on," he yells.

"I promise it'll be delicious. See you soon."

"Alexa, don't hang up. Don't..."

I close my eyes and cut the call.

"I still can't believe you use the *Superman* theme as your ringer for Kent," she snarks while her hands grip the steering wheel so hard that I'm sure her fingernails will cut her skin.

I remain quiet because I don't know what to do. Maybe I'm in panic mode. There's something not quite right with her though. I can't pinpoint it, but the hairs on my arms are standing straight up.

Everything is coming full circle.

Chapter 52

Kent

"Fuck."

My phone rings again as I dash into the station. "Alexa!"

"Kent, it's Griggs. We have the name of the person who bought the tracker. Do you know a Dominic Gargano?"

I run toward Griggs's office. I'm going to kill Dominic and Dani. I should've known all along. How could I have been so stupid? What kind of detective could I ever be?

I barge into his office. "Alexa's in trouble. Dominic's sister just picked her up. I was in the parking lot and found one of my tires flat." I kick the garbage can. "It was a setup. I can track Alexa's phone. We need backup and Dominic's phone number."

Chapter 53

Alexa

She hasn't said a word in the last couple of minutes. We passed my apartment already. "So where are we going? To a store?"

"We're here now," she says as she parks the car on a busy street. "Dominic needs something from our apartment. Well, his apartment."

I twist in my seat. "What do you mean? I thought you lived with him."

She looks in the rearview mirror. "Yeah, but I moved out. I cramped his love life." She winks at me and opens the door.

I'm overreacting. This is her normal weird behavior.

"I'll stay in the car. I don't want to go in with you."

"No way. I would absolutely die if something happened to you. Kent would never forgive me. Don't worry, Dom isn't home."

There's a twang in her voice, like she's mocking me.

I get out of the car and scope out my surroundings as she opens the trunk. There are people everywhere, so I should be safe. Act casual and keep her talking.

"Dominic lives here? These are supposed to be top-notch apartments."

She pulls out a black duffel bag and slams the trunk shut. "Let me show you then," she says, then wraps her arm through mine.

Pay attention to my surroundings, I keep repeating to myself. There's a security officer, but there's no way I can get his attention when she's so close to me. But what would I say?

Okay, Okay. I need to calm down. I'm still jittery from yesterday. It's only paranoia. That's all it is. Everything is fine.

Chapter 54

Kent

I storm back into Griggs's office. "This is where she is." I hand him the address of Dominic's apartment in Hoboken. Vince told me where he lives. "Did you find his phone number?"

He hands it to me. "Let's go. The squad is ready."

As we run out the door, I call his number. He's probably not going to answer if he's got Alexa.

"Hello," he says.

"What did you do to her?" I growl into the phone.

"Who is this? I have no idea what you're talking about."

"It's Kent, and Alexa's in trouble, and I know you're a part of it. We know you put a tracker on Alexa's car."

"Wait a minute. This is fucking nuts. I'm not even in the country. I'm in London. What do you mean, a tracker?"

"Don't play dumb, asshole. Dani took Alexa to your apartment."

"Back up a second. Alexa's with Dani at *my* apartment? I kicked her out weeks ago. I haven't spoken to her since. She was fired from her job, stealing money from me, lying, and acting erratically."

Chapter 55

Alexa

Dani swings her arm out. "Here's the modern, boring as hell, living room. Make yourself at home. It'll only take a few minutes." She tosses the duffel bag by the loaded wet bar and puts her phone on the bar counter.

I wait until she leaves, then search vigorously through my bag for my phone. *Please let the tracker be working.*

"Give me your phone."

My head shoots up.

"Now," she screams shrilly.

I flinch. "What's your problem? Why are you so pissed off?"

"Are you deaf? I said give me your fucking phone." One of her hands is hidden behind her back.

I extend my arm slowly to give it to her. "Is this some kind of sick joke?"

She guffaws obnoxiously and snags the phone out of my hand. She places my phone next to hers on the bar. When she smashes them into little pieces with a hammer on the counter, I bend over and cover my face with my hands. Fragments scatter on the floor.

"Now toss your purse on the floor behind me. I don't want you spraying me with Mace, now do I?"

I toss it, then stand back up straight and try to calm my breathing. Sweat drips down my back under my jacket. I scan the room for an object to protect me. Dominic's apartment is sparsely decorated and depressing. Everything is gray or black. Not what I expected and not helpful.

Dani directs the hammer at me. "Don't you dare move from that spot. I'm not done with you yet."

The doorbell rings. *Kent!* I sigh in relief.

She claps her hands and giggles. "I have a surprise for you. Just you wait and see."

She whips the door open, and in walks *Darren*, of all people. Bile rises in my throat. Just the sight of him makes me furious, not scared.

He strolls in with that cocky smile and tries to capture Dani in his arms, as if to kiss her. *They're together?* She squirms out of his embrace, and a mask of disgust distorts her face.

"What's the matter, Michelle?" he says in utter confusion. "What's with the hammer?" He points to the phone fragments on the floor. "And that?"

Bitter laughter explodes out of my chest. "Michelle? You think her name is Michelle? Or do you mean Michael or Miguel? That's what Natalie told me anyway. It looks like you've been fooled too."

He jerks his head in her direction. "Why is she here, and what's she talking about—" He starts to say Michelle, but stops, then looks at me.

His eyes trace my face and head. "And why are you wearing that ugly thing on your head?"

Dani cocks her hip. "Are you finished with all the questions or do you want to know my bra size too?"

His forehead creases with confusion and unease.

I see red as I stare at Dani. "You are such a bitch. You pretended to be a doctor and fed Darren lies so he'd go back and tell my boss. Acting is your specialty, telling me that you had never seen Darren at the hospital." I clap a couple of times. "You deserve an Oscar."

"You're not a real doctor, Michelle?" His voice cracks.

"Her real name is Dani!" I snap.

She places her forefinger against her lips while twirling the hammer in her other hand. "Shhh, Alexa. Don't tell him all my secrets. It's not his fault he's such an idiot. Even with blond hair, you're pretty smart. Oops. I forgot. You have no hair anymore." She slaps her leg as she bursts out laughing. "Did you like the hairstyle I gave you yesterday? Sorry I left some marks. I got so excited that I pushed down too hard with the electric razor. I hope there wasn't too much blood."

"What the hell did you do to her?" Darren spits with anger.

Dani approaches me with a wicked smile and yanks the scarf off my head, waves it in the air, then tosses it on the floor. "Voilà."

I swiftly cover my head with my hands.

Darren recoils like I'd expected Kent to do.

He then eases toward me. "Alexa, I had nothing to do with this. I swear. She tricked me."

Dani prances to the bar and picks up her duffel bag. "I have something that might help you, Alexa. I bought it for myself a couple of weeks ago. Since the men around here seem to prefer blondes, I thought I'd finally get the attention I deserve." She ducks behind the bar and jumps up wearing a long blond wig. The hair looks like the dirty, knotty kind on a Barbie head. "What do you think? I look just like you now. All I need is a pair of green contacts."

This can't be happening. She's psychotic and horrifying to look at. She was always a bit crazy since Halloween, but never to this point. I have no idea what to do.

Keep her talking.

"How did you break into my car?"

She taps her forehead with the hammerhead. "I'm pretty clever too. Remember how I locked my keys in my car and asked Kent to help me? He showed me how to unlock my car without damaging it. You can thank him for that." She chuckles.

"Darren, you look out of place with nothing on your head. Should I look for another Barbie wig, or should I wrap your head with a dish towel, like Alexa's was?"

"Screw you, you sick bitch." He puffs his chest out and moves forward. He freezes when she lifts the hammer in the air and aims it at him.

"Such harsh language, Darren." She clicks her tongue as she walks back and forth.

"Oh!" she blurts out.

Darren and I startle from her sudden outburst.

"You just reminded me of something. I forgot the best thing. You'll love it, *Sunshine*. Dominic has one. He hides it in this drawer." Next to the sofa is an end table with a small drawer on the side. She puts the hammer on the table and opens it. "I know you love guns. Or did you say you hate them?" She waves the gun in the air, then picks up the hammer again.

Darren and I hunch over. My legs shake like a baby's rattle.

"I personally don't give a shit what you like, and yes, this gun is fully loaded."

"This is getting out of hand. Put the gun and hammer down. Why are you doing this?" Darren says with his hands extended in front of him.

"Stop your bitching." She glances at me. "He's such a girl," she snorts.

"So I guess you were the one who left the box of spiders on my doorstep."

"What spiders?" Darren acts clueless.

She nods with pride. "That was a good one, you have to admit. I would've paid any amount of money to see your reaction when you opened the box. I asked a guy off the street to deliver the package. People will do anything for money."

Her eyes shoot over to Darren. "Right, Darren?"

I stomp toward him. "You had something to do with that? Why?"

He shakes his head. "What? Alexa, I have no clue what she's talking about. Please believe me."

"You are so full of shit. Why do you want my job so badly? You can have it if you'll leave me the hell alone. Wait a second. Dani, how did you know I'm afraid of spiders?"

"As I said, I know everything. I saw your yearbook at James's party. You had it listed as your biggest fear. Anything I found to torture you, I used. Why do you think Darren's here? I know how much you can't stand the sight of him."

Darren shoots daggers at me as I inch away from him.

I had high hopes that Dominic would be home but I found out he's in London. He has no idea what I've been up to. He'll have the shock of his life when he gets back." She shrugs her shoulders. "I don't care. He hates me already."

She paces, turning the gun back and forth like a doorknob.

"Darren's a big, fat alcoholic who's afraid he'll lose his job if someone finds out. He has a lot of debt and can't afford to be jobless. Oh, and he was doing some illegal shit with his old boss. His boss quit his job before they got caught, but Darren didn't. Not yet anyway. Now he's all cozy with your boss. And me at the same time."

"Where the hell did you hear that?" He inches forward.

She points the gun at his face. He freezes. "From you. You can't seem to shut your damn mouth when you're drunk or having sex. And your obnoxious laugh. I wanted to kill myself."

I wrap my arms around my vibrating chest to block my heart if she tries to shoot me. Not that it would do anything. My gut tells me Kent will get here in time. He has the tracker on my phone and hopefully saw—before it was smashed to pieces—that I was here.

"Dani, what does this have to do with you? Why are you doing this to me?"

She waves the gun at me, and I flinch. "Because I fucking hate you. You ruined everything when you showed up on Halloween. I should've never spoken to you."

Darren steps forward in an attempt to protect me.

"Don't move one more inch." She presses the barrel of the gun to his chest. "I have every intention of shooting this gun, but I have a couple of things I need to say first."

His Adam's apple bobbles as his nostrils flare.

She aims the gun at me, and her face transforms into complete evil. Her eyes are onyx black. "You took him from me," she spits out.

I huff. "For fuck's sake. All of this has to do with Vince? I've seen him only a couple times since we met."

"I could give two shits about meathead Vince. I used him to make Kent jealous, to make Kent realize we were meant to be together as a family."

"What?" I shake my head in disbelief. "My Kent? This is beyond fucked up."

"Me, Kent, and Abby. I was waiting for Abby to complete her treatments to confess my love for him. I was so close, but then you pranced in with your never-ending Barbie appeal and ruined everything." She flips the hair of the wig over her shoulders and flutters her eyelashes, trying to imitate me, I guess.

"Barbie and Kent sitting in a tree. Blah blah blah. It makes me want to puke," she says through gritted teeth. She continues to pace back and forth frantically, then stops in front of me again.

"What about all the whining about Vince and your relationship?"

"I pretended to be upset with him to get Kent's attention."

I just can't. This is ridiculous.

I chuckle. "I see that worked out well for ya. You have a strange way of showing your feelings toward someone, by sleeping with his best friend."

"Shut up!" I planned everything out when we met at Kaleidoscope that night. You would hook up with Dominic and live happily ever after. It'd get you out of the picture. But then you left and ended up going to Kent's house. That's when I keyed your princess car. The war was officially on. But Kent was always miserable and so was I. I thought misery loved company. We were perfect for each other."

She rubs under her nose, and a strange, almost regretful look crosses her face. "I even figured out a way to make Abby sicker that day you picked her up at the hospital so I could swoop in and save the day, showing Kent how useless you are."

I gasp. "How could you do that? She's been nothing but nice to you and has suffered enough. You are completely out of your fucking mind."

"Wow." She places the gun over her heart. "Thank you. What a compliment. Unfortunately, being mental cost me my job. As well as the one in California. I'll probably go to jail because of Abby. Dominic kicked me out too. Now I'm living out of my car and am poor, so what do I have to lose since I don't have anything left."

"This isn't even your apartment?" Darren asks. He shakes his head in disbelief and disgust.

"I'm assuming Dominic didn't really like me. That was all your doing."

"He was into you in the beginning, but he's too high on himself to have to beg someone to like him." She rolls her eyes as she walks over to the bar, placing the hammer on it. "I sent the flowers and called your phone from his to distract you from Kent. It makes me sick how Dominic goes out with women who only look like you. I don't know if he even realizes it. What is so fucking special about you?"

She groans loudly, making herself cough, then grabs a small crystal glass off a shelf above the bar. "Want a drink, Darren? You're probably twitching right now." She puts the gun down next to the hammer, unscrews a cap from a vodka bottle and pours herself a generous amount with her shaking hand. Half of it splashes onto the bar. She downs it like it's water, then licks her lips. "That was good. I needed that."

From one second to the next, she slams the glass down so hard, it shatters. Her face crinkles as she shakes her hand. "Poor me. I cut myself." She picks up the gun again with the bloody hand but leaves the hammer there and walks back to us. Blood drips onto the gray carpet.

"So what were we talking about?" She rubs her chin and leaves a streak of blood behind. "Oh right. I remember. I observed everything you did. I listened in on every little conversation you had. How else would I have known you'd be in your car yesterday morning? You told Kent at the Christmas party. It's a good thing Kent wasn't with you when you got into the car. He would've ruined all my plans.

"I thought it'd be fun to stalk you too but make it look like your stalker was doing everything. Then he had to go and die on me. How friggin' rude! Then you were complaining about this guy over here." Gun sways in his direction again. "He gave me another way to fuck with you, hoping that you'd lose your job too."

"So everything you told me was a lie?" Darren says.

She taps her temple with the gun. Droplets of blood cascade down her shirt. "How stupid can you be to believe that just when you needed it, a doctor magically appears complaining about Alexa? And on top of it, you actually thought we were in a relationship."

Darren massages the back of his neck and focuses on the floor.

I almost feel sorry for him. Almost.

She brings her attention back to me. "So my last idea was to shave your hair off. I didn't think Kent would want another reminder of his dead mother and his bald, sick sister. He was supposed to drop you like a sack of potatoes when your beauty was gone." She steps closer and stabs me in the chest with the gun. I stumble backward while I silently pray for a miracle. "But no, he falls in love with you even more. It's like poison on my tongue. I should kill you right now so neither one of us can have him."

A loud crash behind her grabs our attention. The door bursts open, then bounces back off the wall as Kent and several other police officers swarm in the apartment. Darren and I drop to the floor and watch as, in what feels like slow motion, Dani turns and shoots at Kent. He shoots at her in the same instant. Dani lands on the floor, screaming. She drops the gun, and it skitters across the floor toward me. I kick it away, out of her reach.

"Kent is mine!" she screams. "He's all mine. I did this for us. He loves me, not her."

Officers move to restrain her.

I look toward Kent, but all I can see are more officers surrounding him on the floor. And I hear the words, "Officer has been shot."

"No!" I scream. I scramble toward them, but Vince grabs me by the waist and pulls me away.

"Let me go!"

Chapter 56

Kent

Chaos invades the apartment. The air is sucked from my lungs as I'm knocked on my back. A pulsing, fiery pain engulfs the left side of my rib cage. Three officers carry me to the side of the room. I try to get up, but the agony increases tenfold, so I stay where I am.

"I need to talk to Kent. Please. I need to know he's alive," Alexa shouts.

Vince is holding her back, reassuring her. "Alexa, he's okay. He had a vest on. It saved his life."

She wiggles in his arms to break free, but he's too strong.

"Let her go, Vince. She can...can come to me," I say between heavy breaths.

She cries out before she reaches me. "I thought I lost you." She wraps her arms around my neck, and I gasp.

She lets go quickly and looks at my vest. "I'm sorry. Are you in a lot of pain?"

"I don't care how much it hurts. You're...alive, and that's all that matters to me."

She lies on her side next to me.

"It's over now." I catch another breath and try to ignore the pain. "I hate myself for not seeing the signs from Dani. Please forgive me. I didn't...I never guessed she had feelings for me."

Alexa runs her fingers over my head. "You heard that part?"

I nod as another round of sharp pain pierces my side.

Vince approaches us. "I'm sorry too. I should've known. Her moods and streaks of paranoia increased the last week or so. She had us all fooled."

"Well, wait until you hear the entire story. I'm not sure how much you heard, but you won't be happy with what she had admitted. At least Darren can back me up. But he's not off the hook either."

I squeeze my eyes shut. "I need to go to the hospital. My ribs might be broken."

Vince hovers over us. "Paramedics are already on their way up."

I've always wondered what it felt like to be shot with a bulletproof vest on. I've been a cop for years, and I've never had to shoot my gun. But this time, I had to. It was to save someone's life. Alexa's life. I would do it again.

I look over at Dani lying on the ground, moaning. Officers still surround her where she lies. Darren's nearby, being questioned by Detective Griggs.

"Dani'd better go to jail or a mental institution for a very long time," Alexa implies firmly. "I don't know where she was shot."

"Didn't you see? I shot her in the leg. Someone once asked why cops don't shoot the armed person in the knee."

She bawls again. "I love you so much. I knew you'd come." She showers my face with kisses, then sits up on her knees. "Does this mean I can call you Superman now? I think you've earned it."

I crack a smile. "Sounds good to me. I want to take you home and forget all about this."

"Where's my home, Suppy?"

"My house. Where you belong."

Epilogue

One year later

Kent

Felicia giggles as she drops red rose petals down the church aisle. My heart plays the drum as I wait impatiently for Alexa to appear with her father at the back of the church. I readjust my collar for the tenth time and look at my watch. Vince chuckles next to me. *Thirty more seconds.*

Life's a roller-coaster ride. There are ups and downs and unexpected curves that shoot you in different directions. My life has been filled with all kinds of twists, and I assumed they'd only push me in the direction of sadness. The day I met Alexa was a curve I never saw coming.

Timing is everything. Each bend in the path of life makes us who we are. Maybe we won't feel the effects until years later. Life experiences push people down unknown paths, but hopefully the light will overcome the darkness. If my mom hadn't suffered and died and if Abby hadn't gotten sick, would I have ever met Alexa? If I hadn't gone to the hospital that day we met, what would my life be like right now? The answer is, I don't want to know.

This church is full with the best people Alexa and I know. They have their own remarkable stories, proving to me that happiness comes in all shapes and sizes. This past year hasn't been easy for Abby, but Tyler has been by her side for everything. So much so that they eloped in Las Vegas a couple of months ago.

After the fiasco with Alexa's job came to a head, she quit. Instead of searching for a new position in the pharma industry, she went into business with Abby. They own a specialized boutique for head scarves in New York City. Tyler is their investor and has guided them to their success.

I'm a detective now, but it took a long time for Alexa, Vince, and Detective Griggs to convince me to follow through with my dream. I'll always blame myself that I didn't realize Dani was the problem in the end.

It's amazing how much happiness Alexa has brought into my life. She has given me a new family and group of friends that I never thought I'd have and never realized I needed. She's helped me find the happiness I felt I'd lost.

When I look into this crowd of smiling faces, I think about how Lisa met James. Or how Kayla met Matt through Gerry, and how Gerry married Tina, who is also connected to Matt and is Lisa's sister. And then there's Tyler, Kayla's brother. Everything is as crazy as it sounds, but it's exactly how it should be.

Over a year has passed since Alexa and I met. We don't talk about Dani anymore. She's a speck in our crinkled past, and we want to focus only on our new future. One we never dreamed of and couldn't be more thankful for.

I watch Alexa walk toward me with her beautiful, glistening eyes, and imagine the adventures we'll experience as husband and wife. I wait at the end of the aisle for my best friend and the love of my life. I owe all my smiles and laughter to her. She will forever be my sunshine, even when life gets cloudy.

Alexa always says I saved her that day I was shot, but the truth is, she saved me.

Acknowledgments

Wow. I can't believe Alexa's story is finished and the Collide series is complete. It has taken me some time to accept that. Time ran so fast, and so many personal obstacles interrupted my writing schedule. It's a bittersweet moment. I'm emotional as I write this.

I will always start my acknowledgments with the love and appreciation I have for my husband and children. They will never understand how important their support and encouragement is to me and how it has helped me move forward. There were days when I was ready to throw in the towel, but they burned that towel and always said the right things to inspire me.

Souls Collide was the most difficult book to write in the series, but also the most fun. I wanted to get Alexa's story just right. I'd never written a romantic suspense before, so I needed to gather beta readers with different areas of expertise. They didn't disappoint me. My story is stronger because of them. I couldn't be more thankful for Silke Law, Jennifer Kreider, Vicki Motz, Amanda Siegrist, Helen Pryke, and Nadine Kilian. Thank you so much for your support, enthusiasm, and brilliant ideas.

And of course, to my editor, Dori Harrell from Breakout Editing, and proofreader, Rachel Overton from Wordscapes. I loved working with you both again and have learned even more from this experience. I appreciate how patient and detail-oriented you were. Your constant enthusiasm for my books and this series pushes me away from self-doubt. I have learned so much while writing these books. I owe that to you both. Thank you so much!

Sarah Hansen from Okay Creations, you did it again! Thank you for designing another amazing cover for my Collide series. This is one of the most exciting steps in the publishing process. You are awesome at what you do.

Thank you to Rik Hall from Wild Seas Formatting. You've been so easy to work with. Even with stressful timelines, I could always count on you. Thank you for making the formatting process as easy and stress-free as possible.

Many thanks to Cathie Larocca and Amy Wood for sharing their own personal and family experiences with cancer. This book wouldn't have been as authentic without it.

According to Breastcancer.org, about 1 in 8 U.S. women will develop invasive breast cancer over the course of her lifetime. Please be proactive and get annual checkups. It could save your life.

Thanks to Lisa Hemming, who provided me information on law enforcement. I'm so glad we met through the book world.

I have met so many wonderful people within the book community—authors, bloggers, editors, and readers. Saying thank you doesn't describe how much I appreciate every compliment, word of advice, laughter, and encouragement. Thanks for taking a chance on a new indie author. You're the best.

Please follow me on my website or social media for updates on my books.

www.kristinabeck.com
www.facebook.com/krissybeck73
www.twitter.com/krissybeck96
www.instagram.com/krissybeck96
www.goodreads.com/kristina_beck
www.amazon.com/author/kristinabeck
www.bookbub.com/authors/kristina-beck

Books by Kristina Beck

Collide Series
Lives Collide
Dreams Collide
Souls Collide

About the Author

A Jersey Girl herself, Kristina was born and raised in New Jersey, USA, living there for thirty years. She later moved to Germany and has lived there for over fourteen years with her German husband and three children. She is an avid reader of many genres, but romance always takes precedence. She loves coffee, dark chocolate, power naps, and eighties movies. Her hobbies include writing, reading, fitness, and forever trying to improve her German-language skills.

Made in the USA
Monee, IL
20 January 2022